Karl Marx

ON SOCIETY

AND SOCIAL CHANGE

With Selections by Friedrich Engels

Edited and with an Introduction by

NEIL J. SMELSER

THE UNIVERSITY OF CHICAGO PRESS

CHICAGO AND LONDON

NEIL J. SMELSER is University Professor of
Sociology at the University of California,
Berkeley. His many publications include
Social Change in the Industrial Revolution,
Theory of Collective Behavior, and (with Talcott
Parsons) *Economy and Society.*
[1973]

International Standard Book Number: 0-226-50917-6 (clothbound);
                                    0-226-50918-4 (paperbound)
Library of Congress Catalog Card Number: 73-78669

81 80 79 78 77   9 8 7 6 5 4 3 2

Karl Marx

ON SOCIETY AND SOCIAL CHANGE

THE HERITAGE OF SOCIOLOGY

A Series Edited by Morris Janowitz

Contents

v

95451

III. THE MECHANISMS OF CHANGE

Introduction

EVERY INTELLECTUAL PERIOD, Lewis Feuer has observed, has an anthology of Marx and Engels appropriate to itself.[1] He might well have generalized the point: whatever the nature of any person's concern with the human being and his social and cultural condition, he may read many parts of Karl Marx's[2] works with interest and profit. This circumstance arises from two features of Marx's work and life style. First and most important, his thought constitutes one of the most comprehensive theories of man and society ever elaborated. There is a Marxist contribution to, indeed a Marxist explanation for, almost every aspect of individual and social life that one could imagine—human nature, economics, religion, politics, philosophy, social stratification, to name only a few. So extensive were the writings of Marx, moreover, that it has been possible for editors to compile useful collections of his writings on almost all these aspects.[3] Second, Marx was what might

---

[1] Lewis Feuer, Introduction to *Marx and Engels: Basic Writings on Politics and Philosophy* (Garden City, N.Y.: Doubleday, Anchor Books, 1959), p. xx.

[2] Any general references to Karl Marx's works in this introductory essay are intended to include the work of Friedrich Engels as well.

[3] Feuer's anthology, cited in fn. 1, is an example. See also Shlomo Avineri, ed., *Karl Marx on Colonialism and Modernization* (Garden City, N.Y.: Doubleday, 1968); *Selected Writings in Sociology and Social Philosophy*, edited, with translation and notes by T. B. Bottomore and Maximilien Rubel (London: Watts, 1963); Lloyd D. Easton and Kurt H. Guddat, eds., *Writings of the Young Marx on Philosophy and Society* (New York: Harcourt, 1961); Eric Fromm, ed., *Marx's Concept of Man* (New

be called in modern terms a "generalist" in the extreme. His works cannot be assigned to any one scholarly discipline, because he was simultaneously economist, sociologist, political scientist, historian, and philosopher. Nor does this string of disciplinary labels exhaust the significance of the man; he was also a prophet, a moralist, a revolutionist, a journalist, and an agitator. Hence his appeal to the most diverse range of interests and audiences.

Given the scope, complexity, and density of Marx's thought, is it not then illegitimate to separate aspects of his thought into the familiar disciplinary categories of economics, sociology, and political science? Eric Hobsbawm has argued that such separations are "misleading, and entirely contrary to Marx's method."[4] This argument has merit, if one's main aim is to reproduce Marx's method as he himself conceived of it and utilized it. If, however, Marx is regarded as one major contributor to the accumulation of thought and knowledge about society—whose work has been superseded in many ways by subsequent theory and empirical investigation—then it becomes both legitimate and desirable to continuously reassess his insights in the light of the ways we have come to think about man and society since his time.

In this spirit I have collected what I consider to be those writings of Marx that best reveal his contribution to sociology, particularly to the theory of society and social change. This emphasis seems important to me, not only because such selections are appropriate for a series in the heritage of sociology, but also because it has not received adequately focused attention in the past. Inevitably, such an emphasis will ignore many aspects of Marx's work, particularly his early philosophical writings, his ideological polemics, and his technical economics.[5] So interrelated are all

---

York: F. Ungar, 1966); Karl Marx and Friedrich Engels, *On Religion*, introduction by Reinhold Niebuhr (New York: Shocken, 1967); Karl Marx and Friedrich Engels, *Literature and Art* (selections) (New York: International Publishers, 1947).

4   E. J. Hobsbawm, Introduction to *Karl Marx: Pre-Capitalist Economic Formations* (New York: International Publishers, 1964), p. 16.

5   Recently I attempted to assess the theoretical structure developed in volume 1 of *Capital*, in which Marx attempted to derive the major char-

parts of Marx's work, however, that these aspects are in evidence to some degree in the selections. In this introduction I shall develop some comments on Marx's theory of society and social change, in an effort to facilitate a more integrated reading of the selections.

General Notes on Marx's Life and Works

Given the emphasis I have selected, it does not seem appropriate in this introduction to deal very extensively with Marx's biography, or with either the origins of his thought or its subsequent modifications as it has emerged as a worldwide ideological and political force. These aspects are peripheral though not unrelated to my main objective; besides, they have been treated very extensively by others. Nevertheless, a few orienting comments on the important phases of Marx's work and some of its stylistic characteristics are in order.

Karl Marx was born on 5 May 1818 in the German city of Trier. His father was a Jewish lawyer, though early in young Marx's childhood he renounced Judaism and the entire family was baptized into the Christian faith. At the age of seventeen he entered the University of Bonn to study law, but transferred to the University of Berlin one year later. It was at Berlin—Marx remained there for several years—that Marx came under the influence of the philosophy of Hegel, and particularly that variant of Hegelianism that focused on the criticism of law and religion. While at Bonn Marx joined Bruno Bauer, one of the "Young Hegelians," in the publication of a critical journal. About this time, however, the Ministry of Culture, offended and alarmed by the attacks of the Young Hegelians, blocked the promotion of Bauer to a position at the University of Bonn, a move which effectively prevented Marx's appointment at Bonn as well. So while Marx did attain the degree of Doctor of Philosophy—in 1841

---

acteristics of capitalism and the major dynamics of capitalist society from a technical economic basis (the labor theory of value). See Neil J. Smelser, *Sociological Theory: A Contemporary View* (New York: General Learning Press, 1971), pp. 34–50.

from the University of Jena, where he submitted his thesis—his academic career actually ended before it had a chance to begin.

In 1842 Marx became the editor of the *Rheinische Zeitung,* a liberal journal published in Cologne. Again his trenchant criticisms drew the attention of the political authorities, and in early 1843 the paper was suppressed and Marx migrated to Paris. In the next few years, Marx evolved his critique of Hegel's philosophy, a critique which accepted many of the dynamics of Hegel's theory of historical change, but which reinterpreted those dynamics as economic and social realities rather than as development of ideas. In these years, too, partly under the influence of Engels, whom he had come to know in Paris, Marx began to familiarize himself more with economics and to advance his formulations concerning the destructive impact of the capitalist system on the laboring classes and his thesis of the alienation of labor under capitalism.

In 1845 Marx's political expressions in Paris publications once again irritated the German authorities, who persuaded the French government to expel him. Marx went to Brussels. The next four years were among the most productive in his life. He and Engels collaborated closely in these years, and produced the enormous theoretical work, *The German Ideology,* which lays out their materialist philosophy and materialist version of history in elaborate form. They also wrote *The Communist Manifesto,* whose pages cannot be equaled as a compact and comprehensive statement of the communist theory of history and program of action. In addition, Marx continued his philosophical polemics in *The Poverty of Philosophy,* and first set down his version of the labor theory of value, which was to be the foundation stone of the monumental first volume of *Capital,* published almost twenty years later.

Exiled again because of his political activity during the revolutionary uprisings of 1848, Marx moved to England in the summer of 1849 and remained there almost continuously until his death in 1883. During many of these years he was distracted from scholarship by the need to earn money; between 1851 and 1862 he wrote articles for the *New York Daily Tribune* (a few of which are reprinted in this volume). In the 1860s much of his energy was thrown into the politics of the First International. Nevertheless,

Marx's scholarship in the 1850s and 1860s was prodigious. Not only did he complete most of the massive *Capital*, the most fully developed statement of his theory of capitalist society, but he also produced several impressive empirical studies. Most of his historical scholarship is revealed in the pages of *Capital*, in which the conditions of the working classes and their developing conflict with capital are extensively documented. In addition, however, publications such as *The Eighteenth Brumaire of Louis Bonaparte* constituted notable instances of the blending of Marxian theoretical notions on the origins of class conflict with the historical specifics of political conflict.

Marx's theory emerges as a mighty synthesis of an enormous number of ingredients found in various intellectual strands of his day. In a partial account of the origins of Marx's thought, Isaiah Berlin has identified the obvious influences of Hegelian philosophy; of English economic writers such as Smith and Ricardo; of the analyses of class conflict by writers such as Linguet and Saint-Simon; of the analyses of economic crises by Sismondi, and of others.[6]

Yet it would be erroneous to dispose of the question of the originality of Marx's work simply by pointing out his intellectual debts. Marx was able to escape the dangers of eclecticism that arise when so many ingredients are incorporated into a single theory. In fact, his work is a genuine synthesis, precisely because he was able to weld together the diverse ingredients—materialism, alienation and exploitation, class conflict, revolution, and historical process—into a systematic whole. The solder by which this synthesis was effected is the complex series of assumptions and theoretical principles enunciated in his philosophy of history and in his version of economic theory. For example, the theory of contradictions emerges in the first instance from Marx's image of social structure and from the dynamics of the dialectic process; but in addition, this theory was closely derived from Marx's conceptuali-

[6]   Isaiah Berlin, *Karl Marx: His Life and Environment* (London: Oxford University Press, 1963), pp. 13–15. For a more detailed account see George Lichtheim, *Marxism: An Historical and Critical Study* (New York, Praeger, 1963), pp. 3–30.

zations of labor as a commodity; the production of surplus-value; and exploitation of labor as an expression of the production of surplus-value. His theory of revolution was derived from at least three sources—first, from the theory of contradictions; second, from the specific mechanics of capitalist society, which, through competition, innovation, and profit-taking, worsens the objective conditions of the working population as capitalism develops; and third, from the assumptions linking objective conditions, the development of class consciousness, and collective political action. Many parts of Marx's synthesis—most notably the theory of value —have been discredited and are no longer taken seriously even by committed Marxists; many of the specific theoretical links in his synthesis have been questioned, such as the link between objective conditions of exploitation and the growth of revolutionary consciousness; and many of the predictions arising from his synthesis have not been borne out historically. Nevertheless, it must be appreciated that Marx's theory—in contrast to so many of the bodies of thought from which he borrowed and which have borrowed from him—does indeed consist of an attempt to derive all its important ingredients from first theoretical principles, and thereby an attempt to create an original, independent, and integrated *theoretical structure.*

Indebted as Marx was to various bodies of social thought, his attitude toward them was characteristically ambivalent. He aggressively embraced the Hegelian principle of the dialectic, yet he polemicized equally aggressively against its unacceptable emphasis on ideas. He thoroughly incorporated the Ricardian labor theory of value into his treatise on capitalism, yet his pages are filled with bitter diatribes against the "bourgeois economists." Rely as he did on some of the French socialists for his conceptions of political conflict, he nevertheless attacked them repeatedly as misguided romantics. The intensity of Marx's commitment to those ideas which he borrowed and incorporated into his own theory was matched only by the intensity of his hostility toward the *other* ideas of those theories from which he had borrowed.

Another feature of Marx's intellectual style is the notable unity of the scientific and humanistic aspects of his work. Above all,

Marx regarded himself as a scientist of society. In the introduction to *Capital* he noted that he conceived the "ultimate aim" of that work to be a scientific one—"to lay bare the economic law of motion of modern society."[7] Furthermore, he welcomed "every opinion [of his work] based on scientific criticism."[8] Because he regarded the laws of modern society as based on an inevitable world-historical process, moreover, the moral and human implications of these laws were not difficult to discern. It was right to identify with the sufferings of the workers in the present phase of capitalism, because it was historically inevitable, given the laws of economic and social evolution, that the workers were the exploited class and were destined for victorious overthrow of capitalism. Morality is so intricately determined by the process of historical evolution that an understanding of that process virtually dictates the proper moral posture.

All these ingredients of Marx's intellectual style indicate why reading him is often difficult and suggest the spirit in which his work must be read. In the first place, being derived from a number of different intellectual traditions, Marx's writings use several different abstract languages to characterize the same thing. Nowhere is this clearer than in the two selections on the nature of communism in part two below. The first, drawn from the *Economic and Philosophical Manuscripts*, is cast largely in the language deriving from the Hegelian philosophical tradition; the second, drawn from *The Communist Manifesto*, uses the more concrete language of political and economic arrangements. Despite the discontinuity of language, however, the same state of affairs—the character of life in communist society—is being described. Second, Marx often shifts quickly from one style of discourse to another. The same few pages might contain several laborious philosophical distinctions, the citation of extensive historical evidence, an assault on another philosopher or economist (the details of whole intellectual positions may not be revealed), and an ironical jibe at some aspect of the bourgeois mentality. Yet if one understands that in Marx's

7   Karl Marx, *Capital* (London: George Allen and Unwin, 1949), p. xix.
8   Ibid., p. xx.

mind scientific understanding, empirical reality, morality, and passion are integral parts of a unified world view, the apparent obscurity and discontinuity of his style disappears.

Marx's Conception of Society as a Social System

The minimum definitional requirements of the concept of a "social system" are (a) that it have more than one identifiable unit, and that these units be "social" in character (in contrast to biological or physical); (b) that these units stand in some kind of consistent—or "systematic"—relation to one another; and (c) that the system should have some "integrity," that is, its internal relations should differ from those relations between its units and units external to the system. Otherwise the system would have no distinctive character.[9]

By these criteria Marx's view is that society is a social system. Though he never, to my knowledge, developed an exhaustive list of the components of a society, it is clear that he regarded it as a complex of ingredients. In the two selections on "The Material Basis of Society" in part one, Marx distinguished between the "forces of production," or the technological and resource basis of economic activity, and the "social relations of production," which are the interactions (for example, through employment and property arrangements) into which men enter at a given level of the development of the forces of production. Together these compose the mode of production, which is also the material base or the economic infrastructure of a society. In addition, Marx also referred to "legal and political superstructure" and to "social, political and intellectual life process" as ingredients of society.[10] Furthermore, these different ingredients stand in a consistent relationship to one another. According to the classical Marxian

---

[9]   For an extended discussion of the nature of social systems, see Talcott Parsons and Edward A. Shils, "Values, Motives, and Systems of Action," in Parsons and Shils, eds., *Toward a General Theory of Action* (Cambridge: Harvard University Press, 1951), pp. 190–233.

[10]   See chap. 1, sec. II.

formula, "[the] mode of production in material life determines the general character of the social and political process of life."[11] And finally, since Marx held different types of societies to be historically specific to different stages of development, he clearly implied that a society—whatever its historical form—is a distinct, identifiable entity.

The manner in which the "general character" of the superstructure is "determined" by the material forces of production, however, is not altogether clear in Marx's formulations. Do the forces of production affect or "determine" all the other ingredients in society in the same way, or is the structure of society built on more complex principles? The determination of the social relations of production by the forces of production appears to be close and immediate: the "particular form of commerce and consumption" (that is, the social relations of production) depends on the "particular state of development in the productive forces of man."[12] The connection between the forces of production and the various parts of the superstructure appears not to be so direct. In the opening of his letter to P. V. Annenkov, Marx suggested a more complicated hierarchy of determination. The "organization of the family and of the ranks and classes" (part of the superstructure), he argued, depends on the development *both* of production (forces) and of commerce and consumption (social relations). He went on to assert, moreover, that the "particular political conditions" of a given society (also part of the superstructure) depend above all on the "organization of the family and of the ranks and classes" of society.[13] That is to say, the "forces of production" appear as the ultimate determinant, but the mode of determination differs according to the part of society in question. While it is the immediate determinant of the "social relations of production," its determining influence on the higher levels of the superstructure (for example, religion, philosophy) would appear to be more indirect—that is, mediated through the social relations of produc-

11   See chap. 1, sec. II.
12   See chap. 1, sec. I.
13   See chap. 1, sec. I.

tion and through the various political and legal arrangements that reinforce these relations.

The type of causal relationship between the forces of production and the other components of society also seems somewhat ambiguous. The structure of the social relations of production would seem to rest, as almost a kind of immediate necessity, on the forces of production. The pattern of these relations would seem to *reflect* the forces of production; "a certain mode of production . . . is always combined with a certain mode of cooperation, or social stage."[14] The existence of the relations of production, moreover, does not presuppose any particular contradictions within the forces of production; indeed, Marx's concept of "contradiction" rests on a certain *relationship* between the mode of production and the relations of production. Furthermore, when a given economic epoch (for example, capitalism) was in the very earliest phases of its development and was not generating serious contradictions as yet, most of the superstructure could be regarded as *facilitating* the particular mode of production, for example, through legal and political arrangements that facilitated market transactions. Under these circumstances society would appear to stand in stable equilibrium.

In the more advanced phases of a given stage of development, however, when contradictions have become more severe, a different type of causal relationship appears to obtain between the economic structure and the superstructure. Several passages concerning the state, religion, and the family indicate that in Marx's view these owe their existence to *contradictions* between the forces of production and the relations of production, and that their functional significance is to blunt these contradictions. Consider Engels's characterization of the significance of the state:

[The state] is a product of society at a particular stage of development; it is the admission that this society has involved itself in insoluble self-contradiction and is cleft into irreconcilable antagonisms which it is powerless to exorcise. But in order that these antagonisms, classes with conflicting interests, shall not consume themselves and society in

[14]   See chap. 2.

fruitless struggle, a power, apparently standing above society, has become necessary to moderate the conflict and keep it within the bounds of "order"; and this power, arisen out of society, but placing itself above it and increasingly alienating itself from it, is the state.[15]

This formulation, as well as Engels's subsequent assertion that under economic conditions which are based on free and equal association of the producers—that is, conditions free from contradiction—the state will no longer be necessary, suggests that political arrangements owe their existence to contradictions elsewhere in the society, and help subdue them. Marx's famous indictment of religion as "the opium of the people" suggests that religion also operates to subdue contradictions elsewhere in the society.[16]

Consider also the significance of the family, on which I have included a number of selections. Engels treated the monogamous family as a social arrangement which reinforces certain contradictions in society; "wherever the monogamous family remains true to its historical origin and clearly reveals the antagonism between the man and the woman expressed in the man's exclusive supremacy, it exhibits in miniature the same oppositions and contradictions as those in which society has been moving, without power to resolve or overcome them, ever since it split into classes at the beginning of civilization."[17] The bourgeois family, in protecting the institution of property, expresses in different form the same contradictions that are reflected in the class system. Marx's account of the structure of the proletarian family,[18] in which the parents are forced to exploit and degrade their children, is based upon the assumption that the contradictions of the larger society (that is, the exploitation of workers by owners) determine the structure of the family life of the workers.

These formulations suggest that Marx regarded society in part as an equilibrium system tending toward stability. (This is such an unfamiliar view that I should hasten to add that his ultimate posi-

15   See chap. 5.
16   See chap. 3.
17   See chap. 6, sec. I.
18   See chap. 6, sec. II.

tion—to be discussed presently—was that historical forces more powerful than the stabilizing ones are at work, and that society is ultimately unstable.) The principles making for stability, moreover, are three: (1) the necessity for consistency between the forces of production and the social relations of production, for, indeed, men *must* enter into certain definite patterns of cooperation and not others if production at any stage of development can exist at all; (2) the facilitative relations between certain parts of the superstructure and the mode of production at early phases of development of an economic epoch; (3) the softening of contradictions. Since contradictions and antagonisms between the forces of production and the social relations of production inevitably arise, there also arise certain superstructural forms, such as a particular type of state, religion, and family, that stand in a *positive functional relationship* to the contradictions. The superstructural forms tend to prevent these contradictions from breaking into unmanageable conflict.

It is instructive to compare this theme of societal stabilization in Marx with the modern "functionalist" perspective on society, as developed in the works of theorists like Talcott Parsons and Marion J. Levy[19]—a perspective to which Marxist theory is frequently regarded as opposed in almost every respect. The starting theoretical point of functional theorists' analyses is that societies are faced with a number of functional requisites or exigencies, such as recruitment and socialization of new members in society, the production and allocation of means of subsistence, the regulation of conflict, the maintenance of cultural patterns, and so on. It is further held that social life must, in some degree, be organized around meeting these functional exigencies if continuity of the society is to be assured. In fact, the social structure is specialized according to these exigencies: the family specializes in recruitment

[19]   See, for example, D. F. Aberle et al., "The Functional Requisites of a Society," *Ethics* 60 (1950) : 100–111; see also Marion J. Levy, Jr., *The Structure of Society* (Princeton, N.J.: Princeton University Press, 1952), chap. 3; Talcott Parsons, *The Social System* (Glencoe, Ill.: The Free Press, 1951), chap. 2; see also Talcott Parsons and Neil J. Smelser, *Economy and Society* (Glencoe, Ill.: The Free Press, 1956), chap. 2.

and socialization; political structures specialize in the regulation of conflict, among other things; religious and educational structures contribute to the maintenance of cultural patterns, and so on.

A major difference between Marx and the functional theorists is that Marx gives primacy to the economic function—the others being subordinated in various ways to it—whereas the functional theorists regard the various functional exigencies as more nearly cognate. This means that a different set of relationships among the various parts of the social structure is also posed. For Marx the state specializes in dealing with conflict situations, but these situations are of a particular kind—those arising from contradictions in the economic order and the class antagonisms arising from them—and the orientation of the state is subordinated to the interests of the dominant economic class. A functional theorist would agree that much of the functional significance of the political order lies in the management of conflict situations. But these are of no particular kind; they may involve interests other than economic ones. And the state is not conceived as necessarily being aligned with any particular party to the conflict. The functionalist view of structural relations in society, then, is more indeterminate than that of Marx. Marx committed himself to a view of the subordination of other functionally significant structures to the dynamics of the economic system; the functionalists assume that the relations among different structures are characterized by looser interaction, or a "strain toward consistency." Even those functional theorists who emphasize "dysfunctions"[20]—which is a conceptual cousin to notions like "conflict" or "contradiction"—tend to characterize these in general terms and do not give special priority to dysfunctions generated in the economic sphere. All this suggests that Marx, by committing himself to the principle of economic primacy, gave his thought a more determinant theoretical structure than that which characterizes the thought of many functionalists. On the other hand, the functionalists' view of structural relations and social processes is more complex and probably more realistic.

[20] For example, cf. Robert Merton's criticism of the postulate of functional unity in classical functionalists. *Social Theory and Social Structure,* enlarged ed. (New York: The Free Press, 1968), pp. 79–84.

A second difference between the two perspectives arises in the relative emphases given to different kinds of stabilizing and unstabilizing processes. In classical functionalism, structures were regarded as basically congruent with the needs of the system—that is, they fulfilled certain functions and, in the short run, incongruencies tend to set in motion adjustive and restorative processes. In Marxian theory such stabilizing forces do exist, as we have just seen, but in the long run they are overwhelmed by a systematic tendency for the system to generate contradictions that are unresolvable within the confines of the existing social structure. As the actors in a capitalist system carry out activities appropriate to the economic roles in which they find themselves, they build up situations of contradiction, antagonism, and conflict which ultimately overwhelm the superstructural forms geared to subduing them and the economic structure that generated them. On the strength of this line of argument Marx created a second type of equilibrium principle—society as an equilibrium system tending toward breakdown. The Marxian epigram that every society contains the seeds of its own destruction is the most colorful formulation of this principle. It is also forcefully revealed in the opening statement of *The Communist Manifesto*, that the history of all society is the history of class struggles (that is, contradictions), and in the polemic defense of the inevitability of that pattern of history in the pages which follow.[21] Again and again Marx stressed the inevitability of worsening contradictions in the capitalist system, and repeatedly he emphasized the ultimate inability of the bourgeoisie to resolve the conflicts arising from these contradictions. In the end, the two principles of equilibration in the Marxian system—one toward conservation or stability and one toward destruction or instability—are combined in a single equilibrium system of opposing forces.

The differences between the Marxist and the functionalist perspectives, then, appear not to rest on differences in perceptions regarding the *substance* of society. A reading of the two indicates a similar account of the types of institutional structure that consti-

[21]   See chap. 8.

tute a society. The differences lie, rather, in the assumptions concerning the *relations* among the different structures (Marxism opting for the primacy of economic relations, functionalism opting for a principle of mutual interdependence of structures); and in the assumptions regarding the balance of dysfunctions and positive functions in the system (Marxism giving more emphasis to the destructive impact of a single kind of contradiction, and functionalism, while acknowledging dysfunctions, tending to give more emphasis to the adjustive or reconstitutive processes). Both sets of theories contain references to both stabilizing and unstabilizing tendencies. For this reason it seems erroneous to argue that either is "inherently" incapable of analyzing either change or stability. Both have the tools to do both. Marx, however, so organized his assumptions as to build a certain type of direction of change into his system. On occasion functional analysts have also organized their assumptions to create relatively determinate models of change.[22] It is true, however, that as a matter of practice functional analysts have tended to weigh their assumptions in such a way that they do not lead often to the analysis of the destruction of social systems by group conflict.

Part one of this volume contains several statements that reveal Marx and Engels's view on the materialist position; the first selection comments on the relations among the components of society, and the second is Marx's famous summary from *A Contribution to a Critique of Political Economy*. Next follows a brief excerpt from *The German Ideology*, which spells out the material preconditions for the emergence of consciousness, including its expression in philosophy, theology, and ethics. Then comes Marx's famous statement on the functional significance of religion in relation to politics.

It has been remarked that though Marx's theory rests very heavily on the notion of social classes, he never developed a full

---

[22]   See, for example, the model of structural differentiation as developed in Talcott Parsons and Neil J. Smelser, *Economy and Society* (Glencoe, Ill.: The Free Press, 1956), chap. 5.

theoretical statement on that topic.[23] That he intended to do so, however, seems certain. At the end of volume 3 of *Capital*, a major chapter begins, entitled "The Classes," but the manuscript breaks off after only one page. I have included this brief selection. As would be anticipated, Marx first indicated that the composition of classes in capitalist society is to be determined in the first instance by their relations to sources of revenue, which in turn depend on the mode of production of society. In the same selection, however, he posed a dilemma that has plagued Marxist theorists ever since that time: because each of the three great classes—landlords, capitalists, and laborers—are subdivided into so many different kinds of groups, is it appropriate to limit the identification of classes mainly to their sources of revenue?[24]

After an exceptionally clear statement on the origins and nature of the state by Engels, I include several sections on the family. I have given the family rather more attention than other institutional complexes in part one, partly because it is a topic of particular interest to me, and partly because the family has been given rather little attention in many of the commentaries on Marx. The first selection is Engels's statement on the origin and character of the bourgeois family. It reveals Marxian polemic at its sharpest; the sentimental morality on which the bourgeois family is based is revealed as a veneer on social arrangements dedicated to the preservation of property and the systematic exploitation of women. Then follow two lesser-known statements from *Capital* on the impact of capitalism on the proletarian family.

[23]   Cf. Reinhard Bendix and Seymour Martin Lipset, "Karl Marx's Theory of Social Classes," in Bendix and Lipset, eds., *Class, Status and Power*, 2d ed. (New York: The Free Press, 1966), p. 6.

[24]   In a way Dahrendorf's attempt to modify Marx's position on classes might be seen as an attempt to resolve this dilemma. Dahrendorf rejects "source of revenue" or "position in the economic order" as the main basis for class and class conflict in modern society, and substitutes, instead, differential position in an authority system, of which an economic authority system would be only one subtype. Ralf Dahrendorf, *Class and Class Conflict in Industrial Society* (Stanford, Calif.: Stanford University Press, 1959), chap. 5.

One dominant theme in the selections on the family is the exploitation of women. Yet it takes a different form in the proletarian class than among the bourgeoisie. Whereas among the latter women are excluded from access to property by monogamous marital and inheritance arrangements, proletarian women are drawn into the market by the capitalist as a means of expanding the surplus-value to be extracted from the proletarian family. Capital appropriates the labor of children for the same purpose, thereby making the dependents more like chattel than persons, and gradually sinking the family into a state of physical and moral degradation. The same effects, in even more extreme manifestation, are held to characterize the domestic industries as well, though the specific mechanisms are different. In the first stage capital exploits the families by extending the hours of labor and appropriating dependents at low wages. As these strategies of exploitation reach their limits, however, the capitalists begin to introduce machinery into domestic branches of industry to increase their profits further. The impact of this innovation is to set adrift the population of domestic workers, whose labor cannot compete with the more efficient manufacturers.

The two selections by Marx on the proletarian family also reveal the style of his historical scholarship as manifested in *Capital*. Marx was at great pains to demonstrate the laws of capitalism empirically, and to present evidence of the posited historical effects of these laws. Thus, in these selections, Marx wheeled out, in laborious and sometimes tedious detail, dozens of facts testifying to the physical and moral depravity of the working classes. In most cases he relied on data supplied in the reports of Parliamentary investigating committees. In the century since Marx wrote *Capital* many of his conclusions regarding the condition of the working classes—as well as the data on which these conclusions are based—have been called into question. Some subsequent studies indicate considerable economic and other types of advances for laboring people during the British industrial revolution; others tend to reconfirm the Marxist description; and still others show a more mixed or complicated picture. Indeed, this tradition of scholarship on the condition of the working classes is clouded by continuous debate that reflects those very ideological currents—and counter-currents—set into motion by Marxism itself.

Marx's Conception of Social Change

Earlier I suggested that the Marxian conception of society can be regarded as a system expressing the tension between two principles of equilibration: a stabilizing principle, manifested mainly in the superstructural arrangements designed to contain conflicts arising from contradictions in society; and an unstabiliz-ing principle, found in the theory of progressive intensification of contradictions. These two equilibrating principles are set in more definite relation to one another by the principle of the dialectic; the unstabilizing contradictions will, in the end, overwhelm all other societal arrangements, destroy the society, and produce a new social order that will obey the same laws in its turn.

Some of Marx's writings suggest not only that this dialectic principle is a law of history, but that human history manifests a definite number of types of society, and that these types emerge in a definite progression. Summarizing the results of his historical re-search and leaning heavily on Hegel's scheme of periodization, Marx suggested that "in broad outlines we can designate the Asiatic, the ancient, the feudal and the modern bourgeois modes of production as so many epochs in the progress of the economic formation of society."[25] The language of the selection printed in part two from *The German Ideology*—which was Marx's first state-ment on the stages of human history—also suggests the notion of a fixed succession of stages. His subsequent historical writings, how-ever, indicate that while he always held steadfast to the notion that different societies were based on differing modes of production, and that these could be ranked in a progressive series, his views on evolutionary history were less stereotyped and more subtle than some of these earlier and briefer statements might suggest.[26]

[25]   See chap. 1, sec. II.
[26]   See particularly, Marx, *Pre-Capitalist Economic Formations*, espe-

Part two should be read, then, as a sample of the most general and, to some degree, oversimplified versions of Marx's overview of the sweep of historical change. The first selection contains Marx's first statement of the main precapitalist forms of production—as well as the types of property arrangements, divisions of labor, and so on, that accompany them. The second selection, from *The Communist Manifesto*, focuses on capitalism, its contradictions, and its impending destruction. Two brief final selections deal with the nature of communism, particularly on its freedom from the kinds of contradictions that have plagued all earlier forms of societies.

An isolated reading of the selections in part two, particularly the polemics of *The Communist Manifesto*, reveals why Marxist writings lend themselves to vulgarization. The materialist position is enunciated simply and forcefully, and alternative perspectives on society and social change are savagely attacked; the principle of the dialectic is stated in stark and absolute terms; history is depicted as a kind of mechanical unfolding of stages; and the specifics of the historical process are evidently oversimplified by vast generalizations. Many of these features may be understood by appreciating the multiple—particularly the propagandistic—intentions underlying the writings of *The Communist Manifesto*. Nevertheless, it should be acknowledged that these writings possess considerably less sociological merit than Marx's other, more carefully conducted scholarship. As we have seen, an extensive reading of Marx's work yields a more complicated picture of his thought than is found in his grand historical essays. Earlier in this introduction I suggested that the causal avenues by which the material base of society interacts with its other components are by no means simple and that Marx's view of evolution, which on the basis of some statements would seem to be simple and unilinear, is actually more complicated.

But what of the explanatory status of the principle of the dia-

---

cially the Introduction by Hobsbawm. These later writings are often so scattered or obscure, however, that inclusion of brief portions of them in this volume would not seem to be very informative.

lectic itself? In shifting Hegel's version of the dialectic from the realm of ideas to the material realm, Marx conceived of himself as demystifying that principle.[27] Even when thus transformed, however, the principle still retains much of its mystery. It is still a very abstract amalgam of irresistible forces of contradiction, destruction, and recreation, and is singularly lacking in the specification of any particular *mechanisms* by which dialectical convulsions of society occur.

In Marx's writings on social change, however, we discover a discontinuity in his works, not unlike that discontinuity in his writings on materialism. On the one hand some of his work contains statements that suggest he embraced the dialectic as an abstract force. On the other, we find in his historical work quite concrete, detailed discussions of the empirically identifiable mechanisms by which some of the forces posited in the dialectic actually work out. Most of Marx's sociologically valuable contributions, in my estimation, lie in his effort to consistently locate and describe the mechanisms of economic, social, and political change associated with an expanding capitalist system. In fact, one need not accept the dialectic as a world-historical principle to acknowledge the expansive tendencies of capitalism and to identify the mechanisms by which expansion occurs and the consequences of that expansion. Marx's real "demystification" of the dialectic lay not in his "materialization" of the principle, but rather in his effort to analyze in historical detail the mechanisms by which contradictions develop and generate group conflicts. In part three of this volume I have reproduced several parts of Marx's analysis that focus on such mechanisms.

One of the main characteristics of capitalism is that it has a tendency to expand incessantly, to increase the level of exploitation and profits, and to worsen the condition of the working classes and thereby intensify the antagonism between the capitalists and the workers. All these results are clearly consistent with if not derivable from the principle of the dialectic. But the results, if stated in such general terms, reveal little about the *differential* behavior

[27]   *Capital*, 1: xxx.

of capitalists. It remains only as a general tendency of capitalist society, and presumably a basis for predicting the progressive immiserization of the working classes and the ultimate overthrow of the system. As such it yields few specific insights into the variability of the historical process and the behavior of capitalists under different conditions.

Particularly in his work on economics, however, Marx identified another, more specific engine that determines the incessant expansion of capital—the engine of economic competition. Insofar as the capitalist has a competitive advantage over other capitalists, he will be motivated to adopt the mode of production that gives him the advantage, thereby equalizing profits and making the mode of production general. Once equalized, however, the only way for the capitalist to increase profits is to innovate in some way, in order to regain his competitive advantage. Once he gains that advantage, the cycle toward equalization is once again begun. Thus the capitalist, if he is to continue to profit, is forced always to adjust the mode of production—in what ways we shall investigate presently. Furthermore, it is this principle that guarantees the continuous expansion of capitalism—"division of labor necessarily draws after it greater division of labor, the employment of machinery, greater employment of machinery, work upon a large scale works upon a still greater scale."[28]

Note that competition as an explanatory mechanism for the expansion of capital is capable of more specific historical application than the general principle of the dialectic. It is possible to predict the *pattern* of competitive growth by examining the competitive situation—that is, who has a differential advantage, what is the nature of this differential advantage, and so on—of individual industries at different phases of their growth. The dialectic principle would lead one to predict only the overall increase of contradictions, rather than their specific manifestations.

Given the incessant pressure to innovate, what means are available to the capitalist? Marx discussed several of these. The capitalist strives after economies, so that more workers work longer in

[28]   See chap. 10.

relation to a given supply of fixed capital; these economies include overcrowding of the work premises,[29] lengthening of the working day,[30] and others. He also strives to modify the conditions of production so that fewer laborers will have to be employed in relation to a given amount of fixed capital; among these would be modifying the pattern of cooperation among laborers and altering the division of labor,[31] but above all, introducing technologically superior machinery that requires the presence of fewer laborers.[32] Machinery in turn permits still other profitable strategies, such as the appropriation of the supplementary labor of women and children,[33] speeding up machinery, and the like. All these strategies give the capitalist some competitive advantage in his struggle to increase profits and aggravate the exploitation of workers.

Each of the means of increasing profits, moreover, has a kind of "developmental cycle" of its own. The capitalist presses a given strategy until it reaches some kind of natural or social limit. Then, because he can no longer use that strategy as a means for further exploitation, he turns to some new strategy. Consider the search for economies, for example. The crowding of people into small workplaces, neglecting health precautions, and so forth, has a definite set of consequences: it increases the surplus-value of the capitalist, and becomes "a prodigality in the use of the life and health of the laborer himself."[34] Unless, however, the capitalist is bent on physically destroying that on which he depends for profit—the workers' labor power—he must observe some limit to the degree to which he degrades the workers. The extension of the working day, furthermore, has a natural limit imposed by the physiological capacities of the worker; "the limiting of factory labor was dictated by the same necessity which spread guano over the English fields. The same blind eagerness for plunder that in the one case

---

29   See chap. 11.
30   *Capital*, pp. 214–88.
31   Ibid., pp. 311–63.
32   Ibid., pp. 365–515.
33   For a statement of the rationale for the hiring of such labor, see chap 6, sec. II.
34   See chap. 11.

exhausted the soil, had, in the other, torn up by the roots the living force of the nation."[35] Another factor limiting the length of the working day, of course, was the power of the working class, which struggled to resist the extension of the working day.[36] At any rate, whatever the nature of the limits and whatever the exact limits set, the strategy sooner or later loses its effectiveness as a means of extracting surplus-value, and the capitalist is forced to turn to alternative methods. When, for example, the capitalists reached the limits of exploiting domestic workers in England "by sheer abuse of the labor of women and children, by sheer robbery of every normal condition requisite for working and living, and by sheer brutality of overwork and night labor," Marx argued that "the hour has struck for the introduction of machinery."[37] Similarly, when the government of England succeeded in establishing regulations over the length of the working day, one response of the capitalist was to speed up the machinery in the factories, in order to compensate for the surplus-value lost in the shortening of the working day.[38] The capitalist, then, is continuously maneuvering—to press a strategy of exploitation to its limits, to shift strategies when those limits are reached, and to seek forever for new opportunities for exploitation.

This same developmental cycle is repeated with respect to the introduction of machinery. By and large, Marx felt the improvement of productive capacity by the introduction of machinery was the most potent and explosive source of capitalist growth. The improvement of old and the development of new machinery, entailing a continuous increase in the specialization of labor, is "a process which goes on uninterruptedly, with feverish haste, and upon an

---

35   *Capital*, p. 222.

36   Ibid., pp. 256, 269. Marx was not entirely consistent in his reasoning concerning the causes of reducing the length of the working day. On the one hand it would seem to be to the capitalist's advantage, since it preserved the minimum health and welfare of his workers; on the other hand it would seem to be to his disadvantage, because it marked a compromise in the struggle with the working classes.

37   See chap. 6, sec. III.

38   *Capital*, 1: 410–11.

ever more gigantic scale."[39] Any given improvement, however, soon reaches a limit in its ability to increase surplus-value. The limit in this case, however, is found in the decline of competitive advantage that occurs when other capitalists have adopted the improvement. So, again, the capitalist must be ever on the watch for new improvements for himself to gain a momentary edge in the market, and on the watch for new improvements by others, so that he may be quick to adopt them himself to avoid falling behind. This constant struggle for life in the market gives capitalism its quality of "feverish agitation."[40]

Marx regarded the effects of continuous innovation as profound and disastrous. Because industry continues to grow more productive, relatively fewer laborers are needed. This sets laborers in increasingly intense competition with one another for dwindling numbers of jobs.[41] Another way of understanding increasing productivity is that capitalists, by diverting a decreasing proportion of the value of products to the laborers, are able to command an increasing part of that value. This process leads to the famous "law of capital accumulation," which results in an increasing concentration of capital into fewer hands, and the rise of a large industrial reserve army of unemployed workers—unemployed by virtue of the diminished need for them.[42] The process of accumulation also leads to the "unemployment" of some of the smaller capitalists as well, as they are driven out of business by larger competitors. As the scale of capital increases, this group, as well as people living on the interest of capital, will be "precipitated into the ranks of the working class, and they will have nothing else to do than to stretch out their arms alongside of the arms of the workers."[43]

The continuous immiserization of the masses, and the continuous polarization of society into very rich and very poor, is aggravated by one further mechanism—the business cycle. Marx argued that the introduction of new machinery is not a smooth process;

---

[39]   See chap. 10.
[40]   See chap. 10.
[41]   See chap. 10.
[42]   See chap. 12 for an enunciation of the law of capital accumulation.
[43]   See chap. 10.

rather, industrial capitalism has an "enormous power . . . of expanding by jumps."[44] As one major innovation—for example, the steam engine—is adopted, it generates a rush of production based on the new technique and a scramble for the profits made available by its appearance. This period of feverish production, however, necessarily exceeds the capacity of the market to absorb it, so it is typically followed by a contraction of the markets and stagnation of production. "The life of modern industry becomes a series of periods of moderate activity, prosperity, overproduction, crisis and stagnation."[45] These economic crises aggravate the general effects created by the law of capital accumulation. Workers are alternately attracted to and repelled from employment, and the periods of stagnation bankrupt those capitalists unable to survive in the contracted market conditions. It was, in fact, in the severe polarization between classes that was occasioned by the irresistible need for capitalism to expand—and expand irregularly—that Marx found the ultimate contradiction of capitalism, and the ultimate recruiting ground for the revolutionary army that would destroy that system.

The most potent strategy for exploitation available to the capitalists, then, is to increase productivity through technological advance. But before this strategy reaches its ultimate limit, one final strategy is available. Marx found the limits for any given innovation—or set of them—in the size of the market, which cannot sustain the feverish overproduction and thus inhibits industrial expansion. The strategy available under these circumstances is to expand the market and thus increase its capacity to absorb the increased production. Industrial expansion creates the need for more raw materials for itself, and the need for larger markets for its own products. The natural consequence is to internationalize capitalism. With their cheap products capitalists destroy the handicraft industries of backward countries, and force them into the production of raw materials. In this way a "new and international division of labor, a division suited to the requirements of the chief

44   See chap. 13.
45   See chap. 13.

centers of modern industry springs up, and converts one part of the globe into a chiefly agricultural field of production, for supplying the other part which remains a chiefly industrial field."[46] Such is the capitalist basis for the development of international trade, colonization, and international exploitation. Moreover, Marxists widely regard the internationalization of capital as the last defensive strategy available to the capitalists before the ultimate contradictions of capitalism lead to its destruction.[47]

I have included two selections on the internationalization of capitalism. In the first, on India, Marx interpreted the British efforts to unify that country politically and to build a network of railroads as a strategy to convert India into a supplier of cotton and other raw materials for British industries. Marx predicted further that the introduction of railways would set the stage for a more general growth in industry in India, which would, in turn, dissolve the caste system that has posed such obstacles to Indian progress. In the second, on China, Marx attributed the political upheavals in mid-nineteenth-century China to the economic penetration of the mainland by capitalism. In addition, however, Marx commented on the vulnerability of the international dependence that arises from the establishment of trade between the capitalist nations and their economically backward suppliers of raw materials; in fact, Marx ventured the hopeful prediction that the economic crisis occasioned by the contraction of the Chinese market would aggravate the delicate politico-economic conditions in Western Europe and precipitate a revolutionary convulsion there.

So much for the mechanisms of capitalist expansion and domination. These tendencies, however, constitute only a part of Marx's view of the social process. They initiate a number of political changes in the society which, in the end, are the agents of destruction of capitalist society. In the early stages of development of capital, the capitalist classes can easily subdue the workers, because the latter are thoroughly dazed, isolated, and victimized by capitalist exploitation. Marx posited, however, that as the system

[46]   See chap. 13.
[47]   For example, V. I. Lenin, *Imperialism: The Highest Stage of Capitalism* (New York: International Publishers, 1939).

develops and as exploitation worsens, the workers gradually attain greater consciousness of the system that exploits them, and become more readily mobilizable into a political movement. The stages of the worker awakening are sketched in the simplest form in the pages of *The Communist Manifesto*.[48] In the early stages the workers are isolated, in competition with one another, and disorganized; they are capable of only isolated forays against the means of production (for example, machine-breaking) and misguided attacks against the remnants of the feudal ruling classes. As workers are gathered into greater proximity with one another, and as the advance of industry obliterates their differences and homogenizes them, they become more mobilizable into collective action groups, such as trade unions; they are now able to compel their own recognition and to attain certain legislative victories, such as limitations on hours. And finally, as the contradictions of the capitalist system become more extreme, a revolutionary party is formed, consisting of the proletariat and that part of the bourgeoisie that has been driven into the ranks of the workers. It is that party which ultimately overthrows the system and ushers in the communist society which, in the Marxist visions, will not continue to obey the laws of dialectic evolution because it alone will be free from the economic contradictions that have propelled society through its past stages of historical development.[49]

[48]   See chap. 8.
[49]   It is interesting to note some formal parallels in the thought of Karl Marx and Sigmund Freud. Both their theories concern a system that maintains an equilibrium-in-tension between conflicting forces. For Marx the tension is expressed at bottom in contradictions between the mode of production and the social relations of production, but manifests itself in the antagonism between two classes. For Freud the tension is between instinctual impulses (the id), and various personality establishments engaged in the management and control of these impulses (the individual's sense of reality, the superego). Both theorists stress, moreover, that the main strategy of control is a form of repression, politico-economic in one case and psychological in the other. Furthermore, in each case the repressive forces are buttressed by a number of ancillary devices that lead to distortions of reality and consciousness. For Marx, one of the main functions of religion, philosophy, morality, and so on is to disguise the true interests of the workers, and to contribute to a false consciousness in them; for

As in the case of other abstract statements, however, this simplified version of the character of class conflict and its political manifestations gains in qualification and sophistication when we turn to some of Marx's historical analyses and his commentaries on contemporary situations. Consider, for example, his discussion of the different types of conflict that accompany different capitalist strategies.[50] When markets are abundant (as might be the case during a period of colonial expansion) and when extension of the handicraft division of labor serves to provide jobs for displaced agricultural laborers, conflict does not arise between working people and capitalists. Moreover, the absence of conflict traces to the fact that workers have not been displaced by the expansion. Opposition stems rather from the vested guilds and privileged towns. The introduction of machinery, however, does not supply new positions for displaced workers but rather displaces workers from less efficient branches of industry producing the commodity in question. The fact of technological unemployment, plus the fact that machinery disciplines laborers and makes them docile[51] provides the structural basis for the development of worker antagonism toward machinery. While Marx's conclusions regarding technological displacement may be challenged—for example, by the fa-

---

Freud various mechanisms of defense such as projection, isolation, rationalization, and displacement distort the true nature of impulses and obscure them from the individual. For Marx, moreover, the structure of society results from the efforts of the dominant class to save itself from the destructive impact of societal contradictions; for Freud, the structure of the personality (character traits, symptoms, and so forth) is geared in large measure to saving the individual from the destructive impact of his inner conflicts. Finally, for both authors, freedom from repression is gained by an expansion of awareness (consciousness) of the conflicts besetting the system. For Marx, however, freedom expresses itself in the destruction of the system and the creation of a conflict-free one, whereas for Freud freedom expresses itself in the dissolution of symptoms and in the increased capacity of the individual to redirect the previously conflict-bound energy into productive activity.

[50]   See chap. 15, sec. I.

[51]   See chap. 15, sec. I. Note in particular Marx's savage attack on Andrew Ure, the apologist for the capitalist, who acknowledged the "calming" effect of machinery and approved of it.

miliar argument that displaced workers may be absorbed by expansion elsewhere in the system—it remains the case that his structurally grounded explanations of the variations in group conflict are more precise and are open to less objection than the generalized account of unfolding stages of worker consciousness.

According to Marx's general theory, the political orientation of classes is largely determined by their relations to the means of production and according to the stage of development of the society. For example, in the early stages of capitalist development, the bourgeoisie are the primary revolutionaries, the landlords the conservatives; in the later stages of capitalist development, the bourgeoisie's political orientation becomes conservative in relation to the revolutionary posture of the proletariat. In addition, however, any given society at any given time is in a stage of transition, and is characterized by elements of the old order that have not been obliterated by the process of change. Thus, in nineteenth-century Europe the peasants and the landlords, remnants of the feudal era, were still significant political forces. The political situation at any point in time, then, is not a conflict between two forces —though such a conflict may be a dominant one—but rather a complicated balance of forces representing the various groups that characterize the political life of the society. This formulation opens the door to a level of analysis beyond that suggested by the principle of the dialectic. It suggests a political situation that must be analyzed in terms of shifting coalitions among groups, shifting strategies among leaders, political compromise, and the like. In short, it suggests a line of political analysis that relies on a wider range of variables than are available by referring to the economic base of the political groups.

Such a line of analysis is evident in some of Marx's historical essays and political commentaries. In his analysis of the political turmoil between 1848 and 1851 in France, for example,[52] his main focus is on the short-term political strategies and tactics of the leaders of important political groups. True, a sense of the inevitability of the success of the bourgeoisie infuses the analysis in *The*

[52]   See chap. 15, sec. II.

Eighteenth Brumaire; and the general political orientations of the bourgeoisie, the peasants, the petty bourgeoisie, and the rest are in keeping with material positions of these groups. But the behavior of the groups also rests on their short-term strategic relations with other groups. When the proletariat, for example, after a momentary victory in Paris, were crushed by the bourgeoisie and their allies in the June Insurrection, they changed political strategies and began to form temporary and shifting alliances with other classes.[53] To choose another example, the peasantry emerges as the unwitting ally of the bourgeoisie because it has not yet realized that it is no longer opposed to feudal landlords but has slipped under the control of capital.[54] And Bonaparte appears to be a kind of "political man," attempting to shore up his tenuous political position by adopting programs that appeal first to one and then to another of the groups that have coalesced to put him in power.[55] Marx's historical treatment is certainly not above criticism; in particular he seemed to downplay any internal diversity among the various political groups and any divergence between the leaders and the masses in those groups. Yet the analysis in *The Eighteenth Brumaire* provides a more subtle and sophisticated account of the mechanisms of political conflict and political processes than would be suggested by the general theoretical propositions relating economic position and political behavior.

Engels's commentary on the political turmoil in Germany in the same years seems less satisfactory,[56] since its primary explanation of the success of the counterrevolution in Germany rests on the simple argument that the residue of feudalism was greater in Germany than in France or England, and its bourgeoisie and proletariat less developed—in short, that it was at an earlier "stage" than those countries and that a proletarian revolution could not therefore succeed. The same general logic is in the background of *The Eighteenth Brumaire,* but Marx supplemented it with a more detailed account of political maneuverings. Nevertheless, Engels

53   See chap. 15, sec. II.
54   See chap. 15, sec. II.
55   See chap. 15, sec. II.
56   See chap. 15, sec. III.

did attempt to refer to the distinctive political characteristics of Germany, especially its geographical fragmentation and dispersion.

One final selection—from the *Critique of the Gotha Programme*—is included to illustrate further that Marx, while a believer in revolutionary change, was nonetheless in many respects a gradualist. In his and Engels's writings on the turmoil of the mid-nineteenth century, it is clear that the historical movement from one type of society (for example, feudal) to another (for example, capitalistic), while eventuating in a total conquest by the latter, nevertheless consistently retained a layering of the structures and social groups associated with the old order. Similarly, Marx's view of the transition from capitalism to communism is seen not as an immediate or automatic transition, but as requiring a significant period of systematic onslaught on the characteristics of the old order, indeed a dictatorship of the workers to secure the transition.[57] Marx appreciated the tenacity of tradition and vested interests even in periods of revolutionary transition.

Conclusion

If a single purpose has dominated my efforts in collecting this particular group of selections from Marx, it is that most of what is sociologically valuable in Marx is not found in his philosophical critiques, his version of the dialectic, or his polemic defenses of materialism. It is found, instead, in his more concrete discussions of the composition, structure, and functioning of societies; and in his empirically informed—"middle-range" if you will—analyses of the processes and mechanisms of change. These contributions themselves are, of course, subject to criticism and modification. For example, Marx probably exaggerated the lengths to which society would permit capitalists indiscriminately to press strategies of worker exploitation to their physiological limits; he probably also underestimated the degree to which the state would evolve as an agency independent of the capitalist classes, and as-

---

[57] For further discussion of the transition see V. I. Lenin, *The State and Revolution* (New York: International Publishers, 1932), pp. 15–20.

sume an increasingly mediating role between the classes.[58] These and other familiar criticisms should not obscure the fact, however, that these more specific insights and propositions are more amenable to fruitful combination with other knowledge about the functioning of society than are the grand principles of Marxian theory.

Neil J. Smelser

---

[58]   Note Engels's observation (chap. 5), that some exceptional periods occur "when the warring classes are so nearly equal in forces that the state power, as apparent mediator, acquires for the moment a certain independence in relation to both."

Notes on Reproduction and Editing

CHAPTER 1 was reproduced, with minor editorial changes, from a letter from Marx to P. V. Annenkov, dated Brussels, 28 December 1846, in Karl Marx and Friedrich Engels, *Selected Correspondence, 1846–1895,* translated by Donna Torr (New York: International Publishers, 1942), reprinted by permission of International Publishers Co., Inc.; and from the Preface to Karl Marx, *A Contribution to the Critique of Political Economy* ([1859]; Chicago: Kerr, 1913), pp. 11–13. Chapters 2 and 7 were reproduced, with minor editorial changes, from Karl Marx and Friedrich Engels, *The German Ideology,* parts 1 and 2, edited and with an introduction by R. Pascal (New York: International Publishers, 1939), pp. 16–21, 7–13. Chapter 3 was reproduced from Karl Marx, "Contribution to a Critique of Hegel's Philosophy of Right," in Karl Marx, *Early Writings,* translated and edited by T. B. Bottomore, with a foreword by Erich Fromm (New York: McGraw-Hill; London: C. A. Watts, 1964), pp. 43–44. Copyright 1964 by McGraw-Hill. Used with permission of McGraw-Hill Book Company. Chapters 4 and 11 were reproduced, with minor editorial changes, from Karl Marx, *Capital: A Critique of Political Economy,* vol. 3, *The Process of Capitalist Production as a Whole,* edited by Friedrich Engels; translated from the first German edition by Ernest Untermann (Chicago: Kerr, 1909), pp. 1031–32, 100–105. Chapter 5 and chapter 6, section I were reproduced from Friedrich Engels, *The Origin of the Family, Private Property, and the State* (New York: International Publishers, 1969), pp. 154–58, 57–73. Reprinted by permission of International Publishers

Co., Inc. Chapter 6, sections II and III, chapters 12, 13, and chapter 15, section I were reproduced, with minor editorial changes, from Karl Marx, *Capital: A Critique of Political Economy*, vol. 1, *The Process of Capitalistic Production*, edited by Friedrich Engels; translated from the third German edition by Samuel Moore and Edward Aveling (London: George Allen and Unwin, 1949), pp. 391–400, 469–80, 495–97, 642–60, 449–62, 427–38. Chapter 6, section IV, and chapter 8 were reproduced, with minor editorial changes, from Karl Marx and Friedrich Engels, *The Communist Manifesto*, with an introduction by Stefan T. Possony (Chicago: Henry Regnery, 1954), pp. 31–33, 9–25. Chapter 9 was reproduced from Karl Marx, *Economic and Philosophic Manuscripts of 1844*, edited and with an introduction by Dirk J. Struik; translated by Martin Milligan (New York: International Publishers, 1964), pp. 132–35, reprinted by permission of International Publishers Co., Inc.; and from *The Communist Manifesto*, pp. 36–37. Chapter 10 was reproduced, with minor editorial changes, from Karl Marx, *Wage-Labour and Capital* (New York: International Publishers, 1933), pp. 43–48. Chapter 14, section I was reproduced from "The Future Results of British Rule in India," *New York Daily Tribune*, 8 August 1853; section II from "Revolution in China and in Europe," *New York Daily Tribune*, 14 June 1853; both reprinted in *Karl Marx on Colonialism and Modernization*, edited and with an introduction by Shlomo Avineri (Garden City, N.Y.: Doubleday, 1969). Chapter 15, section II was reproduced, with some of the explanatory footnotes, from Karl Marx, *The Eighteenth Brumaire of Louis Bonaparte* (New York: International Publishers, 1969), pp. 15–25, 118–35. Chapter 15, section III was reproduced, with minor omissions, from Friedrich Engels, *Germany: Revolution and Counter-Revolution* (New York: International Publishers, 1933), pp. 9–17. Chapter 16 was reproduced, with minor editorial changes, from Karl Marx, *Critique of the Gotha Programme*, revised translation (New York: International Publishers, 1970), pp. 8–10, 18. Reprinted by permission of International Publishers Co., Inc.

Footnotes signed "N. J. S." are by the editor of this volume;

footnotes signed "Ed." are by the editor of the volume from which the selection was reprinted; all unsigned footnotes are Marx's.

Morris Janowitz, editor of The Heritage of Sociology, gave me very valuable advice on the selections and their organizations. I also received helpful criticisms and suggestions on an earlier draft of the Introduction from Jeff Alexander, Faruk Birtek, and Leo Lowenthal.

If it were the custom for an editor to dedicate an edition of another man's work, then I would dedicate my efforts here to my parents, Joseph and Susie Smelser, in the year of their golden anniversary.

I. The Structure of Society

1

THE MATERIAL BASIS OF SOCIETY

I

WHAT IS SOCIETY, whatever its form may be? The product of men's reciprocal activity. Are men free to choose this or that form of society for themselves? By no means. Assume a particular state of development in the productive forces of man and you will get a particular form of commerce and consumption. Assume particular stages of development in production, commerce, and consumption and you will have a corresponding social order, a corresponding organization of the family and of the ranks and classes, in a word a corresponding civil society. Presuppose a particular civil society and you will get particular political conditions which are only the official expression of civil society. M. Proudhon will never understand this because he thinks he is doing something great by appealing from the State to society—that is to say from the official summary of society to official society.

It is superfluous to add that men are not free to choose their *productive forces*—which are the basis of all their history—for every productive force is an acquired force, the product of former activity.

The productive forces are therefore the result of practical human energy; but this energy is itself conditioned by the circumstances in which men find themselves, by the productive forces already won, by the social form which exists before they do, which

---

Section I of this chapter is from a letter from Marx to P. V. Annenkov, dated Brussels, 28 December 1846; section II is from the Preface to *A Contribution to a Critique of Political Economy*, pp. 11–13, written in 1859.

4 THE STRUCTURE OF SOCIETY

they do not create, which is the product of the former generation. Because of this simple fact that every succeeding generation finds itself in possession of the productive forces won by the previous generation which serve it as the raw material for new production, a connection arises in human history, a history of humanity takes shape which has become all the more a history of humanity since the productive forces of man and therefore his social relations have been extended. Hence it necessarily follows: the social history of men is never anything but the history of their individual development, whether they are conscious of it or not. Their material relations are the basis of all their relations. These material relations are only the necessary forms in which their material and individual activity is realized.

M. Proudhon mixes up ideas and things. Men never relinquish what they have won, but this does not mean that they never relinquish the social form in which they have acquired certain productive forces. On the contrary, in order that they may not be deprived of the result attained, and forfeit the fruits of civilization, they are obliged, from the moment when the form of their intercourse [Fr. *commerce*] no longer corresponds to the productive forces acquired, to change all their traditional social forms. I am using the [French] word *commerce* here in its widest sense, as we use *Verkehr* in German. For example: The institution and privileges of guilds and corporations, the regulatory regime of the Middle Ages, were social relations corresponding only to the acquired productive forces and to the social condition which had previously existed and from which these institutions had arisen. Under the protection of this regime of corporations and regulations capital was accumulated, overseas trade was developed, colonies were founded. But the fruits of this would themselves have been forfeited if men had tried to retain the forms under whose shelter these fruits had ripened. Hence came two thunderclaps—the revolutions of 1640 and 1688.[1] All the old economic forms, the social relations corresponding to them, the political conditions which were the official expression of the old civil society, were destroyed

[1]   In England.

in England. Thus the economic forms in which men produce, consume, exchange, are *transitory and historical*. When new productive forces are won men change their method of production and with the method of production all the economic relations which are merely the necessary conditions of this particular method of production.

II

In the social production of their life, men enter into definite relations that are indispensable and independent of their will, relations of production which correspond to a definite stage of development of their material productive forces. The sum total of these relations of production constitute the economic structure of society, the real foundation, on which rises a legal and political superstructure and to which correspond definite forms of social consciousness. The mode of production of material life conditions the social, political, and intellectual life process in general. It is not the consciousness of men that determines their being, but, on the contrary, their social being that determines their consciousness. At a certain stage of their development, the material productive forces of society come in conflict with the existing relations of production, or—what is but a legal expression for the same thing —with the property relations within which they have been at work hitherto. From forms of development of the productive forces these relations turn into their fetters. Then begins an epoch of social revolution. With the change of the economic foundation the entire immense superstructure is more or less rapidly transformed. In considering such transformations a distinction should always be made between the material transformation of the economic conditions of production, which can be determined with the precision of natural science, and the legal, political, religious, aesthetic, or philosophic—in short, ideological forms in which men become conscious of this conflict and fight it out. Just as our opinion of an individual is not based on what he thinks of himself, so can we not judge of such a period of transformation by its own consciousness; on the contrary, this consciousness must be explained rather from the contradictions of material life, from the existing conflict between the social productive forces and the relations of production. No social order ever perishes before all the productive forces for which there is room in it have developed; and new, higher relations of production never appear before the material conditions of their existence have matured in the womb of the old society itself. Therefore mankind always sets itself only such tasks as it can solve; since, looking at the matter more closely, it will always be found that the task itself arises only when the material conditions for its solution already exist or are at least in the process of formation. In broad outlines Asiatic, ancient, feudal, and modern bourgeois modes of production can be designated as progressive epochs in the economic formation of society. The bourgeois relations of production are the last antagonistic form of the social process of production—antagonistic not in the sense of individual antagonism, but of one arising from the social conditions of life of the individuals; at the same time the productive forces developing in the womb of bourgeois society create the material conditions for the solution of that antagonism. This social formation brings, therefore, the prehistory of human society to a close.

2

THE BASIS OF CONSCIOUSNESS

SINCE we are dealing with the Germans, who do not postulate anything, we must begin by stating the first premise of all human existence, and therefore of all history, the premise namely that men must be in a position to live in order to be able to "make history." But life involves before everything else eating and drinking, a habitation, clothing, and many other things. The first historical act is thus the production of the means to satisfy these needs, the production of material life itself. And indeed this is a historical act, a fundamental condition of all history, which today, as thousands of years ago, must daily and hourly be fulfilled merely in order to sustain human life. Even when the sensuous world is reduced to a minimum, to a stick as with Saint Bruno,[1] it presupposes the action of producing the stick. The first necessity therefore in any theory of history is to observe this fundamental fact in all its significance and all its implications and to accord it its due importance. This, as is notorious, the Germans have never done, and they have never therefore had an earthly basis for history and consequently never a historian. The French and the English, even if they have conceived the relation of this fact with so-called history only in an extremely one-sided fashion, particularly as long as they remained in the toils of political ideology, have nevertheless made the first attempts to give the writing of history a materialistic basis

---

From Karl Marx and Friedrich Engels, *The German Ideology*, pp. 16–21.

[1]   Bruno Bauer.—N.J.S.

by being the first to write histories of civil society, of commerce and industry.

The second fundamental point is that as soon as a need is satisfied (which implies the action of satisfying, and the acquisition of an instrument), new needs are made; and this production of new needs is the first historical act. Here we recognize immediately the spiritual ancestry of the great historical wisdom of the Germans who, when they run out of positive material and when they can serve up neither theological nor political nor literary rubbish, do not write history at all, but invent the "prehistoric era." They do not, however, enlighten us as to how we proceed from this nonsensical "prehistory" to history proper; although, on the other hand, in their historical speculation they seize upon this "prehistory" with especial eagerness because they imagine themselves safe there from interference on the part of "crude facts," and, at the same time, because there they can give full rein to their speculative impulse and set up and knock down hypotheses by the thousand.

The third circumstance which, from the very first, enters into historical development, is that men, who daily remake their own life, begin to make other men, to propagate their kind: the relation between man and wife, parents and children, the family. The family which to begin with is the only social relationship, becomes later, when increased needs create new social relations and the increased population new needs, a subordinate one (except in Germany), and must then be treated and analyzed according to the existing empirical data,[2] not according to "the concept of the family," as is

---

[2]   The building of houses. With savages each family has of course its own cave or hut like the separate family tent of the nomads. This separate domestic economy is made only the more necessary by the further development of private property. With the agricultural peoples a communal domestic economy is just as impossible as a communal cultivation of the soil. A great advance was the building of towns. In all previous periods, however, the abolition of individual economy, which is inseparable from the abolition of private property, was impossible for the simple reason that the material conditions governing it were not present. The setting-up of a communal domestic economy presupposes the development of machinery, of the use of natural forces and of many other productive forces—e.g. of water-

the custom in Germany. These three aspects of social activity are not of course to be taken as three different stages, but just, as I have said, as three aspects or, to make it clear to the Germans, three "moments,"[3] which have existed simultaneously since the dawn of history and the first men, and still assert themselves in history today.

The production of life, both of one's own in labor and of fresh life in procreation, now appears as a double relationship: on the one hand as a natural, on the other as a social relationship. By social we understand the cooperation of several individuals, no matter under what conditions, in what manner and to what end. It follows from this that a certain mode of production, or industrial stage, is always combined with a certain mode of cooperation, or social stage, and this mode of cooperation is itself a "productive force." Further, that the multitude of productive forces accessible to men determines the nature of society, hence that the "history of humanity" must always be studied and treated in relation to the history of industry and exchange. But it is also clear how in Germany it is impossible to write this sort of history, because the Germans lack not only the necessary power of comprehension and the material but also the "evidence of their senses," for across the Rhine you cannot have any experience of these things since history has stopped happening. Thus it is quite obvious from the start that there exists a materialistic connection of men with one another, which is determined by their needs and their mode of production, and which is as old as men themselves. This connec-

---

supplies, of gas-lighting, steam-heating, etc., the removal of the antagonism of town and country. Without these conditions a communal economy would not in itself form a new productive force; lacking any material basis and resting on a purely theoretical foundation, it would be a mere freak and would end in nothing more than a monastic economy. What was possible can be seen in the formation of towns and the erection of communal buildings for various definite purposes (prisons, barracks, etc.). That the abolition of individual economy is inseparable from the abolition of the family is self-evident.

3   *Moment*: A philosophic term which means "a determining active factor."—N.J.S.

tion is ever taking on new forms, and thus presents a "history" independently of the existence of any political or religious nonsense which would hold men together on its own.

Only now, after having considered four moments, four aspects of the fundamental historical relationships, do we find that man also possesses "consciousness"; but, even so, not inherent, not "pure" consciousness. From the start the "spirit" is afflicted with the curse of being "burdened" with matter, which here makes its appearance in the form of agitated layers of air, sounds, in short of language. Language is as old as consciousness, language is practical consciousness, as it exists for other men, and for that reason is really beginning to exist for me personally as well; for language, like consciousness, only arises from the need, the necessity, of intercourse with other men. Where there exists a relationship, it exists for me: the animal has no "relations" with anything, cannot have any. For the animal, its relation to others does not exist as a relation. Consciousness is therefore from the very beginning a social product, and remains so as long as men exist at all. Consciousness is at first, of course, merely consciousness concerning the immediate sensuous environment and consciousness of the limited connection with other persons and things outside the individual who is growing self-conscious. At the same time it is consciousness of nature, which first appears to men as a completely alien, all-powerful and unassailable force, with which men's relations are purely animal and by which they are overawed like beasts; it is thus a purely animal consciousness of nature (natural religion).

We see here immediately: this natural religion or animal behavior towards nature is determined by the form of society and vice versa. Here, as everywhere, the identity of nature and man appears in such a way that the restricted relation of men to nature determines their restricted relation to one another, and their restricted relation to one another determines men's restricted relation to nature, just because nature is as yet hardly modified historically; and, on the other hand, man's consciousness of the necessity of associating with the individuals around him is the beginning of the consciousness that he is living in society at all. This beginning is as animal as social life itself at this stage. It is mere herd-consciousness, and at this point man is only distinguished from sheep by the fact that with him consciousness takes the place of instinct or that his instinct is a conscious one.

This sheeplike or tribal consciousness receives its further development and extension through increased productivity, the increase of needs, and, what is fundamental to both of these, the increase of population. With these there develops the division of labor, which was originally nothing but the division of labor in the sexual act, then that division of labor which develops spontaneously or "naturally" by virtue of natural predisposition (e.g., physical strength), needs, accidents, etc., etc. Division of labor only becomes truly such from the moment when a division of material and mental labor appears. From this moment onwards consciousness *can* really flatter itself that it is something other than consciousness of existing practice, that it is *really* conceiving something without conceiving something *real*; from now on consciousness is in a position to emancipate itself from the world and to proceed to the formation of "pure" theory, theology, philosophy, ethics, etc. But even if this theory, theology, philosophy, ethics, etc. comes into contradiction with the existing relations, this can only occur as a result of the fact that existing social relations have come into contradiction with existing forces of production; this, moreover, can also occur in a particular national sphere of relations through the appearance of the contradiction, not within the national orbit, but between this national consciousness and the practice of other nations, i.e., between the national and the general consciousness of a nation.

Moreover, it is quite immaterial what consciousness starts to do on its own: out of all such muck we get only the one inference that these three moments, the forces of production, the state of society, and consciousness, can and must come into contradiction with one another, because the division of labor implies the possibility, nay the fact that intellectual and material activity—enjoyment and labor, production and consumption—devolve on different individuals, and that the only possibility of their not coming into contradiction lies in the negation in its turn of the division of labor. It is self-evident, moreover, that "spectres," "bonds," "the higher being," "concept," "scruple," are merely the idealistic, spiritual expression, the conception apparently of the isolated individual, the image of very empirical fetters and limitations, within which the mode of production of life, and the form of intercourse coupled with it, move.

3

THE BASIS OF RELIGION

For GERMANY, the *criticism of religion* has been largely completed; and the criticism of religion is the premise of all criticism.

The *profane* existence of error is compromised once its *celestial oratio pro aris et focis* has been refuted. Man, who has found in the fantastic reality of heaven, where he sought a supernatural being, only his own reflection, will no longer be tempted to find only the *semblance* of himself—a nonhuman being—where he seeks and must seek his true reality.

The basis of irreligious criticism is this: *man makes religion;* religion does not make man. Religion is indeed man's self-consciousness and self-awareness so long as he has not found himself or has lost himself again. But *man* is not an abstract being, squatting outside the world. Man is *the human world,* the state, society. This state, this society, produce religion which is an *inverted world consciousness,* because they are an *inverted world.* Religion is the general theory of this world, its encyclopedic compendium, its logic in popular form, its spiritual *point d'honneur,* its enthusiasm, its moral sanction, its solemn complement, its general basis of consolation and justification. It is *the fantastic realization* of the human being inasmuch as the *human being* possesses no true reality. The struggle against religion is, therefore, indirectly a struggle against *that world* whose spiritual *aroma* is religion.

From "Contribution to a Critique of Hegel's Philosophy of Right," pp. 43–44.

Religious suffering is at the same time an *expression* of real suffering and a *protest* against real suffering. Religion is the sigh of the oppressed creature, the sentiment of a heartless world, and the soul of soulless conditions. It is the *opium* of the people.

The abolition of religion as the *illusory* happiness of men, is a demand for their *real* happiness. The call to abandon their illusions about their condition is a *call to abandon a condition which requires illusions.* The criticism of religion is, therefore, *the embryonic criticism of this vale of tears* of which religion is the *halo.*

Criticism has plucked the imaginary flowers from the chain, not in order that man shall bear the chain without caprice or consolation but so that he shall cast off the chain and pluck the living flower. The criticism of religion disillusions man so that he will think, act, and fashion his reality as a man who has lost his illusions and regained his reason; so that he will revolve about himself as his own true sun. Religion is only the illusory sun about which man revolves so long as he does not revolve about himself.

It is the *task of history*, therefore, once the *other-world of truth* has vanished, to establish the *truth of this world*. The immediate *task of philosophy*, which is in the service of history, is to unmask human self-alienation in its *secular form* now that it has been unmasked in its *sacred form*. Thus the criticism of heaven is transformed into the criticism of earth, the *criticism of religion* into the *criticism of law*, and the *criticism of theology* into the *criticism of politics.*

4

THE BASIS OF CLASSES

THE OWNERS of mere labor-power, the owners of capital, and the landlords, whose respective sources of income are wages, profit, and ground-rent, in other words, wage laborers, capitalists, and landlords, form the three great classes of modern society resting upon the capitalist mode of production.

In England, modern society is indisputably developed most highly and classically in its economic structure. Nevertheless the stratification of classes does not appear in its pure form, even there. Middle and transition stages obliterate even here all definite boundaries, although much less in the rural districts than in the cities. However, this is immaterial for our analysis. We have seen that the continual tendency and law of development of capitalist production is to separate the means of production more and more from labor, and to concentrate the scattered means of production more and more in large groups, thereby transforming labor into wage labor and the means of production into capital. In keeping with this tendency we have, on the other hand, the independent separation of private land from capital and labor,[1] or the trans-

---

From *Capital*, 3:1031–32.

1   F. List remarks correctly: "Prevalence of self-management in the case of large estates proves only a lack of civilization, of means of communication, of home industries and rich cities. For this reason it is found everywhere in Russia, Poland, Hungary, Mecklenburg. Formerly it prevailed also in England. But with the rise of commerce and industry came their division into medium-sized farms and their occupancy by tenants" (*The Agrarian Constitution, the Petty Farm, and Emigration* [1842], p. 10).

formation of all property in land into a form of landed property corresponding to the capitalist mode of production.

The first question to be answered is this: What constitutes a class? And this follows naturally from another question, namely: What constitutes wage laborers, capitalists, and landlords into three great social classes?

At first glance it might seem that the identity of their revenues and their sources of revenue does that. They are three great social groups, whose component elements, the individuals forming them, live on wages, profit, and ground-rent, or by the utilization of their labor-power, their capital, and their private land.

However, from this point of view physicians and officials would also form two classes, for they belong to the two distinct social groups, and the revenues of their members flow from the same common source. The same would also be true of the infinite dissipation of interests and positions created by the social division of labor among laborers, capitalists, and landlords. For instance, the landlords are divided into owners of vineyards, farms, forests, miners, fisheries.

5

THE BASIS OF THE STATE

THE THREE main forms in which the state arises on the ruins of the gentile constitution have been examined in detail above. Athens provides the purest, classic form; here the state springs directly and mainly out of the class oppositions which develop within gentile society itself. In Rome, gentile society becomes a closed aristocracy in the midst of the numerous *plebs* who stand outside it, and have duties but no rights; the victory of *plebs* breaks up the old constitution based on kinship, and erects on its ruins the state, into which both the gentile aristocracy and the *plebs* are soon completely absorbed. Lastly, in the case of the German conquerors of the Roman Empire, the state springs directly out of the conquest of large foreign territories, which the gentile constitution provides no means of governing. But because this conquest involves neither a serious struggle with the original population nor a more advanced division of labor; because conquerors and conquered are almost on the same level of economic development, and the economic basis of society remains therefore as before—for these reasons the gentile constitution is able to survive for many centuries in the altered, territorial form of the mark constitution and even for a time to rejuvenate itself in a feebler shape in the later noble and patrician families, and indeed in peasant families, as in Ditmarschen.

The state is therefore by no means a power imposed on society from without; just as little is it "the reality of the moral idea," "the

---

From Friedrich Engels, *The Origin of the Family, Private Property, and the State*, pp. 154–58.

image and the reality of reason," as Hegel maintains. Rather, it is a product of society at a particular stage of development; it is the admission that this society has involved itself in insoluble self-contradiction and is cleft into irreconcilable antagonisms which it is powerless to exorcise. But in order that these antagonisms, classes with conflicting economic interests, shall not consume themselves and society in fruitless struggle, a power, apparently standing above society, has become necessary to moderate the conflict and keep it within the bounds of "order"; and this power, arisen out of society, but placing itself above it and increasingly alienating itself from it, is the state.

In contrast to the old gentile organization, the state is distinguished firstly by the grouping of its members *on a territorial basis*. The old gentile bodies, formed and held together by ties of blood, had, as we have seen, become inadequate largely because they presupposed that the gentile members were bound to one particular locality, whereas this had long ago ceased to be the case. The territory was still there, but the people had become mobile. The territorial division was therefore taken as the starting point and the system introduced by which citizens exercised their public rights and duties where they took up residence, without regard to gens or tribe. This organization of the citizens of the state according to domicile is common to all states. To us, therefore, this organization seems natural; but, as we have seen, hard and protracted struggles were necessary before it was able in Athens and Rome to displace the old organization founded on kinship.

The second distinguishing characteristic is the institution of a *public force* which is no longer immediately identical with the people's own organization of themselves as an armed power. This special public force is needed because a self-acting armed organization of the people has become impossible since their cleavage into classes. The slaves also belong to the population: as against the 365,000 slaves, the 90,000 Athenian citizens constitute only a privileged class. The people's army of the Athenian democracy confronted the slaves as an aristocratic public force, and kept them in check; but to keep the citizens in check as well, a police force was needed, as described above. This public force exists in every state;

it consists not merely of armed men, but also of material appendages, prisons, and coercive institutions of all kinds, of which gentile society knew nothing. It may be very insignificant, practically negligible, in societies with still undeveloped class antagonisms and living in remote areas, as at times and in places in the United States of America. But it becomes stronger in proportion as the class antagonisms within the state become sharper and as adjoining states grow larger and more populous. It is enough to look at Europe today, where class struggle and rivalry in conquest have brought the public power to a pitch that it threatens to devour the whole of society and even the state itself.

In order to maintain this public power, contributions from the state citizens are necessary—*taxes*. These were completely unknown to gentile society. We know more than enough about them today. With advancing civilization, even taxes are not sufficient; the state draws drafts on the future, contracts loans, *state debts*. Our old Europe can tell a tale about these, too.

In possession of the public power and the right of taxation, the officials now present themselves as organs of society standing *above* society. The free, willing respect accorded to the organs of the gentile constitution is not enough for them, even if they could have it. Representatives of a power which estranges them from society, they have to be given prestige by means of special decrees, which invest them with a peculiar sanctity and inviolability. The lowest police officer of the civilized state has more "authority" than all the organs of gentile society put together; but the mightiest prince and the greatest statesman or general of civilization might envy the humblest of the gentile chiefs the unforced and unquestioned respect accorded to him. For the one stands in the midst of society; the other is forced to pose as something outside and above it.

As the state arose from the need to keep class antagonisms in check, but also arose in the thick of the fight between the classes, it is normally the state of the most powerful, economically ruling class, which by its means becomes also the politically ruling class, and so acquires new means of holding down and exploiting the oppressed class. The ancient state was, above all, the state of the slave-owners for holding down the slaves, just as the feudal state was the organ of the nobility for holding down the peasant serfs and bonds-men, and the modern representative state is the instrument for exploiting wage-labor by capital. Exceptional periods, however, occur when the warring classes are so nearly equal in forces that the state power, as apparent mediator, acquires for the moment a certain independence in relation to both. This applies to the abso-lute monarchy of the seventeenth and eighteenth centuries, which balances the nobility and the bourgeoisie against one another; and to the Bonapartism of the First and particularly of the Second French Empire, which played off the proletariat against the bour-geoisie and the bourgeoisie against the proletariat. The latest achievement in this line, in which ruler and ruled look equally comic, is the new German Empire of the Bismarckian nation; here the capitalists and the workers are balanced against one another and both of them fleeced for the benefit of the decayed Prussian cabbage junkers.

Further, in most historical states the rights conceded to citizens are graded on a property basis, whereby it is directly admitted that the state is an organization for the protection of the possessing class against the nonpossessing class. This is already the case in the Athenian and Roman property classes. Similarly in the medieval feudal state, in which the extent of political power was determined by the extent of land-ownership. Similarly, also, in the electoral qualifications in modern parliamentary states. This political recog-nition of property differences is, however, by no means essential. On the contrary, it marks a low stage in the development of the state. The highest form of the state, the democratic republic, which in our modern social conditions becomes more and more an un-avoidable necessity and is the form of state in which alone the last decisive battle between proletariat and bourgeoisie can be fought out—the democratic republic no longer officially recognizes dif-ferences of property. Wealth here employs its power indirectly, but all the more surely. It does this in two ways: by plain corruption of officials, of which America is the classic example, and by an alliance between the government and the stock exchange, which is effected all the more easily the higher the state debt mounts and the more the joint-stock companies concentrate in their hands not only transport but also production itself, and themselves have their own center in the stock exchange. In addition to America, the latest French republic illustrates this strikingly, and honest little Switzerland has also given a creditable performance in this field. But that a democratic republic is not essential to this brotherly bond between government and stock exchange is proved not only by England, but also by the new German Empire, where it is difficult to say who scored most by the introduction of universal suffrage, Bismarck or the Bleichröder bank. And lastly the possessing class rules directly by means of universal suffrage. As long as the oppressed class—in our case, therefore, the proletariat—is not yet ripe for its self-liberation, so long will it, in its majority, recognize the existing order of society as the only possible one and remain politically the tail of the capitalist class, its extreme left wing. But in the measure in which it matures towards its self-emancipation, in the same measure it constitutes itself as its own party and votes for its own representatives, not those of the capitalists. Universal suffrage is thus the gauge of the maturity of the working class. It cannot and never will be anything more in the modern state; but that is enough. On the day when the thermometer of universal suffrage shows boiling-point among the workers, they as well as the capitalists will know where they stand.

The state, therefore, has not existed from all eternity. There have been societies which have managed without it, which had no notion of the state or state power. At a definite stage of economic development, which necessarily involved the cleavage of society into classes, the state became a necessity because of this cleavage. We are now rapidly approaching a stage in the development of production at which the existence of these classes has not only ceased to be a necessity, but becomes a positive hindrance to production. They will fall as inevitably as they once arose. The state inevitably falls with them. The society which organizes production anew on the basis of free and equal association of the producers will put the whole state machinery where it will then belong—into the museum of antiquities, next to the spinning wheel and the bronze ax.

6

THE BASIS OF THE FAMILY

1. *The Economic Origins of Monogamy*

THIS IS the origin of monogamy as far as we can trace it back among the most civilized and highly developed people of antiquity. It was not in any way the fruit of individual sex-love, with which it had nothing whatever to do; marriages remained as before marriages of convenience. It was the first form of the family to be based, not on natural, but on economic conditions—on the victory of private property over primitive, natural communal property. The Greeks themselves put the matter quite frankly: the sole exclusive aims of monogamous marriage were to make the man supreme in the family, and to propagate, as the future heirs to his wealth, children indisputably his own. Otherwise, marriage was a burden, a duty which had to be performed, whether one liked it or not, to gods, state, and one's ancestors. In Athens the law exacted from the man not only marriage but also the performance of a minimum of so-called conjugal duties.

Thus when monogamous marriage first makes its appearance in history, it is not as the reconciliation of man and woman, still less as the highest form of such a reconciliation. Quite the contrary. Monogamous marriage comes on the scene as the subjugation of the one sex by the other; it announces a struggle between

---

Section I of this chapter is from Friedrich Engels, *The Origin of The Family, Private Property, and the State*, pp. 57–73; section II from *Capital*, 1:391–400; section III from *Capital*, 1:469–80, 495–97; and section IV from *The Communist Manifesto*, pp. 31–33.

the sexes unknown throughout the whole previous prehistoric period. In an old unpublished manuscript, written by Marx and myself in 1846,[1] I find the words: "The first division of labor is that between man and woman for the propagation of children." And today I can add: The first class opposition that appears in history coincides with the development of the antagonism between man and woman in monogamous marriage, and the first class oppression coincides with that of the female sex by the male. Monogamous marriage was a great historical step forward; nevertheless, together with slavery and private wealth, it opens the period that has lasted until today in which every step forward is also relatively a step backward, in which prosperity and development for some is won through the misery and frustration of others. It is the cellular form of civilized society, in which the nature of the oppositions and contradictions fully active in that society can be already studied.

The old comparative freedom of sexual intercourse by no means disappeared with the victory of pairing marriage or even of monogamous marriage: "The old conjugal system, now reduced to narrower limits by the gradual disappearance of the punaluan groups, still environed the advancing family, which it was to follow to the verge of civilization. . . . It finally disappeared in the new form of hetaerism, which still follows mankind in civilization as a dark shadow upon the family."[2]

By "hetaerism" Morgan understands the practice, *co-existent with monogamous marriage*, of sexual intercourse between men and unmarried women outside marriage, which, as we know, flourishes in the most varied forms throughout the whole period of civilization and develops more and more into open prostitution. This hetaerism derives quite directly from group marriage, from the ceremonial surrender by which women purchased the right of chastity. Surrender for money was at first a religious act; it took

[1]   The reference here is to the *German Ideology* written by Marx and Engels in Brussels in 1845–46.—Ed.
[2]   Lewis H. Morgan, *Ancient Society, or Researches in the Lives of Human Progress from Savagery through Barbarism to Civilization* (London: Macmillan, 1877), p. 511.—N.J.S.

place in the temple of the goddess of love, and the money originally went into the temple treasury. The temple slaves of Anaitis in Armenia and of Aphrodite in Corinth, like the sacred dancing-girls attached to the temples of India, the so-called *bayaderes* (the word is a corruption of the Portuguese word *bailadeira*, meaning female dancer), were the first prostitutes. Originally the duty of every woman, this surrender was later performed by these priestesses alone as representatives of all other women. Among other peoples, hetaerism derives from the sexual freedom allowed to girls before marriage—again, therefore, a relic of group marriage, but handed down in a different way. With the rise of the inequality of property —already at the upper stage of barbarism, therefore—wage-labor appears sporadically side by side with slave labor, and at the same time, as its necessary correlate, the professional prostitution of free women side by side with the forced surrender of the slave. Thus the heritage which group marriage has bequeathed to civilization is double-edged, just as everything civilization brings forth is double-edged, double-tongued, divided against itself, contradictory: here monogamy, there hetaerism, with its most extreme form, prostitution. For hetaerism is as much a social institution as any other; it continues the old sexual freedom—to the advantage of the men. Actually not merely tolerated, but gaily practiced, by the ruling classes particularly, it is condemned in words. But in reality this condemnation never falls on the men concerned, but only on the women; they are despised and outcast, in order that the unconditional supremacy of men over the female sex may be once more proclaimed as a fundamental law of society.

But a second contradiction thus develops within monogamous marriage itself. At the side of the husband who embellishes his existence with hetaerism stands the neglected wife. And one cannot have one side of this contradiction without the other, any more than a man has a whole apple in his hand after eating half. But that seems to have been the husbands' notion, until their wives taught them better. With monogamous marriage, two constant social types, unknown hitherto, make their appearance on the scene— the wife's attendant lover and the cuckold husband. The husbands had won the victory over the wives, but the vanquished magnanimously provided the crown. Together with monogamous marriage and hetaerism, adultery became an unavoidable social institution —denounced, severely penalized, but impossible to suppress. At best, the certain paternity of the children rested on moral conviction as before, and to solve the insoluble contradiction the *Code Napoléon*, Art. 312, decreed: *"L'enfant conçu pendant le mariage a pour père le mari,"* the father of a child conceived during marriage is—the husband. Such is the final result of three thousand years of monogamous marriage.

Thus, wherever the monogamous family remains true to its historical origin and clearly reveals the antagonism between the man and the woman expressed in the man's exclusive supremacy, it exhibits in miniature the same oppositions and contradictions as those in which society has been moving, without power to resolve or overcome them, ever since it split into classes at the beginning of civilization. I am speaking here, of course, only of those cases of monogamous marriage where matrimonial life actually proceeds according to the original character of the whole institution, but where the wife rebels against the husband's supremacy. Not all marriages turn out thus, as nobody knows better than the German philistine, who can no more assert his rule in the home than he can in the state, and whose wife, with every right, wears the trousers he is worthy of. But, to make up for it, he considers himself far above his French companion in misfortune, to whom, oftener than to him, something much worse happens.

However, monogamous marriage did not by any means appear always and everywhere in the classically harsh form it took among the Greeks. Among the Romans, who, as future world-conquerors, had a larger, if a less fine, vision than the Greeks, women were freer and more respected. A Roman considered that his power of life and death over his wife sufficiently guaranteed her conjugal fidelity. Here, moreover, the wife equally with the husband could dissolve the marriage at will. But the greatest progress in the development of individual marriage certainly came with the entry of the Germans into history, and for the reason that the Germans— on account of their poverty, very probably—were still at a stage where monogamy seems not yet to have become perfectly distinct from pairing marriage. We infer this from three facts mentioned by Tacitus. First, though marriage was held in great reverence—"they content themselves with one wife, the women live hedged round with chastity"—polygamy was the rule for the distinguished members and the leaders of the tribe, a condition of things similar to that among the Americans, where pairing marriage was the rule. Secondly, the transition from mother-right to father-right could only have been made a short time previously, for the brother on the mother's side—the nearest gentile male relation according to mother-right—was still considered almost closer of kin than the father, corresponding again to the standpoint of the American Indians, among whom Marx, as he often said, found the key to the understanding of our own primitive age. And, thirdly, women were greatly respected among the Germans, and also influential in public affairs, which is in direct contradiction to the supremacy of men in monogamy. In almost all these points the Germans agree with the Spartans, among whom also, as we saw, pairing marriage had not yet been completely overcome. Thus, here again an entirely new influence came to power in the world with the Germans. The new monogamy, which now developed from the mingling of peoples amid the ruins of the Roman world, clothed the supremacy of the men in milder forms and gave women a position which, outwardly at any rate, was much more free and respected than it had ever been in classical antiquity. Only now were the conditions realized in which through monogamy—within it, parallel to it, or in opposition to it, as the case might be—the greatest moral advance we owe to it could be achieved: modern individual sex-love, which had hitherto been unknown to the entire world.

This advance, however, undoubtedly sprang from the fact that the Germans still lived in pairing families and grafted the corresponding position of women onto the monogamous system, so far as that was possible. It most decidedly did not spring from the legendary virtue and wonderful moral purity of the German character, which was nothing more than the freedom of the pairing family from the crying moral contradictions of monogamy. On the contrary, in the course of their migrations the Germans had morally much deteriorated, particularly during their southeasterly wanderings among the nomads of the Black Sea steppes, from whom they acquired, not only equestrian skill, but also gross, unnatural vices, as Ammianus expressly states of the Taifalians and Procopius of the Herulians.

But if monogamy was the only one of all the known forms of the family through which modern sex-love could develop, that does not mean that within monogamy modern sexual love developed exclusively or even chiefly as the love of husband and wife for each other. That was precluded by the very nature of strictly monogamous marriage under the rule of the man. Among all historically active classes—that is, among all ruling classes—matrimony remained what it had been since the pairing marriage, a matter of convenience which was arranged by the parents. The first historical form of sexual love as passion, a passion recognized as natural to all human beings (at least if they belonged to the ruling classes), and as the highest form of the sexual impulse—and that is what constitutes its specific character—this first form of individual sexual love, the chivalrous love of the Middle Ages, was by no means conjugal. Quite the contrary. In its classic form among the Provençals, it heads straight for adultery, and the poets of love celebrated adultery. The flower of Provençal love poetry are the Albas (*aubades*, songs of dawn). They describe in glowing colors how the knight lies in bed beside his love—the wife of another man—while outside stands the watchman who calls to him as soon as the first gray of dawn (*alba*) appears, so that he can get away unobserved; the parting scene then forms the climax of the poem. The northern French and also the worthy Germans adopted this kind of poetry together with the corresponding fashion of chivalrous love; old Wolfram of Eschenbach has left us three wonderfully beautiful songs of dawn on this same improper subject, which I like better than his three long heroic poems.

Nowadays there are two ways of concluding a bourgeois marriage. In Catholic countries the parents, as before, procure a suitable wife for their young bourgeois son, and the consequence is, of course, the fullest development of the contradiction inherent in monogamy: the husband abandons himself to hetaerism and the wife to adultery. Probably the only reason why the Catholic Church abolished divorce was because it had convinced itself that there is no more a cure for adultery than there is for death. In Protestant countries, on the other hand, the rule is that the son of a bourgeois family is allowed to choose a wife from his own class with more or less freedom; hence there may be a certain element of love in the marriage, as, indeed, in accordance with Protestant hypocrisy, is always assumed, for decency's sake. Here the husband's hetaerism is a more sleepy kind of business, and adultery by the wife is less the rule. But since, in every kind of marriage, people remain what they were before, and since the bourgeois of Protestant countries are mostly philistines, all that this Protestant monogamy achieves, taking the average of the best cases, is a conjugal partnership of leaden boredom, known as "domestic bliss." The best mirror of these two methods of marrying is the novel—the French novel for the Catholic manner, the German for the Protestant. In both, the hero "gets" them: in the German, the young man gets the girl; in the French, the husband gets the horns. Which of them is worse off is sometimes questionable. This is why the French bourgeois is as much horrified by the dullness of the German novel as the German philistine is by the "immorality" of the French. However, now that "Berlin is a world capital," the German novel is beginning with a little less timidity to use as part of its regular stock-in-trade the hetaerism and adultery long familiar to that town.

In both cases, however, the marriage is conditioned by the class position of the parties and is to that extent always a marriage of convenience. In both cases this marriage of convenience turns often enough into crassest prostitution—sometimes of both partners, but far more commonly of the woman, who only differs from the ordinary courtesan in that she does not let out her body on piece-work as a wage-worker, but sells it once and for all into slavery. And of all marriages of convenience Fourier's words hold true: "As in grammar two negatives make an affirmative, so in matrimonial morality two prostitutions pass for a virtue."[3] Sex-love in the relationship with a woman becomes, and can only become, the

---

[3]   Charles Fourier, *Théorie de l'unité universelle* (Paris, 1841–45) 3:120.—Ed.

real rule among the oppressed classes, which means today among the proletariat—whether this relation is officially sanctioned or not. But here all the foundations of typical monogamy are cleared away. Here there is no property, for the preservation and inheritance of which monogamy and male supremacy were established; hence there is no incentive to make this male supremacy effective. What is more, there are no means of making it so. Bourgeoisie law, which protects this supremacy, exists only for the possessing class and their dealings with the proletarians. The law costs money and, on account of the worker's poverty, it has no validity for his relation to his wife. Here quite other personal and social conditions decide. And now that large-scale industry has taken the wife out of the home onto the labor market and into the factory, and made her often the bread-winner of the family, no basis for any kind of male supremacy is left in the proletarian household—except, perhaps, for something of the brutality towards women that has spread since the introduction of monogamy. The proletarian family is therefore no longer monogamous in the strict sense, even where there is passionate love and firmest loyalty on both sides, and maybe all the blessings of religious and civil authority. Here, therefore, the eternal attendants of monogamy, hetaerism and adultery, play only an almost vanishing part. The wife has in fact regained the right to dissolve the marriage, and if two people cannot get on with one another, they prefer to separate. In short, proletarian marriage is monogamous in the etymological sense of the word, but not at all in its historical sense.

Our jurists, of course, find that progress in legislation is leaving women with no further ground of complaint. Modern civilized systems of law increasingly acknowledge, first, that for a marriage to be legal, it must be a contract freely entered into by both partners, and, secondly, that also in the married state both partners must stand on a common footing of equal rights and duties. If both these demands are consistently carried out, say the jurists, women have all they can ask.

This typically legalist method of argument is exactly the same as that which the radical republican bourgeois uses to put the proletarian in his place. The labor contract is to be freely entered into by both partners. But it is considered to have been freely entered into as soon as the law makes both parties equal on *paper*. The power conferred on the one party by the difference of class position, the pressure thereby brought to bear on the other party—the real economic position of both—that is not the law's business. Again, for the duration of the labor contract both parties are to have equal rights, insofar as one or the other does not expressly surrender them. That economic relations compel the worker to surrender even the last semblance of equal rights—here again, that is no concern of the law.

In regard to marriage, the law, even the most advanced, is fully satisfied as soon as the partners have formally recorded that they are entering into the marriage of their own free consent. What goes on in real life behind the juridical scenes, how this free consent comes about—that is not the business of the law and the jurist. And yet the most elementary comparative jurisprudence should show the jurist what this free consent really amounts to. In the countries where an obligatory share of the paternal inheritance is secured to the children by law and they cannot therefore be disinherited—in Germany, in the countries with French law, and elsewhere—the children are obliged to obtain their parents' consent to their marriage. In the countries with English law, where parental consent to a marriage is not legally required, the parents on their side have full freedom in the testamentary disposal of their property and can disinherit their children at their pleasure. It is obvious that, in spite and precisely because of this fact, freedom of marriage among the classes with something to inherit is in reality not a whit greater in England and America than it is in France and Germany.

As regards the legal equality of husband and wife in marriage, the position is no better. The legal inequality of the two partners, bequeathed to us from earlier social conditions, is not the cause but the effect of the economic oppression of the woman. In the old communistic household, which comprised many couples and their children, the task entrusted to the women of managing the household was as much a public and socially necessary industry as the procuring of food by the men. With the patriarchal family, and still more with the single monogamous family, a change came. Household management lost its public character. It no longer concerned society. It became a *private service;* the wife became the head servant, excluded from all participation in social production. Not until the coming of modern large-scale industry was the road to social production opened to her again—and then only to the proletarian wife. But it was opened in such a manner that, if she carries out her duties in the private service of her family, she remains excluded from public production and unable to earn; and if she wants to take part in public production and earn independently, she cannot carry out family duties. And the wife's position in the factory is the position of women in all branches of business, right up to medicine and the law. The modern individual family is founded on the open or concealed domestic slavery of the wife, and modern society is a mass composed of these individual families as its molecules.

In the great majority of cases today, at least in the possessing classes, the husband is obliged to earn a living and support his family, and that in itself gives him a position of supremacy, without any need for special legal titles and privileges. Within the family he is bourgeois and the wife represents the proletariat. In the industrial world, the specific character of the economic oppression burdening the proletariat is visible in all its sharpness only when all special legal privileges of the capitalist class have been abolished and complete legal equality of both classes established. The democratic republic does not do away with the opposition of the two classes; on the contrary, it provides the clear field on which the fight can be fought out. And in the same way, the peculiar character of the supremacy of the husband over the wife in the modern family, the necessity of creating real social equality between them, and the way to do it, will only be seen in the clear light of day when both possess legally complete equality of rights. Then it will be plain that the first condition for the liberation of the wife is to bring the whole female sex back into public industry, and that this in turn demands the abolition of the monogamous family as the economic unit of society.

We thus have three principal forms of marriage which correspond broadly to the three principal stages of human development. For the period of savagery, group marriage; for barbarism, pairing marriage; for civilization, monogamy, supplemented by adultery and prostitution. Between pairing marriage and monogamy intervenes a period in the upper stage of barbarism when men have female slaves at their command and polygamy is practiced.

As our whole presentation has shown, the progress which manifests itself in these successive forms is connected with the peculiarity that women, but not men, are increasingly deprived of the sexual freedom of group marriage. In fact, for men group marriage actually still exists even to this day. What for the woman is a crime, entailing grave legal and social consequences, is considered honorable in a man or, at the worse, a slight moral blemish which he cheerfully bears. But the more the hetaerism of the past is changed in our time by capitalist commodity production and brought into conformity with it, the more, that is to say, it is transformed into undisguised prostitution, the more demoralizing are its effects. And it demoralizes men far more than women. Among women, prostitution degrades only the unfortunate ones who become its victims, and even these by no means to the extent commonly believed. But it degrades the character of the whole male world. A long engagement, particularly, is in nine cases out of ten a regular preparatory school for conjugal infidelity.

We are now approaching a social revolution in which the economic foundations of monogamy as they have existed hitherto will disappear just as surely as those of its complement—prostitution. Monogamy arose from the concentration of considerable wealth in the hands of a single individual—a man—and from the need to bequeath this wealth to the children of that man and of no other. For this purpose, the monogamy of the woman was required, not that of the man, so this monogamy of the woman did not in any way interfere with open or concealed polygamy on the part of the man. But by transforming by far the greater portion, at any rate, of permanent, heritable wealth—the means of production—into social property, the coming social revolution will reduce to a minimum all this anxiety about bequeathing and inheriting. Having arisen from economic causes, will monogamy then disappear when these causes disappear?

One might answer, not without reason: far from disappearing,

it will, on the contrary, be realized completely. For with the transformation of the means of production into social property there
will disappear also wage-labor, the proletariat, and therefore the
necessity for a certain—statistically calculable—number of women
to surrender themselves for money. Prostitution disappears; monogamy, instead of collasping, at last becomes a reality—also for
men.

In any case, therefore, the position of men will be very much
altered. But the position of women, of *all* women, also undergoes
significant change. With the transfer of the means of production
into common ownership, the single family ceases to be the economic unit of society. Private housekeeping is transformed into a
social industry. The care and education of the children becomes a
public affair; society looks after all children alike, whether they
are legitimate or not. This removes all the anxiety about the "consequences," which today is the most essential social—moral as well
as economic—factor that prevents a girl from giving herself completely to the man she loves. Will not that suffice to bring about the
gradual growth of unconstrained sexual intercourse and with it a
more tolerant public opinion in regard to a maiden's honor and a
woman's shame? And, finally, have we not seen that in the modern
world monogamy and prostitution are indeed contradictions, but
inseparable contradictions, poles of the same state of society? Can
prostitution disappear without dragging monogamy with it into
the abyss?

Here a new element comes into play, an element which, at the
time when monogamy was developing, existed at most in germ:
individual sex-love.

Before the Middle Ages we cannot speak of individual sex-love.
That personal beauty, close intimacy, similarity of tastes and so
forth awakened in people of opposite sex the desire for sexual intercourse, that men and women were not totally indifferent regarding the partner with whom they entered into this most intimate
relationship—that goes without saying. But it is still a very long
way to our sexual love. Throughout the whole of antiquity, marriages were arranged by the parents, and the partners calmly accepted their choice. What little love there was between husband

and wife in antiquity is not so much subjective inclination as objective duty, not the cause of the marriage, but its corollary. Love relationships in the modern sense only occur in antiquity outside official society. The shepherds of whose joys and sorrows in love Theocritus and Moschus sing, the Daphnis and Chloe of Longus are all slaves who have no part in the state, the free citizen's sphere of life. Except among slaves, we find love affairs only as products of the disintegration of the old world and carried on with women who also stand outside official society, with *hetairai*—that is, with foreigners or freed slaves: in Athens from the eve of its decline, in Rome under the Caesars. If there were any real love affairs between free men and free women, these occurred only in the course of adultery. And to the classical love poet of antiquity, old Anacreon, sexual love in our sense mattered so little that it did not even matter to him which sex his beloved was.

Our sexual love differs essentially from the simple sexual desire, the Eros, of the ancients. In the first place, it assumes that the person loved returns the love; to this extent the woman is on an equal footing with the man, whereas in the Eros of antiquity she was often not even asked. Secondly, our sexual love has a degree of intensity and duration which makes both lovers feel that nonpossession and separation are a great, if not the greatest, calamity; to possess one another, they risk high stakes, even life itself. In the ancient world this happened only, if at all, in adultery. And, finally, there arises a new moral standard in the judgment of a sexual relationship. We do not only ask, was it within or outside marriage? but also, did it spring from love and reciprocated love or not? Of course, this new standard has fared no better in feudal or bourgeois practice than all the other standards of morality—it is ignored. But neither does it fare any worse. It is recognized just as much as they are—in theory, on paper. And for the present it cannot ask anything more.

At the point where antiquity broke off its advance to sexual love, the Middle Ages took it up again: in adultery. We have already described the knightly love which gave rise to the songs of dawn. From the love which strives to break up marriage to the love which is to be its foundation there is still a long road, which chivalry never fully traversed. Even when we pass from the frivolous Latins to the virtuous Germans, we find in the *Nibelungenlied* that, although in her heart Kriemhild is as much in love with Siegfried as he is with her, yet when Gunther announces that he has promised her to a knight he does not name, she simply replies: "You have no need to ask me; as you bid me, so will I ever be; whom you, lord, give me as husband, him will I gladly take in troth." It never enters her head that her love can be even considered. Gunther asks for Brünhild in marriage, and Etzel for Kriemhild, though they have never seen them. Similarly, in *Gutrun*, Sigebant of Ireland asks for the Norwegian Ute, whom he has never seen, Hetel of Hegelingen for Hilde of Ireland, and, finally, Siegfried of Moorland, Hartmut of Ormany, and Herwig of Seeland for Gutrun, and here Gutrun's acceptance of Herwig is for the first time voluntary. As a rule, the young prince's bride is selected by his parents, if they are still living, or, if not, by the prince himself, with the advice of the great feudal lords, who have a weighty word to say in all these cases. Nor can it be otherwise. For the knight or baron, as for the prince of the land himself, marriage is a political act, an opportunity to increase power by new alliances; the interest of the *house* must be decisive, not the wishes of an individual. What chance then is there for love to have the final word in the making of a marriage?

The same thing holds for the guild member in the medieval towns. The very privileges protecting him, the guild charters with all their clauses and rubrics, the intricate distinctions legally separating him from other guilds, from the members of his own guild or from his journeymen and apprentices, already made the circle narrow enough within which he could look for a suitable wife. And who in the circle was the most suitable was decided under this complicated system most certainly not by his individual preference but by the family interests.

In the vast majority of cases, therefore, marriage remained, up to the close of the Middle Ages, what it had been from the start—a matter which was not decided by the partners. In the beginning, people were already born married—married to an entire group of the opposite sex. In the later forms of group marriage similar relations probably existed, but with the group continually contracting. In the pairing marriage it was customary for the mothers to settle the marriages of their children; here, too, the decisive considerations are the new ties of kinship, which are to give the young pair a stronger position in the gens and tribe. And when, with the preponderance of private over communal property and the interest in its bequeathal, father-right and monogamy gained supremacy, the dependence of marriages on economic considerations became complete. The *form* of marriage by purchase disappears, the actual practice is steadily extended until not only the woman but also the man acquires a price—not according to his personal qualities, but according to his property. That the mutual affection of the people concerned should be the one paramount reason for marriage, outweighing everything else, was and always had been absolutely unheard of in the practice of the ruling classes; that sort of thing only happened in romance—or among the oppressed classes, who did not count.

Such was the state of things encountered by capitalist production when it began to prepare itself, after the epoch of geographical discoveries, to win world power by world trade and manufacture. One would suppose that this manner of marriage exactly suited it, and so it did. And yet—there are no limits to the irony of history—capitalist production itself was to make the decisive breach in it. By changing all things into commodities, it dissolved all inherited and traditional relationships, and, in place of time-honored custom and historic right, it set up purchase and sale, "free" contract. And the English jurist, H. S. Maine, thought he had made a tremendous discovery when he said that our whole progress in comparison with former epochs consisted in the fact that we had passed "from status to contract," from inherited to freely contracted conditions—which, insofar as it is correct, was already in *The Communist Manifesto.*

But a contract requires people who can dispose freely of their persons, actions, and possessions, and meet each other on the footing of equal rights. To create these "free" and "equal" people was one of the main tasks of capitalist production. Even though at the start it was carried out only half-consciously, and under a religious disguise at that, from the time of the Lutheran and Calvinist Reformation the principle was established that man is only fully responsible for his actions when he acts with complete freedom of will, and that it is a moral duty to resist all coercion to an immoral act. But how did this fit in with the hitherto existing practice in the arrangement of marriages? Marriage, according to the bourgeois conception, was a contract, a legal transaction, and the most important one of all, because it disposed of two human beings, body and mind, for life. Formally, it is true, the contract at that time was entered into voluntarily: without the assent of the persons concerned, nothing could be done. But everyone knew only too well how this assent was obtained and who were the real contracting parties in the marriage. But if real freedom of decision was required for all other contracts, then why not for this? Had not the two young people to be coupled also the right to dispose freely of themselves, of their bodies and organs? Had not chivalry brought sex-love into fashion, and was not its proper bourgeois form, in contrast to chivalry's adulterous love, the love of husband and wife? And if it was the duty of married people to love each other, was it not equally the duty of lovers to marry each other and nobody else? Did not this right of the lovers stand higher than the right of parents, relations, and other traditional marriage-brokers and matchmakers? If the right of free, personal discrimination broke boldly into the Church and religion, how should it halt before the intolerable claim of the older generation to dispose of the body, soul, property, happiness, and unhappiness of the younger generation?

These questions inevitably arose at a time which was loosening all the old ties of society and undermining all traditional conceptions. The world had suddenly grown almost ten times bigger; instead of one quadrant of a hemisphere, the whole globe lay before the gaze of the West Europeans, who hastened to take the other seven quadrants into their possession. And with the old narrow barriers of their homeland fell also the thousand-year-old barriers of the prescribed medieval way of thought. To the outward and the inward eye of man opened an infinitely wider horizon. What did a young man care about the approval of respectability, or honorable guild privileges handed down for generations, when the wealth of India beckoned to him, the gold and the silver mines of Mexico and Potosi? For the bourgeoisie, it was the time of knight-errantry; they, too, had their romance and their raptures of love, but on a bourgeois footing and, in the last analysis, with bourgeois aims.

So it came about that the rising bourgeoisie, especially in Protestant countries, where existing conditions had been most severely shaken, increasingly recognized freedom of contract also in marriage, and carried it into effect in the manner described. Marriage remained class marriage, but within the class the partners were conceded a certain degree of freedom of choice. And on paper, in ethical theory and in poetic description, nothing was more immutably established than that every marriage is immoral which does not rest on mutual sexual love and really free agreement of husband and wife. In short, the love marriage was proclaimed as a human right, and indeed not only as a *droit de l'homme,* one of the rights of man, but also, for once in a way, as *droit de la femme,* one of the rights of woman.

This human right, however, differed in one respect from all other so-called human rights. While the latter, in practice, remain restricted to the ruling class (the bourgeoisie), and are directly or indirectly curtailed for the oppressed class (the proletariat), in the case of the former the irony of history plays another of its tricks. The ruling class remains dominated by the familiar economic influences and therefore only in exceptional cases does it provide instances of really freely contracted marriages, while among the oppressed class, as we have seen, these marriages are the rule.

Full freedom of marriage can therefore only be generally established when the abolition of capitalist production and of the property relations created by it has removed all the accompanying economic considerations which still exert such a powerful influence on the choice of a marriage partner. For then there is no other motive left except mutual inclination.

And as sexual love is by its nature exclusive—although at present this exclusiveness is fully realized only in the woman—the marriage based on sexual love is by its nature individual marriage. We have seen how right Bachofen was in regarding the advance from group marriage to individual marriage as primarily due to the women. Only the step from pairing marriage to monogamy can be put down to the credit of the men, and historically the essence of this was to make the position of the women worse and the infidelities of the men easier. If now the economic considerations also disappear which made women put up with the habitual infidelity of their husbands—concern for their own means of existence and still more for their children's future—then, according to all previous experience, the equality of woman thereby achieved will tend infinitely more to make men really monogamous than to make women polyandrous.

But what will quite certainly disappear from monogamy are all the features stamped upon it through its origin in property relations; these are, in the first place, supremacy of the man, and, secondly, indissolubility. The supremacy of the man in marriage is the simple consequence of his economic supremacy, and with the abolition of the latter will disappear of itself. The indissolubility of marriage is partly a consequence of the economic situation in which monogamy arose, partly tradition from the period when the connection between this economic situation and monogamy was not yet fully understood and was carried to extremes under a religious form. Today it is already broken through at a thousand points. If only the marriage based on love is moral, then also only the marriage in which love continues. But the intense emotion of individual sex-love varies very much in duration from one individual to another, especially among men, and if affection definitely comes to an end or is supplanted by a new passionate love, separation is a benefit for both partners as well as for society— only people will then be spared having to wade through the useless mire of a divorce case.

What we can now conjecture about the way in which sexual relations will be ordered after the impending overthrow of capitalist production is mainly of a negative character, limited for the most part to what will disappear. But what will there be new? That will be answered when a new generation has grown up: a generation of men who never in their lives have known what it is to buy a woman's surrender with money or any other social instrument of power; a generation of women who have never known what it is to give themselves to a man from any other considerations than real love, or to refuse to give themselves to their lover from fear of the economic consequences. When these people are in the world, they will care precious little what anybody today thinks they ought to do; they will make their own practice and their corresponding public opinion about the practice of each individual—and that will be the end of it.

II. The Effects of Machinery on the Family Life of the Factory Worker

The starting point of Modern Industry is, as we have shown, the revolution in the instruments of labor, and this revolution attains its most highly developed form in the organized system of machinery in a factory. Before we inquire how human material is incorporated with this objective organism, let us consider some general effects of this revolution on the laborer himself.

Insofar as machinery dispenses with muscular power, it becomes a means of employing laborers of slight muscular strength, and those whose bodily development is incomplete, but whose limbs are all the more supple. The labor of women and children was, therefore, the first thing sought for by capitalists who used machinery. That mighty substitute for labor and laborers was forthwith changed into a means for increasing the number of wage-laborers by enrolling, under the direct sway of capital, every member of the workman's family, without distinction of age or sex. Compulsory work for the capitalist usurped the place, not only of the children's play, but also of free labor at home within moderate limits for the support of the family.[4]

---

[4]   Dr. Edward Smith, during the cotton crisis caused by the American Civil War, was sent by the English Government to Lancashire, Cheshire, and other places, to report on the sanitary condition of the cotton operatives. He reported, that from a hygienic point of view, and apart from the banishment of the operatives from the factory atmosphere, the crisis had several advantages. The women now had sufficient leisure to give their

The value of labor-power was determined, not only by the labor-time necessary to maintain the individual adult laborer, but also by that necessary to maintain his family. Machinery, by throwing every member of that family onto the labor market, spreads the value of the man's labor-power over his whole family. It thus depreciates his labor-power. To purchase the labor-power of a family of four workers may, perhaps, cost more than it formerly did to purchase the labor-power of the head of the family, but, in return, four days' labor takes the place of one, and their price falls in proportion to the excess of the surplus-labor of four over the surplus-labor of one. In order that the family may live, four people must now, not only labor, but expend surplus-labor for the capitalist. Thus we see, that machinery, while augmenting the human material that forms the principal object of capital's exploiting power,[5] at the same time raises the degree of exploitation.

---

infants the breast, instead of poisoning them with "Godfrey's cordial." They had time to learn to cook. Unfortunately the acquisition of this art occurred at a time when they had nothing to cook. But from this we see how capital, for the purposes of its self-expansion, has usurped the labor necessary in the home of the family. This crisis was also utilized to teach sewing to the daughters of the workmen in sewing schools. An American revolution and a universal crisis, in order that the working girls, who spin for the whole world, might learn to sew!

5   "The numerical increase of labourers has been great, through the growing substitution of female for male, and above all, of childish for adult labour. Three girls of 13, at wages from 6 shillings to 8 shillings a week, have replaced the one man of mature age, of wages varying from 18 shillings to 45 shillings." (Th. de Quincey, "The Logic of Political Econ., London, 1845." Note to p. 147.) Since certain family functions, such as nursing and suckling children, cannot be entirely suppressed, the mothers confiscated by capital, must try substitutes of some sort. Domestic work, such as sewing and mending, must be replaced by the purchase of ready-made articles. Hence, the dimished expenditure of labor in the house is accompanied by an increased expenditure of money. The cost of keeping the family increases, and balances the greater income. In addition to this, economy and judgment in the consumption and preparation of the means of subsistence becomes impossible. Abundant material relating to these facts, which are concealed by official political economy, is to be found in the Reports of the Inspectors of Factories, of the Children's Employment Commission, and more especially in the Reports on Public Health.

Machinery also revolutionizes out and out the contract between the laborer and the capitalist, which formally fixes their mutual relations. Taking the exchange of commodities as our basis, our first assumption was that capitalist and laborer met as free persons, as independent owners of commodities; the one possessing money and means of production, the other labor-power. But now the capitalist buys children and young persons under age. Previously, the workman sold his own labor-power, which he disposed of nominally as a free agent. Now he sells wife and child. He has become a slave dealer.[6] The demand for children's labor often resembles in form the inquiries for negro slaves, such as were formerly to be read among the advertisements in American journals. "My attention," says an English factory inspector, "was drawn to an advertisement in the local paper of one of the most important manufacturing towns of my district, of which the following is a copy: Wanted, 12 to 20 young persons, not younger than what can pass for 13 years. Wages, 4 shillings a week. Apply etc."[7] The phrase "what can pass for 13 years," has reference to the fact, that by the Factory Act, children under 13 years may work only 6 hours. A surgeon officially appointed must certify their age. The manufacturer, therefore, asks for children who look as if they

---

[6]   In striking contrast with the great fact, that the shortening of the hours of labor of women and children in English factories was exacted from capital by the male operatives, we find in the latest reports of the Children's Employment Commission traits of the operative parents in relation to the traffic in children, that are truly revolting and thoroughly like slave-dealing. But the Pharisee of a capitalist, as may be seen from the same reports, denounces this brutality which he himself creates, perpetuates, and exploits, and which he moreover baptizes "Freedom of labor." "Infant labor has been called into aid . . . even to work for their own daily bread. Without strength to endure such disproportionate toil, without instruction to guide their future life, they have been thrown into a situation physically and morally polluted. The Jewish historian has remarked upon the overthrow of Jerusalem by Titus that it was no wonder it should have been destroyed, with such a signal destruction, when an inhuman mother sacrificed her own offspring to satisfy the cravings of absolute hunger." ("Public Economy Concentrated." Carlisle, 1833, p. 56.)

[7]   A. Redgrave in "Reports of Insp. of Fact. for 31st October, 1858," pp. 40, 41.

were already 13 years old. The decrease, often by leaps and bounds in the number of children under 13 years employed in factories, a decrease that is shown in an astonishing manner by the English statistics of the last 20 years, was for the most part, according to the evidence of the factory inspectors themselves, the work of the certifying surgeons, who overstated the age of the children, agreeably to the capitalist's greed for exploitation, and the sordid trafficking needs of the parents. In the notorious district of Bethnal Green, a public market is held every Monday and Tuesday morning, where children of both sexes from 9 years of age upwards, hire themselves out to the silk manufacturers. "The usual terms are 1s. 8d. a week (this belongs to the parents) and '2d. for myself and tea.' The contract is binding only for the week. The scene and language while this market is going on are quite disgraceful."[8] It has also occurred in England, that women have taken "children from the workhouse and let any one have them out for 2s. 6d. a week."[9] In spite of legislation, the number of boys sold in Great Britain by their parents to act as live chimney-sweeping machines (although there exist plenty of machines to replace them) exceeds 2000.[10] The revolution effected by machinery in the juridical relations between the buyer and the seller of labor-power, causing the transaction as a whole to lose the appearance of a contract between free persons, afforded the English Parliament an excuse, founded on juridical principles, for the interference of the state with factories. Whenever the law limits the labor of children to 6 hours in industries not before interfered with, the complaints of the manufacturers are always renewed. They allege that numbers of the parents withdraw their children from the industry brought under the Act, in order to sell them where "freedom of labor" still rules, i.e., where children under 13 years are compelled to work like grown-up people, and therefore can be got rid of at a higher price. But since capital is by nature a leveller, since it exacts in every

[8]   Children's Employment Commission, Fifth Report London, 1866, p. 81, n. 31.
[9]   Children's Employment Commission, Third Report, London, 1864, p. 53, n. 15.
[10]   L. c., Fifth Report, p. 22, n. 137.

sphere of production equality in the conditions of the exploitation of labor, the limitation by law of children's labor, in one branch of industry, becomes the cause of its limitation in others.

We have already alluded to the physical deterioration as well of the children and young persons as of the women, whom machinery, first directly in the factories that shoot up on its basis, and then indirectly in all the remaining branches of industry, subjects to the exploitation of capital. In this place, therefore, we dwell only on one point, the enormous mortality, during the first few years of their life, of the children of the operatives. In sixteen of the registration districts into which England is divided, there are, for every 100,000 children alive under the age of one year, only 9000 deaths in a year on an average (in one district only 7047); in 24 districts the deaths are over 10,000, but under 11,000; in 39 districts, over 11,000, but under 12,000; in 48 districts over 12,000, but under 13,000; in 22 districts over 20,000; in 25 districts over 21,000; in 17 over 22,000; in 11 over 23,000; in Hoo, Wolverhampton, Ashton-under-Lyne, and Preston, over 24,000; in Nottingham, Stockport, and Bradford, over 25,000; in Wisbeach, 26,000; and in Manchester, 26,125.[11] As was shown by an official medical inquiry in the year 1861, the high death-rates are, apart from local causes, principally due to the employment of the mothers away from their homes, and to the neglect and maltreatment consequent on her absence, such as, among others, insufficient nourishment, unsuitable food, and dosing with opiates; besides this, there arises an unnatural estrangement between mother and child, and as a consequence intentional starving and poisoning of the children.[12] In those agricultural districts, "where a minimum in the employment of women exists, the death-rate is

11   Sixth Report on Public Health. Lond., 1864, p. 34.
12   "It (the inquiry of 1861) . . . showed, moreover, that while, with the described circumstances, infants perish under the neglect and mismanagement which their mothers' occupations imply, the mothers become to a grievous extent denaturalized towards their offspring—commonly not troubling themselves much at the death, and even sometimes . . . taking direct measures to insure it." (l. c.)

on the other hand very low."[13] The Inquiry Commission of 1861 led, however, to the unexpected result, that in some purely agricultural districts bordering on the North Sea, the death-rate of children under one year old almost equalled that of the worst factory districts. Dr. Julian Hunter was therefore commissioned to investigate this phenomenon on the spot. His report is incorporated with the "Sixth Report on Public Health."[14] Up to that time it was supposed, that the children were decimated by malaria, and other diseases peculiar to low-lying and marshy districts. But the inquiry showed the very opposite, namely, that the same cause which drove away malaria, the conversion of the land, from a morass in winter and a scanty pasture in summer, into fruitful corn land, created the exceptional death-rate of the infants.[15] The 70 medical men, whom Dr. Hunter examined in that district, were "wonderfully in accord" on this point. In fact, the revolution in the mode of cultivation had led to the introduction of the industrial system. Married women, who work in gangs along with boys and girls, are, for a stipulated sum of money, placed at the disposal of the farmer, by a man called the "undertaker," who contracts for the whole gang. "These gangs will sometimes travel many miles from their own village; they are to be met morning and evening on the roads, dressed in short petticoats with suitable coats and boots, and sometimes trousers, looking wonderfully strong and healthy, but tainted with a customary immorality, and heedless of the fatal results which their love of this busy and independent life is bringing on their unfortunate offspring who are pining at home."[16] Every phenomenon of the factory districts is here reproduced, including, but to a greater extent, ill-disguised infanticide, and dosing children with opiates.[17] "My knowledge of

13   L. c., p. 454.
14   L. c., p. 454–63. "Report by Dr. Henry Julian Hunter on the excessive mortality of infants in some rural districts of England."
15   L. c., p. 35 and pp. 455, 456.
16   L. c., p. 456.
17   In the agricultural as well as in the factory districts the consumption of opium among the grown-up laborers, both male and female, is

such evils," says Dr. Simon, the medical officer of the Privy Council and editor in chief of the Reports on Public Health, "may excuse the profound misgiving with which I regard any large industrial employment of adult women."[18] "Happy indeed," exclaims Mr. Baker, the factory inspector, in his official report, "happy indeed will it be for the manufacturing districts of England, when every married woman having a family is prohibited from working in any textile works at all."[19]

The moral degradation caused by the capitalistic exploitation of women and children has been so exhaustively depicted by F. Engels in his "Lage der Arbeitenden Klasse Englands," and other writers, that I need only mention the subject in this place. But the intellectual desolation, artifically produced by converting immature human beings into mere machines for the fabrication of surplus-value, a state of mind clearly distinguishable from that natural ignorance which keeps the mind fallow without destroying its capacity for development, its natural fertility, this desolation finally compelled even the English Parliament to make elementary education a compulsory condition to the "productive" employment of children under 14 years, in every industry subject to the Factory Acts. The spirit of capitalist production stands out clearly in the ludicrous wording of the so-called education clauses in the Factory Acts, in the absence of an administrative machinery, an absence that again makes the compulsion illusory, in the opposition of the manufacturers themselves to these education clauses, and in the tricks and dodges they put in practice for evading them. "For this the legislature is alone to blame, by having passed a delusive law, which, while it would seem to provide that the children employed in factories shall be *educated*, contains no enactment by

---

extending daily. "To push the sale of opiate . . . is the great aim of some enterprising wholesale merchants. By druggists it is considered the leading article." (l. c., p. 459.) Infants that take opiates "shrank up into little old men," or "wizzened like little monkeys." (l. c., p. 460). We here see how India and China avenged themselves on England.

[18]   L. c., p. 37.
[19]   "Rep. of Insp. of Fact. for 31st Oct., 1862," p. 59. Mr. Baker was formerly a doctor.

which that professed end can be secured. It provides nothing more than that the children shall on certain days of the week, and for a certain number of hours (three) in each day, be inclosed within the four walls of a place called a school, and that the employer of the child shall receive weekly a certificate to that effect signed by a person designated by the subscriber as a schoolmaster or school-mistress."[20] Previous to the passing of the amended Factory Act, 1844, it happened, not unfrequently, that the certificates of attendance at school were signed by the schoolmaster or schoolmistress with a cross, as they themselves were unable to write. "On one occasion, on visiting a place called a school, from which certificates of school attendance had issued, I was so struck with the ignorance of the master, that I said to him: "Pray, sir, can you read?" His reply was: "Aye, summat!" and as a justification of his right to grant certificates, he added: "At any rate, I am before my scholars." The inspectors, when the Bill of 1844 was in preparation, did not fail to represent the disgraceful state of the places called schools, certificates from which they were obliged to admit as a compliance with the laws, but they were successful only in obtaining thus much, that since the passing of the Act of 1844, the figures in the school certificate must be filled up in the handwriting of the schoolmaster, who must also sign his Christian and surname in full."[21] Sir John Kincaid, factory inspector for Scotland, relates experiences of the same kind. "The first school we visited was kept by a Mrs. Ann Killin. Upon asking her to spell her name, she straightway made a mistake, by beginning with the letter C, but correcting herself immediately, she said her name began with a K. On looking at her signature, however, in the school certificate books, I noticed that she spelt it in various ways, while her handwriting left no doubt as to her unfitness to teach. She herself also acknowledged that she could not keep the register . . . . In a second school I found the schoolroom 15 feet long, and 10 feet wide, and counted in this space 75 children, who were gabbling something

---

[20]   Leonard Horner in "Reports of Insp. of Fact. for 30th June, 1857," p. 17.

[21]   L. Horner in "Rep. of Insp. of Fact. for 31st Oct., 1855," pp. 18, 19.

unintelligible."[22] "But it is not only in the miserable places above
referred to that the children obtain certificates of school attendance without having received instruction of any value, for in many
schools where there is a competent teacher, his efforts are of little
avail from the distracting crowd of children of all ages, from infants of 3 years old and upwards; his livelihood, miserable at the
best, depending on the pence received from the greatest number
of children whom it is possible to cram into the space. To this is
to be added scanty school furniture, deficiency of books, and other
materials for teaching, and the depressing effect upon the poor
children themselves of a close, noisome atmosphere. I have been
in many such schools, where I have seen rows of children doing
absolutely nothing; and this is certified as school attendance, and,
in statistical returns, such children are set down as being educated."[23] In Scotland the manufacturers try all they can to do
without the children that are obliged to attend school. "It requires
no further argument to prove that the educational clauses of the
Factory Act, being held in such disfavour among mill owners, tend
in a great measure to exclude that class of children alike from the
employment and the benefit of education contemplated by this
Act."[24] Horribly grotesque does this appear in print works, which
are regulated by a special Act. By that Act,

every child, before being employed in a print work must have attended
school for at least 30 days, and not less than 150 hours, during the six
months immediately preceding such first day of employment, and during the continuance of its employment in the print works, it must attend
for a like period of 30 days, and 150 hours during every successive
period of six months. . . . The attendance at school must be between
8 a.m. and 6 p.m. No attendance less than $2\frac{1}{2}$ hours, nor more than 5
hours on any one day, shall be reckoned as part of the 150 hours.
Under ordinary circumstances the children attend school morning and
afternoon for 30 days, for at least 5 hours each day, and upon the
expiration of the 30 days, the statutory total of 150 hours having been

[22]   Sir John Kincaid in "Rep. of Insp. of Fact. for 31st Oct., 1858,"
pp. 31, 32.
[23]   L. Horner in "Reports, etc. for 31st Oct., 1857," pp. 17, 18.
[24]   Sir J. Kincaid in "Reports, etc. 31st Oct., 1856," p. 66.

attained, having, in their language, made up their book, they return to the print work, where they continue until the six months have expired, when another instalment of school attendance becomes due, and they again seek the school until the book is again made up. . . . Many boys having attended school for the required number of hours, when they return to school after the expiration of their six months' work in the print work, are in the same condition as when they first attended school as print-work boys, that they have lost all they gained by their previous school attendance. . . . In other print works the children's attendance at school is made to depend altogether upon the exigencies of the work in the establishment. The requisite number of hours is made up each six months, by instalments consisting of from 3 to 5 hours at a time, spreading over, perhaps, the whole six months. . . . For instance, the attendance on one day might be from 8 to 11 a.m., on another day from 1 p.m. to 4 p.m., and the child might not appear at school again for several days, when it would attend from 3 p.m. to 6 p.m.; then it might attend for 3 or 4 days consecutively, or for a week, then it would not appear in school for 3 weeks or a month, after that upon some odd days at some odd hours when the operative who employed it chose to spare it; and thus the child was, as it were, buffeted from school to work, from work to school, until the tale of 150 hours was told.[25]

By the excessive addition of women and children to the ranks of the workers, machinery at last breaks down the resistance which the male operatives in the manufacturing period continued to oppose to the despotism of capital.[26]

[25]   A. Redgrave in "Rep. of Insp. of Fact., 31st Oct., 1857," pp. 41–42. In those industries where the Factory Act proper (not the Print Works Act referred to in the text) has been in force for some time, the obstacles in the way of the education clauses have, in recent years, been overcome. In industries not under the Act, the views of Mr. J. Geddes, a glass manufacturer, still extensively prevail. He informed Mr. White, one of the Inquiry Commissioners: "As far as I can see, the greater amount of education which a part of the working class has enjoyed for some years past is an evil. It is dangerous, because it makes them independent." (Children's Empl. Comm., Fourth Report, Lond., 1865, p. 253.)
[26]   "Mr. E., a manufacturer . . . informed me that he employed females exclusively at his power-looms . . . gives a decided preference to married females, especially those who have families at home dependent on them for support; they are attentive, docile, more so than unmarried females, and are compelled to use their utmost exertions to procure the necessaries

III. The Effects of Machinery on Family Life in the Domestic Industries

I now come to the so-called domestic industry. In order to get an idea of the horrors of this sphere, in which capital conducts its exploitation in the background of modern mechanical industry, one must go to the apparently quite idyllic trade of nail-making,[27] carried on in a few remote villages of England. In this place, however, it will be enough to give a few examples from those branches of the lace-making and straw-plaiting industries that are not yet carried on by the aid of machinery and that as yet do not compete with branches carried on in factories or in manufactories.

Of the 150,000 persons employed in England in the production of lace, about 10,000 fall under the authority of the Factory Act, 1861. Almost the whole of the remaining 140,000 are women, young persons, and children of both sexes, the male sex, however, being weakly represented. The state of health of this cheap material for exploitation will be seen from the following table, computed by Dr. Trueman, physician to the Nottingham General Dispensary. Out of 686 female patients who were lace makers, most of them between the ages of 17 and 24, the number of consumptive ones were:

1852—1 in 45	1857—1 in 13
1853—1 in 28	1858—1 in 15
1854—1 in 17	1859—1 in 9
1855—1 in 18	1860—1 in 8
1856—1 in 15	1861—1 in 8[28]

---

of life. Thus are the virtues, the peculiar virtues of the female character to be perverted to her injury—thus all that is most dutiful and tender in her nature is made a means of her bondage and suffering." (Ten Hours' Factory Bill. The Speech of Lord Ashley, March 15th, Lond., 1844, p. 20.)

[27]   I allude here to hammered nails, as distinguished from nails cut out and made by machinery. See Child. Empl. Comm., Third Rep., p. xi, p. xix. n. 125–130, p. 53, n. 11, p. 114, n. 487, p. 137, n. 674.

[28]   Ch. Empl. Comm., II. Rep., p. xxii, n. 166.

This progress in the rate of consumption ought to suffice for the most optimist of progressists, and for the biggest hawker of lies among the Free Trade bagmen of Germany.

The Factory Act of 1861 regulates the actual making of the lace, so far as it is done by machinery, and this is the rule in England. The branches that we are about to examine, solely with regard to those of the workpeople who work at home, and not those who work in manufactories or warehouses, fall into two divisions, viz. (1) finishing; (2) mending. The former gives the finishing touches to the machine-made lace, and includes numerous subdivisions.

The lace finishing is done either in what are called "Mistresses' Houses," or by women in their own houses, with or without the help of their children. The women who keep the "Mistresses' Houses" are themselves poor. The workroom is in a private house. The mistresses take orders from manufacturers, or from warehousemen, and employ as many women, girls, and young children as the size of their rooms and the fluctuating demand of the business will allow. The number of the workwomen employed in these workrooms varies from 20 to 40 in some, and from 10 to 20 in others. The average age at which the children commence work is six years, but in many cases it is below five. The usual working hours are from 8 in the morning till 8 in the evening, with 1½ hours for meals, which are taken at irregular intervals, and often in the foul workrooms. When business is brisk, the labor frequently lasts from 8 or even 6 o'clock in the morning till 10, 11, or 12 o'clock at night. In English barracks the regulation space allotted to each soldier is 500–600 cubic feet, and in the military hospitals 1200 cubic feet. But in those finishing styes there are but 67 to 100 cubic feet to each person. At the same time the oxygen of the air is consumed by gas-lights. In order to keep the lace clean, and although the floor is tiled or flagged, the children are often compelled, even in winter, to pull off their shoes.

It is not at all uncommon in Nottingham to find 14 to 20 children huddled together in a small room, of, perhaps, not more than 12 feet square, and employed for 15 hours out of the 24, at work that of itself is exhausting, from its weariness and monotony, and is besides carried on under every possible unwholesome condition. . . . Even the very youngest children work with a strained attention and a rapidity that is astonishing, hardly ever giving their fingers rest or slowering their motion. If a question be asked them, they never raise their eyes from their work from fear of losing a single moment.

The "long stick" is used by the mistresses as a stimulant more and more as the working hours are prolonged. "The children gradually tire and become as restless as birds towards the end of their long detention at an occupation that is monotonous, eye-straining, and exhausting from the uniformity in the posture of the body. Their work is like slavery."[29] When women and their children work at home, which nowadays means in a hired room, often in a garret, the state of things is, if possible, still worse. This sort of work is given out within a circle of 80 miles radius from Nottingham. On leaving the warehouses at 9 or 10 o'clock at night, the children are often given a bundle of lace to take home with them and finish. The Pharisee of a capitalist represented by one of his servants, accompanies this action, of course, with the unctuous phrase: "That's for mother," yet he knows well enough that the poor children must sit up and help.[30]

Pillow lace making is chiefly carried on in England in two agricultural districts; one, the Honiton lace district, extending from 20 to 30 miles along the south coast of Devonshire, and including a few places in North Devon; the other comprising a great part of the counties of Buckingham, Bedford, and Northampton, and also the adjoining portions of Oxfordshire and Huntingdonshire. The cottages of the agricultural laborers are the places where the work is usually carried on. Many manufacturers employ upwards of 3000 of these lace makers, who are chiefly children and young persons of the female sex exclusively. The state of things described as incidental to lace finishing is here repeated, save that instead of the "mistresses' houses," we find what are called "lace schools," kept by poor women in their cottages. From their fifth year and

[29]   Ch. Empl. Comm., II. Rep., 1864, pp. xix, xx., xxi.
[30]   L. c., pp. xxi, xxvi.

often earlier, until their twelfth or fifteenth year, the children work in these schools; during the first year the very young ones work from four to eight hours, and later on, from six in the morning till eight and ten o'clock at night.

The rooms are generally the ordinary living rooms of small cottages, the chimney stopped up to keep out the draughts, inmates kept warm by their own animal heat alone, and this frequently in winter. In other cases, these so-called school-rooms are like small store-rooms without fire-places. . . . The overcrowding in these dens and the consequent vitiation of the air are often extreme. Added to this is the injurious effect of drains, privies, decomposing substances, and other filth usual in the purlieus of the smaller cottages.

With regard to space: "In one lace school 18 girls and a mistress, 35 cubic feet to each person; in another, where the smell was unbearable, 18 persons and 24½ cubic feet per head. In this industry are to be found employed children of 2 and 2½ years."[31]

Where lace-making ends in the counties of Buckingham and Bedford, straw-plaiting begins, and extends over a large part of Hertfordshire and the westerly and northerly parts of Essex. In 1861, there were 40,043 persons employed in straw-plaiting and straw-hat making; of these 3815 were males of all ages, the rest females, of whom 14,913, including 7000 children, were under 20 years of age. In the place of the lace-schools we find here the "straw-plait schools." The children commence their instruction in straw-plaiting generally in their 4th, often between their 3rd and 4th year. Education, of course, they get none. The children themselves call the elementary schools, "natural schools," to distinguish them from these blood-sucking institutions, in which they are kept at work simply to get through the task, generally 30 yards daily, prescribed by their half-starved mothers. These same mothers often make them work at home, after school is over, till 10, 11, and 12 o'clock at night. The straw cuts their mouths, with which they constantly moisten it, and their fingers. Dr. Ballard gives it as the general opinion of the whole body of medical officers in London, that 300 cubic feet is the minimum space proper for each

31 L. c., pp. xxix, xxx.

person in a bedroom or work-room. But in the straw-plait schools space is more sparingly allotted than in the lace-schools, "12⅔, 17, 18½ and below 22 cubic feet for each person." The smaller of these numbers, says one of the commissioners, Mr. White, represents less space than the half of what a child would occupy if packed in a box measuring 3 feet in each direction. Thus do the children enjoy life till the ages of 12 or 14. The wretched half-starved parents think of nothing but getting as much as possible out of their children. The latter, as soon as they are grown up, do not care a farthing, and naturally so, for their parents, and leave them. "It is no wonder that ignorance and vice abound in a population so brought up. . . . Their morality is at the lowest ebb, . . . a great number of the women have illegitimate children, and that at such an immature age that even those most conversant with criminal statistics are astounded."[32] And the native land of these model families is the pattern Christian country for Europe; so says at least Count Montalembert, certainly a competent authority on Christianity!

Wages in the above industries, miserable as they are (the maximum wages of a child in the straw-plait schools rising in rare cases to 3 shillings), are reduced far below their nominal amount by the prevalance of the truck system everywhere, but especially in the lace districts.[33]

The cheapening of labor-power, by sheer abuse of the labor of women and children, by sheer robbery of every normal condition requisite for working and living, and by the sheer brutality of overwork and night-work, meets at last with natural obstacles that cannot be overstepped. So also, when based on these methods, do the cheapening of commodities and capitalist exploitation in general. So soon as this point is at last reached—and it takes many years —the hour has struck for the introduction of machinery, and for the thenceforth rapid conversion of the scattered domestic industries and also of manufactures into factory industries.

32   L. c., pp. xl, xli.
33   Child. Empl. Comm. I. Rep. 1863, p. 185.

An example, on the most colossal scale, of this movement is afforded by the production of wearing apparel. This industry, according to the classification of the Childrens' Employment Commission, comprises straw-hat makers, ladies'-hat makers, cap-makers, tailors, milliners and dressmakers, shirt-makers, corset-makers, glove-makers, shoemakers, besides many minor branches, such as the making of neck-ties, collars, etc. In 1861, the number of females employed in these industries, in England and Wales, amounted to 586,299, of these 115,242 at the least were under 20, and 16,650 under 15 years of age. The number of these work-women in the United Kingdom in 1861, was 750,334. The number of males employed in England and Wales, in hat-making, shoe-making, glove-making, and tailoring was 437,969; of these 14,964 under 15 years, 89,285 between 15 and 20, and 333,117 over 20 years. Many of the smaller branches are not included in these fig-ures. But take the figures as they stand; we then have for England and Wales alone, according to the census of 1861, a total of 1,024,277 persons, about as many as are absorbed by agriculture and cattle breeding. We begin to understand what becomes of the immense quantities of goods conjured up by the magic of ma-chinery, and of the enormous masses of workpeople, which that machinery sets free.

The production of wearing apparel is carried on partly in manufactories in whose workrooms there is but a reproduction of that division of labor, the membra disjecta of which were found ready to hand; partly by small master-handicraftsmen; these, how-ever, do not, as formerly, work for individual consumers, but for manufactories and warehouses, and to such an extent that often whole towns and stretches of country carry on certain branches, such as shoe-making, as a speciality; finally, on a very great scale by the so-called domestic workers, who form an external depart-ment of the manufactories, warehouses, and even of the work-shops of the smaller masters.[34]

---

[34] In England millinery and dressmaking are for the most part car-ried on, on the premises of the employer, partly by workwomen who live there, partly by women who live off the premises.

The raw material, etc., is supplied by mechanical industry, the mass of cheap human material (taillable à merci et miséricorde) is composed of the individuals "liberated" by mechanical industry and improved agriculture. The manufactures of this class owed their origin chiefly to the capitalist's need of having at hand an army ready equipped to meet any increase of demand.[35] These manufactures, nevertheless, allowed the scattered handicrafts and domestic industries to continue to exist as a broad foundation. The great production of surplus-value in these branches of labor, and the progressive cheapening of their articles, were and are chiefly due to the minimum wages paid, no more than requisite for a miserable vegetation, and to the extension of working time up to the maximum endurable by the human organism. It was in fact by the cheapness of the human sweat and the human blood, which were converted into commodities, that the markets were constantly being extended, and continue daily to be extended; more especially was this the case with England's colonial markets, where, besides, English tastes and habits prevail. At last the critical point was reached. The basis of the old method, sheer brutality in the exploitation of the workpeople, accompanied more or less by a systematic division of labor, no longer sufficed for the extending markets and for the still more rapidly extending competition of the capitalists. The hour struck for the advent of machinery. The decisively revolutionary machine, the machine which attacks in an equal degree the whole of the numberless branches of this sphere of production, dressmaking, tailoring, shoe-making, sewing, hat-making, and many others, is the sewing machine.

Its immediate effect on the workpeople is like that of all machinery, which, since the rise of modern industry, has seized upon new branches of trade. Children of too tender an age are sent adrift. The wage of the machine hands rises compared with that of the house-workers, many of whom belong to the poorest of the poor. That of the better situated handicraftsmen, with whom the ma-

[35]   Mr. White, a commissioner, visited a military clothing manufactory that employed 1000 to 1200 persons, almost all females, and a shoe manufactory with 1300 persons, of these nearly one half were children and young persons.

chine competes, sinks. The new machine hands are exclusively girls and young women. With the help of mechanical force, they destroy the monopoly that male labor had of the heavier work, and they drive off from the lighter work numbers of old women and very young children. The overpowering competition crushes the weakest of the manual laborers. The fearful increase in death from starvation during the last 10 years in London runs parallel with the extension of machine sewing.[36] The new workwomen turn the machines by hand and foot, or by hand alone, sometimes sitting, sometimes standing, according to the weight, size, and special make of the machine, and expend a great deal of labor-power. Their occupation is unwholesome, owing to the long hours, although in most cases they are not so long as under the old system. Wherever the sewing machine locates itself in narrow and already overcrowded workrooms, it adds to the unwholesome influences. "The effect," says Mr. Lord, "on entering low-ceiled workrooms in which 30 to 40 machine hands are working is unbearable. . . . The heat, partly due to the gas stoves used for warming the irons, is horrible. . . . Even when moderate hours of work, i.e., from 8 in the morning till 6 in the evening, prevail in such places, yet 3 or 4 persons fall into a swoon regularly every day."[37]

The revolution in the industrial methods which is the necessary result of the revolution in the instruments of production, is effected by a medley of transition forms. These forms vary according to the extent to which the sewing machine has become prevalent in one branch of industry or the other, to the time during which it has been in operation, to the previous condition of the workpeople, to the preponderance of manufacture, of handicrafts or of domestic industry, to the rent of the workrooms, etc.[38] In dressmaking, for

36   An instance. The weekly report of deaths by the Registrar General dated 26th Feb., 1864, contains 5 cases of death from starvation. On the same day the "Times" reports another case. Six victims of starvation in one week!

37   Child. Empl. Comm., Second Rep., 1864, p. lxvii, n. 406–9, p. 84 n. 124, p. xxiii, n. 441, p. 66, n. 6, p. 84, n. 126, p. 78, n. 85, p. 76, n. 69, p. lxxii, n. 483.

38   "The rental of premises required for workrooms seems the element which ultimately determines the point; and consequently it is in the me-

instance, where the labor for the most part was already organized, chiefly by simple cooperation, the sewing machine at first formed merely a new factor in that manufacturing industry. In tailoring, shirt-making, shoe-making, etc., all the forms are intermingled. Here the factory system proper. There middlemen receive the raw material from the capitalist *en chef*, and group around their sewing machines, in "chambers" and "garrets," from 10 to 50 or more workwomen. Finally, as is always the case with machinery when not organized into a system, and when it can also be used in dwarfish proportions, handicraftsmen and domestic workers, along with their families, or with a little extra labor from without, make use of their own sewing machines.[39] The system actually prevalent in England is, that the capitalist concentrates a large number of machines on his premises, and then distributes the produce of those machines for further manipulation among the domestic workers.[40] The variety of the transition forms, however, does not conceal the tendency to conversion into the factory system proper. This tendency is nurtured by the very nature of the sewing machine, the manifold uses of which push on the concentration, under one roof, and one management, of previously separated branches of a trade. It is also favored by the circumstance that preparatory needlework, and certain other operations, are most conveniently done on the premises where the machine is at work; as well as by the inevitable expropriation of the hand sewers, and of the domestic workers who work with their own machines. This fate has already in part overtaken them. The constantly increasing amount of capital invested in sewing machines,[41] gives the spur to the production

tropolis, that the old system of giving work out to small employers and families has been longest retained, and earliest returned to." (l. c. p. 83, n. 123.) The concluding statement in this quotation refers exclusively to shoe-making.

[39] In glove-making and other industries where the condition of the workpeople is hardly distinguishable from that of paupers, this does not occur.

[40] L. c., p. 2, n. 122.

[41] In the wholesale boot and shoe trade of Leicester alone, there were in 1864, 800 sewing machines already in use.

of, and gluts the markets with, machine-made articles, thereby giving the signal to the domestic workers for the sale of their machines. The overproduction of sewing machines themselves, causes their producers, in bad want of a sale, to let them out for so much a week, thus crushing by their deadly competition the small owners of machines.[42] Constant changes in the construction of the machines, and their ever-increasing cheapness, depreciate day by day the older makes, and allow of their being sold in great numbers, at absurd prices, to large capitalists, who alone can thus employ them at a profit. Finally, the substitution of the steam-engine for man gives in this, as in all similar revolutions, the finishing blow. At first, the use of steam power meets with mere technical difficulties, such as unsteadiness in the machines, difficulty in controlling their speed, rapid wear and tear of the lighter machines, etc., all of which are soon overcome by experience.[43] If, on the one hand, the concentration of many machines in large manufactories leads to the use of steam power, on the other hand, the competition of steam with human muscles hastens on the concentration of workpeople and machines in large factories. Thus England is at present experiencing, not only in the colossal industry of making wearing apparel, but in most of the other trades mentioned above, the conversion of manufacture, of handicrafts, and of domestic work into the factory system, after each of those forms of production, totally changed and disorganized under the influence of modern industry, has long ago reproduced, and even overdone, all the horrors of the factory system, without participating in any of the elements of social progress it contains.[44]

[42]   L. c., p. 84, n. 124.

[43]   Instances: The Army Clothing Depot at Pimlico, London, the shirt factory of Tillie and Henderson at Londonderry, and the clothes factory of Messrs. Tait at Limerick, which employs about 1200 hands.

[44]   "Tendency to factory system" (l. c., p. lxvii). "The whole employment is at this time in a state of transition, and is undergoing the same change as that effected in the lace trade, weaving, etc." (l. c., n. 405.) "A complete revolution" (l. c., p. xlvi, n. 318). At the date of the Child. Empl. Comm. of 1840, stocking making was still done by manual labor. Since 1846 various sorts of machines have been introduced, which are now driven by steam. The total number of persons of both sexes and of all ages from

This industrial revolution which takes place spontaneously, is artificially helped on by the extension of the Factory Acts to all industries in which women, young persons, and children are employed. The compulsory regulation of the working day as regards its length, pauses, beginning and end, the system of relays of children, the exclusion of all children under a certain age, etc., necessitate on the one hand more machinery[45] and the substitution of steam as a motive power in the place of muscles.[46] On the other hand, in order to make up for the loss of time, an expansion occurs of the means of production used in common, of the furnaces, buildings, etc.; in one word, greater concentration of the means of production and a correspondingly greater concourse of workpeople. The chief objection, repeatedly and passionately urged on behalf of each manufacture threatened with the Factory Act, is in fact this, that in order to continue the business on the old scale a greater outlay of capital will be necessary. But as regards labor in the so-called domestic industries and the intermediate forms between them and Manufacture, so soon as limits are put to the working day and to the employment of children, those industries go to the wall. Unlimited exploitation of cheap labor-power is the sole foundation of their power to compete.

So long as Factory legislation is confined to regulating the labor in factories, manufactories, etc., it is regarded as a mere interference with the exploiting rights of capital. But when it comes to reg-

---

3 years upwards, employed in stocking making in England, was in 1862 about 129,000. Of these only 4063 were, according to the Parliamentary Return of the 11th February, 1862, working under the Factory Acts.

[45] Thus, e.g., in the earthenware trade, Messrs. Cochrane, of the Britain Pottery, Glasgow, report: "To keep up our quantity we have gone extensively into machines wrought by unskilled labor, and every day convinces us that we can produce a greater quantity than by the old method." ("Rep. of Insp. of Fact., 31st Oct., 1865," p. 13.) "The effect of the Fact. Acts is to force on the further introduction of machinery" (l. c., p. 13–14).

[46] Thus, after the extension of the Factory Act to the potteries, great increase of power-jiggers in place of hand-moved jiggers.

ulating the so-called home-labor,[47] it is immediately viewed as a direct attack on the patria potestas, on parental authority. The tender-hearted English Parliament long affected to shrink from taking this step. The force of facts, however, compelled it at last to acknowledge that modern industry, in overturning the economical foundation on which was based the traditional family, and the family labor corresponding to it, had also unloosened all traditional family ties. The rights of the children had to be proclaimed. The final report of the Ch. Empl. Comm. of 1866, states: "It is unhappily, to a painful degree, apparent throughout the whole of the evidence, that against no persons do the children of both sexes so much require protection as against their parents." The system of unlimited exploitation of children's labor in general and the so-called home-labor in particular is

maintained only because the parents are able, without check or control, to exercise this arbitrary and mischievous power over their young and tender offspring. . . . Parents must not possess the absolute power of making their children mere "machines to earn so much weekly wage." . . . The children and young persons, therefore, in all such cases may justifiably claim from the legislature, as a natural right, that an exemption should be secured to them, from what destroys prematurely their physical strength, and lowers them in the scale of intellectual and moral beings.[48]

It was not, however, the misuse of parental authority that created the capitalistic exploitation, whether direct or indirect, of children's labor; but, on the contrary, it was the capitalistic mode of exploitation which, by sweeping away the economical basis of parental authority, made its exercise degenerate into a mischievous misuse of power. However terrible and disgusting the dissolution, under the capitalist system, of the old family ties may appear, nevertheless, modern industry, by assigning as it does an important

---

47   This sort of labor goes on mostly in small workshops, as we have seen in the lace-making and straw-plaiting trades, and as could be shown more in detail from the metal trades of Sheffield, Birmingham, etc.

48   Ch. Empl. Comm., V. Rep., p. xxv, n. 162, and II. Rep., p. xxxviii, n. 285, 289, p. xxv, xxvi, n. 191.

part in the process of production, outside the domestic sphere, to women, to young persons, and to children of both sexes, creates a new economical foundation for a higher form of the family and of the relations between the sexes. It is, of course, just as absurd to hold the Teutonic-Christian form of the family to be absolute and final as it would be to apply that character to the ancient Roman, the ancient Greek, or the Eastern forms, which moreover, taken together form a series in historic development. Moreover, it is obvious that the fact of the collective working group being composed of individuals of both sexes and all ages, must necessarily, under suitable conditions, become a source of humane development; although in its spontaneously developed, brutal, capitalistic form, where the laborer exists for the process of production, and not the process of production for the laborer, that fact is a pestiferous source of corruption and slavery.[49]

The necessity for a generalization of the Factory Acts, for transforming them from an exceptional law relating to mechanical spinning and weaving—those first creations of machinery—into a law affecting social production as a whole, arose, as we have seen, from the mode in which Modern Industry was historically developed. In the rear of that industry, the traditional form of manufacture, of handicraft, and of domestic industry, is entirely revolutionized; manufactures are constantly passing into the factory system, and handicrafts into manufactures; and lastly, the spheres of handicraft and of the domestic industries become, in a, comparatively speaking, wonderfully short time, dens of misery in which capitalistic exploitation obtains free play for the wildest excesses. There are two circumstances that finally turn the scale: first, the constantly recurring experience that capital, so soon as it finds itself subject to legal control at one point, compensates itself all the more recklessly at other points;[50] secondly, the cry of the capitalists for equality in the conditions of competition, i.e., for equal restraint on all exploitation of labor.[51]

[49] "Factory labor may be as pure and as excellent as domestic labor, and perhaps more so." (Rep. Insp. Fact., 31st October, 1865, p. 127.)
[50] Rep. Insp. of Fact., 31st October, 1865, p. 27–32.
[51] Numerous instances will be found in Rep. of Insp. of Fact.

IV. The Family under Capitalism and Communism

Abolition of the family! Even the most radical flare up at this infamous proposal of the Communists.

On what foundation is the present family, the bourgeois family, based? On capital, on private gain. In its completely developed form this family exists only among the bourgeoisie. But this state of things finds its complement in the practical absence of the family among the proletarians, and in public prostitution.

The bourgeois family will vanish as a matter of course when its complement vanishes, and both will vanish with the vanishing of capital.

Do you charge us with wanting to stop the exploitation of children by their parents? To this crime we plead guilty.

But, you will say, we destroy the most hallowed of relations, when we replace home education by social.

And your education! Is not that also social, and determined by the social conditions under which you educate, by the intervention, direct or indirect, of society by means of schools, etc.? The Communists have not invented the intervention of society in education; they do but seek to alter the character of that intervention, and to rescue education from the influence of the ruling class.

The bourgeois clap-trap about the family and education, about the hallowed co-relation of parent and child, becomes all the more disgusting, the more, by the action of Modern Industry, all family ties among the proletarians are torn asunder, and their children transformed into simple articles of commerce and instruments of labor.

But you Communists would introduce community of women, screams the whole bourgeoisie in chorus.

The bourgeoisie sees in his wife a mere instrument of production. He hears that the instruments of production are to be exploited in common, and, naturally, can come to no other conclusion, than that the lot of being common to all will likewise fall to the women.

He has not even a suspicion that the real point aimed at is to do away with the status of women as mere instruments of production.

For the rest, nothing is more ridiculous than the virtuous in- dignation of our bourgeois at the community of women which, they pretend, is to be openly and officially established by the Commu- nists. The Communists have no need to introduce community of women; it has existed almost from time immemorial.

Our bourgeois, not content with having the wives and daughters of their proletarians at their disposal, not to speak of common prostitutes, take the greatest pleasure in seducing each others' wives.

Bourgeois marriage is in reality a system of wives in common and thus, at the most, what the Communists might possibly be reproached with, is that they desire to introduce, in substitution for a hypocritically concealed, an openly legalized community of women. For the rest, it is self-evident, that the abolition of the pres- ent system of production must bring with it the abolition of the community of women springing from that system, i.e., of prostitu- tion both public and private.

II. The Sweep of Historical Change

7

PRECAPITALIST STAGES OF
DEVELOPMENT

THE WAY in which men produce their means of subsistence
depends first of all on the nature of the actual means they find in
existence and have to reproduce. This mode of production must
not be considered simply as being the reproduction of the physical
existence of the individuals. Rather it is a definite form of activity
of these individuals, a definite form of expressing their life, a definite *mode of life* on their part. As individuals express their life, so
they are. What they are, therefore, coincides with their production,
both with *what* they produce and with *how* they produce. The nature of individuals thus depends on the material conditions determining their production.

This production only makes its appearance with the increase
of population. In its turn this presupposes the intercourse of individuals with one another. The form of this intercourse is again
determined by production.

The relations of different nations among themselves depend
upon the extent to which each has developed its productive forces,
the division of labor, and internal intercourse. This statement is
generally recognized. But not only the relation of one nation to
others, but also the whole internal structure of the nation itself depends on the stage of development reached by its production and
its internal intercourse. How far the productive forces of a nation
are developed is shown most manifestly by the degree to which the
division of labor has been carried. Each new productive force,

From Marx and Engels, *The German Ideology*, pp. 7–13.

insofar as it is not merely a quantitative extension of productive forces already known (for instance the bringing into cultivation of fresh land), brings about a further development of the division of labor.

The division of labor inside a nation leads at first to the separation of industrial and commercial from agricultural labor, and hence to the separation of town and country and a clash of interests between them. Its further development leads to the separation of commercial from industrial labor. At the same time through the division of labor there develop further, inside these various branches, various divisions among the individuals cooperating in definite kinds of labor. The relative position of these individual groups is determined by the methods employed in agriculture, industry, and commerce (patriarchalism, slavery, estates, classes). These same conditions are to be seen (given a more developed intercourse) in the relations of different nations to one another.

The various stages of development in the division of labor are just so many different forms of ownership; i.e., the existing stage in the division of labor determines also the relations of individuals to one another with reference to the material, instrument, and product of labor.

The first form of ownership is tribal ownership. It corresponds to the undeveloped stage of production, at which a people lives by hunting and fishing, by the rearing of beasts or, in the highest stage, agriculture. In the latter case it presupposes a great mass of uncultivated stretches of land. The division of labor is at this stage still very elementary and is confined to a further extension of the natural division of labor imposed by the family. The social structure is therefore limited to an extension of the family; patriarchal family chieftains; below them the members of the tribe; finally slaves. The slavery latent in the family only develops gradually with the increase of population, the growth of wants, and with the extension of external relations, of war or of trade.

The second form is the ancient communal and State ownership which proceeds especially from the union of several tribes into a city by agreement or by conquest, and which is still accompanied by slavery. Beside communal ownership we already find movable, and later also immovable, private property developing, but as an abnormal form subordinate to communal ownership. It is only as a community that the citizens hold power over their laboring slaves, and on this account alone, therefore, they are bound to the form of communal ownership. It is the communal private property which compels the active citizens to remain in this natural form of association over against their slaves. For this reason the whole structure of society based on this communal ownership, and with it the power of the people, decays in the same measure as immovable private property evolves. The division of labor is already more developed. We already find the antagonism of town and country; later the antagonism between those states which represent town interests and those which represent country, and inside the towns themselves the antagonism between industry and maritime commerce. The class relation between citizens and slaves is now completely developed.

This whole interpretation of history appears to be contradicted by the fact of conquest. Up till now violence, war, pillage, rape, and slaughter, etc. have been accepted as the driving force of history. Here we must limit ourselves to the chief points and take therefore only a striking example—the destruction of an old civilization by a barbarous people and the resulting formation of an entirely new organization of society (Rome and the barbarians; Feudalism and Gaul; the Byzantine Empire and the Turks). With the conquering barbarian people war itself is still, as hinted above, a regular form of intercourse, which is the more eagerly exploited as the population increases, involving the necessity of new means of production to supersede the traditional and, for it, the only possible, crude mode of production. In Italy it was, however, otherwise. The concentration of landed property (caused not only by buying-up and indebtedness but also by inheritance, since loose living being rife and marriage rare, the old families died out and their possessions fell into the hands of a few) and its conversion into grazing-land (caused not only by economic forces still operative today but by the importation of plundered and tribute-corn and the resultant lack of demand for Italian corn) brought about the almost total disappearance of the free population. The very slaves died out again and again, and had constantly to be replaced by new ones. Slavery remained the basis of the whole productive system. The plebians, mid-way between freemen and slaves, never succeeded in becoming more than a proletarian rabble. Rome indeed never became more than a city; its connection with the provinces was almost exclusively political and could therefore easily be broken again by political events.

With the development of private property, we find here for the first time the same conditions which we shall find again, only on a more extensive scale, with modern private property. On the one hand the concentration of private property, which began very early in Rome (as the Licinian agrarian law proves),[1] and proceeded very rapidly from the time of the civil wars and especially under the Emperors; on the other hand, coupled with this, the transformation of the plebian small peasantry into a proletariat, which, however, owing to its intermediate position between propertied citizens and slaves, never achieved an independent development.

The third form of ownership is feudal or estate-property. If antiquity started out from the town and its little territory, the Middle Ages started out from the country. This different starting-point was determined by the sparseness of the population at that time, which was scattered over a large area and which received no large increase from the conquerors. In contrast to Greece and Rome, feudal development therefore extends over a much wider field, prepared by the Roman conquests and the spread of agriculture at first associated with it. The last centuries of the declining Roman Empire and its conquest by the barbarians destroyed a number of productive forces; agriculture had declined, industry had decayed for want of a market, trade had died out or been violently suspended, the rural and urban population had decreased. From these conditions and the mode of organization of the conquest determined by them, feudal property developed under the influence of the Germanic military constitution. Like tribal and communal own-

---

[1]   The Licinian agrarian law, passed 367 B.C., limited the amount of common land which a single Roman citizen could hold, and is a sign of the growth of private ownership in Rome.—N.J.S.

ership, it is based again on a community; but the directly producing class standing over against it is not, as in the case of the ancient
community, the slaves, but the enserfed small peasantry. As soon
as feudalism is fully developed, there also arises antagonism to the
towns. The hierarchical system of land ownership, and the armed
bodies of retainers associated with it, gave the nobility power over
the serfs. This feudal organization was, just as much as the ancient
communal ownership, an association against a subjected producing class; but the form of association and the relation to the direct
producers were different because of the different conditions of
production.

This feudal organization of land-ownership had its counterpart
in the towns in the shape of corporative property, the feudal organization of trades. Here property consisted chiefly in the labor of
each individual person. The necessity for association against the
organized robber-nobility, the need for communal covered markets
in an age when the industrialist was at the same time a merchant,
the growing competition of the escaped serfs swarming into the rising towns, the feudal structure of the whole country: these combined to bring about the guilds. Further, the gradually accumulated capital of individual craftsmen and their stable numbers, as
against the growing population, evolved the relation of journeyman
and apprentice, which brought into being in the towns a hierarchy
similar to that in the country.

Thus the chief form of property during the feudal epoch consisted on the one hand of landed property with serf-labor chained to
it, and on the other of individual labor with small capital commanding the labor of journeymen. The organization of both was
determined by the restricted conditions of production—the small-
scale and primitive cultivation of the land, and the craft type of
industry. There was little division of labor in the heyday of feudalism. Each land bore in itself the conflict of town and country
and the division into estates was certainly strongly marked; but
apart from the differentiation of princes, nobility, clergy, and
peasants in the country, and masters, journeymen, apprentices,
and soon also the rabble of casual laborers in the towns, no division of importance took place. In agriculture it was rendered diffi-

cult by the strip-system, beside which the cottage industry of the peasants themselves emerged as another factor. In industry there was no division of labor at all in the individual trades themselves, and very little between them. The separation of industry and commerce was found already in existence in older towns; in the newer it only developed later, when the towns entered into mutual relations.

The grouping of larger territories into feudal kingdoms was a necessity for the landed nobility as for the towns. The organization of the ruling class, the nobility, had, therefore, everywhere a monarch at its head.

8

CAPITALISM'S CONQUEST

THE HISTORY of all hitherto existing society[1] is the history of class struggles.

Freeman and slave, patrician and plebeian, lord and serf, guild-master[2] and journeyman; in a word, oppressor and oppressed, stood in constant opposition to one another, carried on an uninterrupted, now hidden, now open fight, a fight that each time ended, either in a revolutionary reconstitution of society at large, or in the common ruin of the contending classes.

In the early epochs of history, we find almost everywhere a complicated arrangement of society into various orders, a manifold graduation of social rank. In ancient Rome we have patricians,

From *Communist Manifesto*, pp. 9–25.

1   That is, all written history. In 1847, the prehistory of society, the social organization existing previous to recorded history, was all but unknown. Since then, Haxthausen discovered common ownership of land in Russia. Maurer proved it to be the social foundation from which all Teutonic races started in history, and by and by village communities were found to be, or to have been, the primitive form of society everywhere from India to Ireland. The inner organization of this primitive Communistic society was laid bare, in its typical form, by Morgan's crowning discovery of the true nature of the gens and its relation to the tribe. With the dissolution of these primeval communities society begins to be differentiated into separate and finally antagonistic classes I [Engels] have attempted to retrace this process of dissolution in "The Origin of the Family, Private Property and the State" (Chicago, Charles H. Kerr & Co.).

2   Guild-master, that is a full member of a guild, a master within, not a head of, a guild.

knights, plebeians, slaves; in the Middle Ages, feudal lords, vassals, guild-masters, journeymen, apprentices, serfs; in almost all of these classes, again, subordinate gradations.

The modern bourgeois society that has sprouted from the ruins of feudal society, has not done away with class antagonisms. It has but established new classes, new conditions of oppression, new forms of struggle in place of the old ones.

Our epoch, the epoch of the bourgeoisie, possesses, however, this distinctive feature: it has simplified the class antagonisms. Society as a whole is more and more splitting up into two great hostile camps, into two great classes directly facing each other: Bourgeoisie and Proletariat.

From the serfs of the Middle Ages sprang the chartered burghers of the earliest towns. From these burgesses the first elements of the bourgeoisie were developed.

The discovery of America, the rounding of the Cape, opened up fresh ground for the rising bourgeoisie. The East-Indian and Chinese markets, the colonization of America, trade with the colonies, the increase in the means of exchange and in commodities, generally, gave to commerce, to navigation, to industry, an impulse never before known, and thereby, to the revolutionary element in the tottering feudal society, a rapid development.

The feudal system of industry, under which industrial production was monopolized by closed guilds, now no longer sufficed for the growing wants of the new markets. The manufacturing system took its place. The guild-masters were pushed on one side by the manufacturing middle-class; division of labor between the different corporate guilds vanished in the face of division of labor in each single workshop.

Meantime the markets kept ever growing, the demand, ever rising. Even manufacturing no longer sufficed. Thereupon, steam and machinery revolutionized industrial production. The place of manufacture was taken by the giant, Modern Industry, the place of the industrial middle-class, by industrial millionaires, the leaders of whole industrial armies, the modern bourgeoisie.

Modern Industry has established the world-market, for which the discovery of America paved the way. This market has given an immense development to commerce, to navigation, to communication by land. This development has, in its turn, reacted on the extension of industry; and in proportion as industry, commerce, navigation, railways extended in the same proportion the bourgeoisie developed, increased its capital, and pushed into the background every class handed down from the Middle Ages.

We see, therefore, how the modern bourgeoisie is itself the product of a long course of development, of a series of revolutions in the modes of production and of exchange.

Each step in the development of the bourgeoisie was accompanied by a corresponding political advance of that class. An oppressed class under the sway of the feudal nobility, an armed and self-governing association in the medieval commune,[3] here independent urban republic (as in Italy and Germany), there taxable "third estate" of the monarchy (as in France), afterwards, in the period of manufacturing proper, serving either the semifeudal or the absolute monarchy as a counterpoise against the nobility, and in fact, cornerstone of the great monarchies in general, the bourgeoisie has at last, since the establishment of Modern Industry and of the world-market, conquered for itself, in the modern representative State, exclusive political sway. The executive of the modern State is but a committee for managing the common affairs of the whole bourgeoisie.

The bourgeoisie, historically, has played a most revolutionary part.

The bourgeoisie, wherever it has got the upper hand, has put an end to all feudal, patriarchal, idyllic relations. It has pitilessly torn asunder the motley feudal ties that bound man to his "natural superiors," and has left remaining no other nexus between man and man than naked self-interest, than callous "cash payment." It has drowned the most heavenly ecstasies of religious fervor, of chivalrous enthusiasm, of philistine sentimentalism, in the icy

---

3   "Commune" was the name taken, in France, by the nascent towns even before they had conquered from their feudal lords and masters, local self-government and political rights as "the Third Estate." Generally speaking, for the economical development of the bourgeoisie, England is here taken as the typical country, for its political development, France.

water of egotistical calculation. It has resolved personal worth into exchange value, and in place of the numberless indefeasible chartered freedoms, has set up that single, unconscionable freedom—Free Trade. In one word, for exploitation, veiled by religious and political illusions, it has substituted naked, shameless, direct, brutal exploitation.

The bourgeoisie has stripped of its halo every occupation hitherto honored and looked up to with reverent awe. It has converted the physician, the lawyer, the priest, the poet, the man of science, into its paid wage-laborers.

The bourgeoisie has torn away from the family its sentimental veil, and has reduced the family relation to a mere money relation.

The bourgeoisie has disclosed how it came to pass that the brutal display of vigor in the Middle Ages, which Reactionists so much admire, found its fitting complement in the most slothful indolence. It has been the first to show what man's activity can bring about. It his accomplished wonders far surpassing Egyptian pyramids, Roman aqueducts, and Gothic cathedrals; it has conducted expeditions that put in the shade all former Exoduses of nations and crusades.

The bourgeoisie cannot exist without constantly revolutionizing the instruments of production, and thereby the relations of production, and with them the whole relations of society. Conservation of the old modes of production in unaltered form, was, on the contrary, the first condition of existence for all earlier industrial classes. Constant revolutionizing of production, uninterrupted disturbance of all social conditions, everlasting uncertainty and agitation distinguish the bourgeois epoch from all earlier ones. All fixed, fast-frozen relations, with their train of ancient and venerable prejudices and opinions, are swept away, all newly-formed ones become antiquated before they can ossify. All that is solid melts into air, all that is holy is profaned, and man is at last compelled to face with sober senses, his real conditions of life, and his relations with his kind.

The need of a constantly expanding market for its products chases the bourgeoisie over the whole surface of the globe. It must nestle everywhere, settle everywhere, establish connections everywhere.

The bourgeoisie has through its exploitation of the world-market given a cosmopolitan character to production and consumption in every country. To the great chagrin of Reactionists, it has drawn from under the feet of industry the national ground on which it stood. All old-established national industries have been destroyed or are daily being destroyed. They are dislodged by new industries, whose introduction becomes a life and death question for all civilized nations, by industries that no longer work up indigenous raw material, but raw material drawn from the remotest zones; industries whose products are consumed, not only at home, but in every quarter of the globe. In place of the old wants, satisfied by the productions of the country, we find new wants, requiring for their satisfaction the products of distant lands and climes. In place of the old local and national seclusion and self-sufficiency, we have intercourse in every direction, universal interdependence of nations. And as in material, so also in intellectual production. The intellectual creations of individual nations become common property. National one-sidedness and narrow-mindedness become more and more impossible, and from the numerous national and local literatures there arises a world-literature.

The bourgeoisie, by the rapid improvement of all instruments of production, by the immensely facilitated means of communication, draws all, even the most barbarian, nations into civilization. The cheap prices of its commodities are the heavy artillery with which it batters down all Chinese walls, with which it forces the barbarians' intensely obstinate hatred of foreigners to capitulate. It compels all nations, on pain of extinction, to adopt the bourgeois mode of production; it compels them to introduce what it calls civilization into their midst, i.e., to become bourgeois themselves. In a word, it creates a world after its own image.

The bourgeoisie has subjected the country to the rule of the towns. It has created enormous cities, has greatly increased the urban population as compared with the rural, and has thus rescued a considerable part of the population from the idiocy of rural life. Just as it has made the country dependent on the towns, so it has made barbarian and semibarbarian countries dependent on the civilized ones, nations of peasants on nations of bourgeois, the East on the West.

The bourgeoisie keeps more and more doing away with the scattered state of the population, of the means of production, and of property. It has agglomerated population, centralized means of production, and has concentrated property in a few hands. The necessary consequence of this was political centralization. Independent, or but loosely connected provinces, with separate interests, laws, governments, and systems of taxation, became lumped together in one nation, with one government, one code of laws, one national class-interest, one frontier, and one customs-tariff.

The bourgeoisie, during its rule of scarce one hundred years, has created more massive and more colossal productive forces than have all preceding generations together. Subjection of Nature's forces to man, machinery, application of chemistry to industry and agriculture, steam-navigation, railways, electric telegraphs, clearing of whole continents for cultivation, canalization of rivers, whole populations conjured out of the ground—what earlier century had even a presentiment that such productive forces slumbered in the lap of social labor?

We see then: the means of production and of exchange on whose foundations the bourgeoisie built itself up, were generated in feudal society. At a certain stage in the development of these means of production and of exchange, the conditions under which feudal society produced and exchanged, the feudal organization of agriculture and manufacturing industry, in one word, the feudal relations of property became no longer compatible with the already developed productive forces; they became so many fetters. They had to be burst asunder; they were burst asunder.

Into their places stepped free competition, accompanied by a social and political constitution adapted to it, and by the economical and political sway of the bourgeois class.

A similar movement is going on before our own eyes. Modern bourgeois society with its relations of production, of exchange, and of property, a society that has conjured up such gigantic means of production and of exchange, is like the sorcerer, who is no longer able to control the powers of the nether world whom he has called up by his spells. For many a decade past the history of industry and commerce is but the history of the revolt of modern productive

forces against modern conditions of production, against the property relations that are the condition for the existence of the bourgeoisie and of its rule. It is enough to mention the commercial
crises that by their periodical return put on trial, each time more
threateningly, the existence of the entire bourgeois society. In these
crises a great part not only of the existing products, but also of the
previously created productive forces, are periodically destroyed.
In these crises there breaks out an epidemic that, in all earlier
epochs, would have seemed an absurdity—the epidemic of overproduction. Society suddenly finds itself put back into a state of
momentary barbarism; it appears as if a famine, a universal war of
devastation had cut off the supply of every means of subsistence; industry and commerce seem to be destroyed; and why? Because
there is too much civilization, too much means of subsistence, too
much industry, too much commerce. The productive forces at the
disposal of society no longer tend to further the development of the
conditions of bourgeois property; on the contrary, they have become too powerful for these conditions, by which they are fettered,
and so soon as they overcome these fetters, they bring disorder
into the whole of bourgeois society, endangering the existence of
bourgeois property. The conditions of bourgeois society are too
narrow to comprise the wealth created by them. And how does the
bourgeoisie get over these crises? On the one hand by enforced
destruction of a mass of productive forces; on the other, by the conquest of new markets, and by the more thorough exploitation of the
old ones. That is to say, by paving the way for more extensive and
more destructive crises, and by diminishing the means whereby
crises are prevented.

The weapons with which the bourgeoisie felled feudalism to
the ground are now turned against the bourgeoisie itself.

But not only has the bourgeoisie forged the weapons that bring
death to itself; it has also called into existence the men who are to
wield those weapons—the modern working-class—the proletarians.

In proportion as the bourgeoisie, i.e., capital, is developed, in
the same proportion is the proletariat, the modern working-class,
developed, a class of laborers, who live only so long as they find
work, and who find work only so long as their labor increases

capital. These laborers, who must sell themselves piecemeal, are a commodity, like every other article of commerce, and are consequently exposed to all the vicissitudes of competition, to all the fluctuations of the market.

Owing to the extensive use of machinery and to division of labor, the work of the proletarians has lost all individual character, and, consequently, all charm for the workman. He becomes an appendage of the machine, and it is only the most simple, most monotonous, and most easily acquired knack that is required of him. Hence, the cost of production of a workman is restricted, almost entirely, to the means of subsistence that he requires for his maintenance, and for the propagation of his race. But the price of a commodity, and also of labor, is equal to its cost of production. In proportion, therefore, as the repulsiveness of the work increases, the wage decreases. Nay more, in proportion as the use of machinery and division of labor increases, in the same proportion the burden of toil also increases, whether by prolongation of the working hours, by increase of the work enacted in a given time, or by increased speed of the machinery, etc.

Modern Industry has converted the little workshop of the patriarchal master into the great factory of the industrial capitalist. Masses of laborers, crowded into the factory, are organized like soldiers. As privates of the industrial army they are placed under the command of a perfect hierarchy of officers and sergeants. Not only are they the slaves of the bourgeois class, and of the bourgeois State, they are daily and hourly enslaved by the machine, by the overlooker, and, above all, by the individual bourgeois manufacturer himself. The more openly this despotism proclaims gain to be its end and aim, the more petty, the more hateful, and the more embittering it is.

The less the skill and exertion or strength implied in manual labor, in other words, the more modern industry becomes developed, the more is the labor of men superseded by that of women. Differences of age and sex have no longer any distinctive social validity for the working class. All are instruments of labor, more or less expensive to use, according to their age and sex.

No sooner is the exploitation of the laborer by the manufacturer so far at an end, that he receives his wages in cash, than he is set upon by the other portions of the bourgeoisie, the landlord, the shopkeeper, the pawnbroker, etc.

The low strata of the middle class—the small trades-people, shopkeepers, and retired tradesmen generally, the handicraftsmen and peasants—all these sink gradually into the proletariat, partly because their diminutive capital does not suffice for the scale on which Modern Industry is carried on, and is swamped in the competition with the large capitalists, partly because their specialized skill is rendered worthless by new methods of production. Thus the proletariat is recruited from all classes of the population.

The proletariat goes through various stages of development. With its birth begins its struggle with the bourgeoisie. At first the contest is carried on by individual laborers, then by the workpeople of a factory, then by the operatives of one trade, in one locality, against the individual bourgeois who directly exploits them. They direct their attacks not against the bourgeois conditions of production, but against the instruments of production themselves; they destroy imported wares that compete with their labor, they smash to pieces machinery, they set factories ablaze, they seek to restore by force the vanished status of the workman of the Middle Ages.

At this stage the laborers still form an incoherent mass scattered over the whole country, and broken up by their mutual competition. If anywhere they unite to form more compact bodies, this is not yet the consequence of their own active union, but of the union of bourgeoisie, which class, in order to attain its own political ends, is compelled to set the whole proletariat in motion, and is moreover yet, for a time, able to do so. At this stage, therefore, the proletarians do not fight their enemies, but the enemies of their enemies, the remnants of absolute monarchy, the landowners, the nonindustrial bourgeoisie, the petty bourgeoisie. Thus the whole historical movement is concentrated in the hands of the bourgeoisie; every victory so obtained is a victory for the bourgeoisie.

But with the development of industry the proletariat not only increases in number, it becomes concentrated in great masses, its strength grows, and it feels that strength more. The various interests and conditions of life within the ranks of the proletariat are more and more equalized, in proportion as machinery obliterates all distinction of labor, and nearly everywhere reduces wages to the same low level. The growing competition among the bourgeoisie, and the resulting commercial crises, make the wages of the worker ever more fluctuating. The unceasing improvement of machinery, even more rapidly developing, makes their livelihood more and more precarious, the collisions between individual workmen and individual bourgeois take more and more the character of collision between two classes. Thereupon the workers begin to form combinations (Trades Unions) against the bourgeoisie; they club together in order to keep up the rate of wages; they found permanent associations in order to make provision beforehand for these occasional revolts. Here and there the contest breaks out into riots.

Now and then the workers are victorious, but only for a time. The real fruits of their battles lie, not in the immediate result, but in the ever expanding union of the workers. This union is helped on by the improved means of communication that are created by modern industry, and that place the workers of different localities in contact with one another. It was just this contact that was needed to centralize the numerous local struggles, all of the same character, into one national struggle between classes. But every class struggle is a political struggle. And that union, to attain which the burghers of the Middle Ages, with their miserable highways, required centuries, the modern proletarians, thanks to railways, achieve in a few years.

This organization of the proletarians into a class, and consequently into a political party, is continually being upset again by the competition between the workers themselves. But it ever rises up again, stronger, firmer, mightier. It compels legislative recognition of particular interests of the workers, by taking advantage of the divisions among the bourgeoisie itself. Thus the ten-hour bill in England was carried.

Altogether collisions between the classes of the old society further, in many ways, the course of development of the proletariat. The bourgeoisie finds itself involved in a constant battle. At first with the aristocracy; later on, with those portions of the bourgeoisie itself, whose interests have become antagonistic to the progress of industry; at all times, with the bourgeoisie of foreign countries. In all these battles it sees itself compelled to appeal to the proletariat, to ask for its help, and thus, to drag it into the political arena. The bourgeoisie itself, therefore, supplies the proletariat with its own elements of political and general education, in other words, it furnishes the proletariat with weapons for fighting the bourgeoisie.

Further, as we have already seen, entire sections of the ruling classes are, by the advance of industry, precipitated into the proletariat, or are at least threatened in their conditions of existence. These also supply the proletariat with fresh elements of enlightenment and progress.

Finally, in times when the class-struggle nears the decisive hour, the process of dissolution going on within the ruling class, in fact, within the whole range of old society, assumes such a violent, glaring character, that a small section of the ruling class cuts itself adrift, and joins the revolutionary class, the class that holds the future in its hands. Just as, therefore, at an earlier period, a section of the nobility went over to the bourgeoisie, so now a portion of the bourgeoisie goes over to the proletariat, and in particular, a portion of the bourgeois ideologists, who have raised themselves to the level of comprehending theoretically the historical movements as a whole.

Of all the classes that stand face to face with the bourgeoisie today, the proletariat alone is a really revolutionary class. The other classes decay and finally disappear in the face of Modern Industry; the proletariat is its special and essential product.

The lower middle-class, the small manufacturer, the shopkeeper, the artisan, the peasant, all these fight against the bourgeoisie, to save from extinction their existence as fractions of the middle class. They are, therefore, not revolutionary, but conservative. Nay more, they are reactionary, for they try to roll back the wheel of history. If by chance they are revolutionary, they are so, only in view of their impending transfer into the proletariat, they thus defend not their present, but their future interests, they desert their own standpoint to place themselves at that of the proletariat.

The "dangerous class," the social scum, that passively rotting mass thrown off by the lowest layers of old society, may, here and there, be swept into the movement by a proletarian revolution; its conditions of life, however, prepare it far more for the part of a bribed tool of reactionary intrigue.

In the conditions of the proletariat, those of old society at large are already virtually swamped. The proletarian is without property; his relation to his wife and children has no longer anything in common with the bourgeois family-relations; modern industrial labor, modern subjugation to capital, the same in England as in France, in America as in Germany, has stripped him of every trace of national character. Law, morality, religion, are to him so many bourgeois prejudices, behind which lurk in ambush just as many bourgeois interests.

All the preceding classes that got the upper hand, sought to fortify their already acquired status by subjecting society at large to their conditions of appropriation. The proletarians cannot become masters of the productive forces of society, except by abolishing their own previous mode of appropriation, and thereby also every other previous mode of appropriation. They have nothing of their own to secure and to fortify; their mission is to destroy all previous securities for, and insurances of, individual property.

All previous historical movements were movements of minorities, or in the interests of minorities. The proletarian movement is the self-conscious, independent movement of the immense majority, in the interest of the immense majority. The proletariat, the lowest stratum of our present society, cannot stir, cannot raise itself up, without the whole superincumbent strata of official society being sprung into the air.

Though not in substance, yet in form, the struggle of the proletariat with the bourgeoisie is at first a national struggle. The proletariat of each country must, of course, first of all settle matters with its own bourgeoisie.

In depicting the most general phases of the development of the proletariat, we traced the more or less veiled civil war, raging within existing society, up to the point where that war breaks out into open revolution, and where the violent overthrow of the bourgeoisie lays the foundation for the sway of the proletariat.

Hitherto, every form of society has been based, as we have already seen, on the antagonism of oppressing and oppressed classes. But in order to oppress a class, certain conditions must be assured to it under which it can, at least, continue its slavish existence. The serf, in the period of serfdom, raised himself to membership in the commune, just as the petty bourgeois, under the yoke of feudal absolutism, managed to develop into a bourgeois.

The modern laborer, on the contrary, instead of rising with the progress of industry, sinks deeper and deeper below the conditions of existence of his own class. He becomes a pauper, and pauperism develops more rapidly than population and wealth. And here it becomes evident that the bourgeoisie is unfit any longer to be the ruling class in society, and to impose its conditions of existence upon society as an overriding law. It is unfit to rule, because it is incompetent to assure an existence to its slave within his slavery, because it cannot help letting him sink into such a state that it has to feed him, instead of being fed by him. Society can no longer live under this bourgeoisie, in other words, its existence is no longer compatible with society.

The essential condition for the existence, and for the sway of the bourgeois class, is the formation and augmentation of capital; the condition for capital is wage-labor. Wage-labor rests exclusively on competition between the laborers. The advance of industry, whose involuntary promoter is the bourgeoisie, replaces the isolation of the laborers, due to competition, by their revolutionary combination, due to association. The development of Modern Industry, therefore, cuts from under its feet the very foundation on which the bourgeoisie produces and appropriates products. What the bourgeoisie therefore produces, above all, are its own gravediggers. Its fall and the victory of the proletariat are equally inevitable.

9

THE NATURE OF COMMUNISM

I

THE TRANSCENDENCE of self-estrangement follows the same course as self-estrangement. *Private property* is first considered only in its objective aspect—but nevertheless with labor as its essence. Its form of existence is therefore *capital,* which is to be annulled "as such" (Proudhon). Or a *particular form* of labor—labor leveled down, parceled, and therefore unfree—is conceived as the source of private property's *perniciousness* and of its existence in estrangement from men. For instance, *Fourier,* who, like the physiocrats, also conceived *agricultural labor* to be at least the *exemplary* type, whilst *Saint-Simon* declares in contrast that *industrial labor* as such is the essence, and only aspires to the *exclusive* rule of the industrialists and the improvement of the workers' condition. Finally, *communism* is the *positive* expression of annulled private property—at first as *universal* private property. By embracing this relation as a *whole,* communism is:

1. In its first form only a *generalization* and *consummation* of this relationship. As such it appears in a twofold form: on the one hand, the dominion of *material* property bulks so large that it wants to destroy *everything* which is not capable of being possessed by all as *private property.* It wants to do away *by force* with talent, etc. For it the sole purpose of life and existence is direct, physical *possession.* The task of the *laborer* is not done away with, but ex-

---

Section I of this chapter is from *Economic and Philosophical Manuscripts,* pp. 132–35; section II is from *Communist Manifesto,* pp. 36–37.

tended to all men. The relationship of private property persists as the relationship of the community to the world of things.

Finally, this movement of opposing universal private property to private property finds expression in the animal form of opposing to *marriage* (certainly a *form of exclusive private property*) the *community of women,* in which a woman becomes a piece of *communal* and *common* property. It may be said that this idea of the *community of women* gives away the *secret* of this as yet completely crude and thoughtless communism.[1] Just as woman passes from marriage to general prostitution, so the entire world of wealth (that is, of man's objective substance) passes from the relationship of exclusive marriage with the owner of private property to a state of universal prostitution with the community. In negating the *personality* of man in every sphere, this type of communism is really nothing but the logical expression of private property, which is its negation. General *envy* constituting itself as a power is the disguise in which *greed* reestablishes itself and satisfies itself, only in *another* way. The thought of every piece of private property—inherent in each piece as such—is *at least* turned against all *wealthier* private property in the form of envy and the urge to reduce things to a common level, so that this envy and urge even constitute the essence of competition. The crude communism is only the culmination of this envy and of this leveling-down proceeding from the *preconceived* minimum. It has a *definite, limited* standard. How little this annulment of private property is really an appropriation is in fact proved by the abstract negation of the entire world of culture and civilization, the regression to the *unnatural* simplicity of the *poor and undemanding* man who has not only failed to go beyond private property, but has not yet even reached it.

The community is only a community of *labor,* and of equality of *wages* paid out by communal capital—the *community* as the universal capitalist. Both sides of the relationship are raised to an *imagined* universality—*labor* as a state in which every person is

[1]   Prostitution is only a *specific* expression of the *general* prostitution of the *laborer*, and since it is a relationship in which falls not the prostitute alone, but also the one who prostitutes—and the latter's abomination is still greater—the capitalist, etc., also comes under this head.

placed, and *capital* as the acknowledged universality and power of the community.

In the approach to *woman* as the spoil and handmaid of communal lust is expressed the infinite degradation in which man exists for himself, for the secret of this approach has its *unambiguous*, decisive, *plain* and undisguised expression in the relation of *man* to *woman* and in the manner in which the *direct* and *natural* species relationship is conceived. This direct, natural, and necessary relation of person to person is the *relation of man to woman*. In this *natural* species relationship man's relation to nature is immediately his relation to man, just as his relation to man is immediately his relation to nature—his own *natural* destination. In this relationship, therefore, is *sensuously manifested*, reduced to an observable *fact*, the extent to which the human essence has become nature to man, or to which nature to him has become the human essence of man. From this relationship one can therefore judge man's whole level of development. From the character of this relationship follows how much *man* as a *species being*, as *man*, has come to be himself and to comprehend himself; the relation of man to woman is *the most natural* relation of human being to human being. It therefore reveals the extent to which man's *natural* behavior has become *human*, or the extent to which the *human* essence in him has become a *natural* essence—the extent to which his *human nature* has come to be *nature to him*. In this relationship is revealed, too, the extent to which man's *need* has become a *human* need; the extent to which, therefore, the *other* person as a person has become for him a need—the extent to which he in his individual existence is at the same time a social being.

The first positive annulment of private property—*crude* communism—is thus merely one *form* in which the vileness of private property, which wants to set itself up as the *positive community*, comes to the surface.

2. Communism (*a*) still political in nature—democratic or despotic; (*b*) with the abolition of the state, yet still incomplete, and being still affected by private property (i.e., by the estrangement of man). In both forms communism already is aware of being reintegration or return of man to himself, the transcendence of hu-

man self-estrangement; but since it has not yet grasped the positive essence of private property, and just as little the *human* nature of need, it remains captive to it and infected by it. It has, indeed, grasped its concept, but not its essence.

3. *Communism* as the *positive* transcendence of *private property*, as *human self-estrangement*, and therefore as the real *appropriation of the human* essence by and for man; communism therefore as the complete return of man to himself as a *social* (i.e., human) being—a return become conscious, and accomplished within the entire wealth of previous development. This communism, as fully developed naturalism, equals humanism, and as fully developed humanism equals naturalism; it is the genuine resolution of the conflict between man and nature and between man and man —the true resolution of the strife between existence and essence, between objectification and self-confirmation, between freedom and necessity, between the individual and the species. Communism is the riddle of history solved, and it knows itself to be this solution.

II

The proletariat will use its political supremacy, to wrest, by degrees, all capital from the bourgeoisie, to centralize all instruments of production in the hands of the State, i.e., of the proletariat organized as the ruling class; and to increase the total of productive forces as rapidly as possible.

Of course, in the beginning, this cannot be effected except by means of despotic inroads on the rights of property, and on the conditions of bourgeois production, by means of measures, therefore, which appear economically insufficient and untenable, but which, in the course of the movement, outstrip themselves, necessitate further inroads upon the old social order, and are unavoidable as a means of entirely revolutionizing the mode of production.

These measures will of course be different in different countries.

Nevertheless in the most advanced countries the following will be pretty generally applicable:

1. Abolition of property in land and application of all rents of land to public purposes.

2. A heavy progressive or graduated income tax.

3. Abolition of all right of inheritance.

4. Confiscation of the property of all emigrants and rebels.

5. Centralization of credit in the hands of the State, by means of a national bank with State capital and an exclusive monopoly.

6. Centralization of the means of communication and transport in the hands of the State.

7. Extension of factories and instruments of production owned by the State, the bringing into cultivation of waste lands, and the improvement of the soil generally in accordance with a common plan.

8. Equal liability of all to labor. Establishment of industrial armies, especially for agriculture.

9. Combination of agriculture with manufacturing industries; gradual abolition of the distinction between town and country, by a more equable distribution of population over the country.

10. Free education for all children in public schools. Abolition of children's factory labor in its present form. Combination of education with industrial production, etc., etc.

When, in the course of development, class distinctions have disappeared, and all production has been concentrated in the hands of a vast association of the whole nation, the public power will lose its political character. Political power, property so called, is merely the organized power of one class for suppressing another. If the proletariat during its contest with the bourgeoisie is compelled, by the force of circumstances, to organize itself as a class, if, by means of a revolution, it makes itself the ruling class, and, as such, sweeps away by force the old conditions of production, then it will, along with these conditions, have swept away the conditions for the existence of class antagonisms, and of classes generally, and will thereby have abolished its own supremacy as a class.

In place of the old bourgeois society, with its classes and class antagonisms, we shall have an association, in which the free development of each is the condition for the free development of all.

III. The Mechanisms of Change

10

COMPETITION AND ITS EFFECTS
ON THE VARIOUS CLASSES

WE THUS SEE how the method of production and the means of production are constantly enlarged, revolutionized, how *division of labor necessarily draws after it greater division of labor, the employment of machinery greater employment of machinery, work upon a large scale work upon a still greater scale.* This is the law that continually throws capitalist production out of its old ruts and compels capital to strain ever more the productive forces of labor *for the very reason* that it has already strained them—the law that grants it no respite, and constantly shouts in its ear: March! March! This is no other law than that which, within the periodical fluctuations of commerce, necessarily *adjusts the price of a commodity to its cost of production.*

No matter how powerful the means of production which a capitalist may bring into the field, competition will make their adoption general; and from the moment that they have been generally adopted, the sole result of the greater productiveness of his capital will be that he must furnish *at the same price*, ten, twenty, one hundred times as much as before. But since he must find a market for, perhaps, a thousand times as much, in order to outweigh the lower selling price by the greater quantity of the sales; since now a more extensive sale is necessary not only to gain a greater profit, but also in order to replace the cost of production (the instrument of production itself grows always more costly, as we have seen), and since this more extensive sale has become a question of life and death not only for him, but also for his rivals, the old struggle must begin again, and it is all the more violent the more powerful the means of production already invented are. *The division of labor and the application of machinery will therefore take a fresh start, and upon an even greater scale.*

Whatever be the power of the means of production which are employed, competition seeks to rob capital of the golden fruits of this power by reducing the price of commodities to the cost of production; in the same measure in which production is cheapened, i.e., in the same measure in which more can be produced with the same amount of labor, it compels by a law which is irresistible a still greater cheapening of production, the sale of even greater masses of product for smaller prices. Thus the capitalist will have gained nothing more by his efforts than the obligation to furnish a greater product in the same labor-time; in a word, more difficult conditions for the profitable employment of his capital. While competition, therefore, constantly pursues him with its law of the cost of production and turns against himself every weapon that he forges against his rivals, the capitalist continually seeks to get the best of competition by restlessly introducing further subdivision of labor and new machines, which, though more expensive, enable him to produce more cheaply, instead of waiting until the new machines shall have been rendered obsolete by competition.

If we now conceive this feverish agitation as it operates in the *market of the whole world,* we shall be in a position to comprehend how the growth, accumulation, and concentration of capital bring in their train an ever more detailed subdivision of labor, an ever greater improvement of old machines, and a constant application of new machines—a process which goes on uninterruptedly, with feverish haste, and upon an ever more gigantic scale.

But what effect do these conditions, which are inseparable from the growth of productive capital, have upon the determination of wages?

The greater *division of labor* enables one laborer to accomplish the work of five, ten, or twenty laborers; it therefore increases competition among the laborers fivefold, tenfold, or twentyfold. The laborers compete not only by selling themselves one cheaper than the other, but also by one doing the work of five, then ten, or twenty; and they are forced to compete in this manner by the division of labor, which is introduced and steadily improved by capital.

Furthermore, to the same degree in which the division of labor increases, is the labor simplified. The special skill of the laborer becomes worthless. He becomes transformed into a simple monotonous force of production, with neither physical nor mental elasticity. His work becomes accessible to all; therefore competitors press upon him from all sides. Moreover, it must be remembered that the more simple, the more easily learned the work is, so much the less is its cost of production, the expense of its acquisition, and so much the lower must the wages sink—for, like the price of any other commodity, they are determined by the cost of production. Therefore, *in the same measure in which labor becomes more unsatisfactory, more repulsive, do competition increase and wages decrease.*

The laborer seeks to maintain the total of his wages for a given time by performing more labor, either by working a greater number of hours, or by accomplishing more in the same number of hours. Thus, urged on by want, he himself multiplies the disastrous effects of division of labor. The result is: *the more he works, the less wages he receives.* And for this simple reason: the more he works, the more he competes against his fellow workmen, the more he compels them to compete against him, and to offer themselves on the same wretched conditions as he does; so that, in the last analysis, *he competes against himself as a member of the working class.*

Machinery produces the same effects, but upon a much larger scale. It supplants skilled laborers by unskilled, men by women, adults by children; where newly introduced, it throws workers upon the streets in great masses; and as it becomes more highly developed and more productive it discards them in additional though smaller numbers.

We have hastily sketched in broad outlines the *industrial war of capitalists among themselves. This war has the peculiarity that the battles in it are won less by recruiting than by discharging the army of workers. The generals (the capitalists) vie with one an-*

other as to who can discharge the greatest number of industrial soldiers.

The economists tell us, to be sure, that those laborers who have been rendered superfluous by machinery find new avenues of employment. They dare not assert directly that the same laborers that have been discharged find situations in new branches of labor. Facts cry out too loudly against this lie. Strictly speaking, they only maintain that new means of employment will be found *for other sections of the working class;* for example, for that portion of the young generation of laborers who were about to enter upon that branch of industry which had just been abolished. Of course, this is a great satisfaction to the disabled laborers. There will be no lack of fresh exploitable blood and muscle for the Messrs. Capitalists—the dead may bury their dead. This consolation seems to be intended more for the comfort of the capitalists themselves than of their laborers. If the whole class of the wage-laborer were to be annihilated by machinery, how terrible that would be for capital, *which, without wage-labor, ceases to be capital!*

But even if we assume that all who are directly forced out of employment by machinery, as well as all of the rising generation who were waiting for a chance of employment in the same branch of industry, do actually find some new employment—are we to believe that this new employment will pay as high wages as did the one they have lost? If it did, *it would be in contradiction to all the laws of political economy.* We have seen how modern industry always tends to the substitution of the simpler and more subordinate employments for the higher and more complex ones. How, then, could a mass of workers thrown out of one branch of industry by machinery find refuge in another branch, unless they were to be paid more poorly?

An exception to the law has been adduced, namely, the workers who are employed in the manufacture of machinery itself. As soon as there is in industry a greater demand for and a greater consumption of machinery, it is said that the number of machines must necessarily increase; consequently, also, the manufacture of machines; consequently, also, the employment of workers in machine manufacture; and the workers employed in this branch of industry are skilled, even educated, workers.

Since the year 1840[1] this assertion, which even before that date was only half true, has lost all semblance of truth; for the most diverse machines are now applied to the manufacture of the machines themselves on quite as extensive a scale as in the manufacture of cotton yarn, and the laborers employed in machine factories can but play the role of very stupid machines alongside of the highly ingenious machines.

But in place of the man who has been dismissed by the machine, the factory may employ, perhaps, three children and one woman! And must not the wages of the man have previously sufficed for the three children and one woman? Must not the minimum wages have sufficed for the preservation and propagation of the race? What, then, do these beloved bourgeois phrases prove? Nothing more than that now four times as many workers' lives are used up as there were previously, in order to obtain the livelihood of one working family.

To sum up: *the more productive capital grows, the more it extends the division of labor and the application of machinery; the more the division of labor and the application of machinery extend, the more does competition extend among the workers, the more do their wages shrink together.*

In addition, the working class is also recruited from the *higher strata* of society; a mass of small businessmen and of people living upon the interest of their capitals is precipitated into the ranks of the working class, and they will have nothing else to do than to stretch out their arms alongside of the arms of the workers. Thus the forest of outstretched arms, begging for work, grows ever thicker, while the arms themselves grow ever leaner.

It is evident that the small manufacturer cannot survive in a struggle in which the first condition of success is production upon an ever greater scale. It is evident that the small manufacturer cannot at the same time be a big manufacturer.

That the interest on capital decreases in the same ratio in which the mass and number of capitals increase, that it diminishes with the growth of capital, that therefore the small capitalist can no longer live on his interest, but must consequently throw himself

[1]   *Wage-Labor and Capital* was originally written in 1849.—N.J.S.

upon industry by joining the ranks of the small manufacturers and thereby increasing the number of candidates for the proletariat— all this requires no further elucidation.

Finally, in the same measure in which the capitalists are compelled, by the movement described above, to exploit the already existing gigantic means of production on an ever-increasing scale, and for this purpose to set in motion all the mainsprings of credit, in the same measure do they increase the industrial earthquakes, in the midst of which the commercial world can preserve itself only by sacrificing a portion of its wealth, its products, and even its forces of production, to the gods of the lower world—in short, the *crises* increase. They become more frequent and more violent, if for no other reason, than for this alone, that in the same measure in which the mass of products grows, and therefore the needs for extensive markets, in the same measure does the world market shrink ever more, and ever fewer markets remain to be exploited, since every previous crisis has subjected to the commerce of the world a hitherto unconquered or but superficially exploited market.

But capital not only lives upon labor. Like a master, at once distinguished and barbarous, it drags with it into its grave the corpses of its slaves, whole hecatombs of workers, who perish in the crises.

We thus see that *if capital grows rapidly, competition among the workers grows with even greater rapidity, i.e., the means of employment and subsistence for the working class decrease in proportion even more rapidly; but, this notwithstanding, the rapid growth of capital is the most favorable condition for wage-labor.*

11

THE CAPITALIST'S SEARCH FOR
ECONOMIES, AND THE EFFECTS
OF ECONOMIES ON LABOR

THE FANATIC hankering of the capitalist after economies in means of production is . . . intelligible. That nothing is lost or wasted, that the means of production are consumed only in the manner required by production itself, depends partly on the skill and intelligence of the laborers, partly on the discipline exerted over them by the capitalist. This discipline will become superfluous under a social system in which the laborers work for their own account, as it has already become practically superfluous in piece-work. This fanatic love of the capitalist for profit is expressed, on the other hand, by the adulteration of the elements of production, which is one of the principal means of reducing the value of the

---

From *Capital*, 3:100–105. For this selection, the reader should keep the following technical definitions in mind:

Constant capital: "that part of capital which is represented by the means of production, by the raw material, auxiliary material, and the instruments of labor" (*Capital*, 1:191).

Variable capital: "that part of capital, represented by labor power" (*Capital*, 1:191).

Use-value: "Use-values become a reality only by use or consumption: they also constitute the substance of all wealth. . . . A commodity, such as iron, corn, or a diamond, is, so far as it is a material thing, a use-value, something useful" (*Capital*, 1:2–3).

Necessary labor and *surplus-value:* Marx divided labor into two parts: (1) necessary, which was the amount of labor required to reproduce the value of commodities necessary to keep the worker and his family alive; (2) surplus labor, or the amount of labor imparted to the productive process above and beyond necessary labor time. This surplus, when appropriated by the capitalist, becomes "surplus-value" (*Capital*, 1:145–55). —N.J.S.

constant capital in comparison with the variable capital, and thus of raising the rate of profit. In addition to this, the sale of these elements of production above their value, so far as this value reappears in the product, plays a considerable role in cheating. This practice plays an essential part particularly in German industry, whose maxim seems to be: People will surely appreciate getting first good samples and then inferior goods from us. . . .

It should be noted that this raising of the rate of profit by means of a depreciation in the value of the constant capital, in other words, by a reduction of its expensiveness, is entirely independent of the fact whether the line of industry, in which this takes place, produces articles of luxury, necessities of life for the individual consumption of laborers, or means of production. This circumstance would be of material importance only in the case that it would be a question of the rate of surplus-value, which depends essentially on the value of labor-power, and consequently on the value of the customary necessities of the laborer. But in the present case the surplus-value and the rate of surplus-value have been assumed as given. The proportion of the surplus-value to the total capital, which determines the rate of profit, depends under these circumstances exclusively on the value of the constant capital, and in no way on the use-value of the elements of which this capital is composed.

A relative cheapening of the means of production does not, of course, exclude the absolute increase of their aggregate values. For the absolute scope of their application grows extraordinarily with the development of the productive power of labor and the parallel extension of the scale of production. The economies in the use of constant capital, from whatever point of view they may be considered, are the result, either exclusively of the fact that the means of production serve as cooperative materials for the combined laborers, so that the resulting economies appear as products of the social nature of directly productive labor itself; or, in part, of the fact that the productivity of labor is developed in those spheres which supply capital with means of production, and in that case these economies present themselves once more as products of the development of the productive forces of social labor, provided only that the total labor is compared with the total capital, and not simply with the laborers employed by the individual capitalist owning this particular constant capital. The difference in this case is merely that the capitalist takes advantage not only of the productivity of labor in his own establishment, but also of that in other establishments. Nevertheless, the capitalist presumes that the economies of his constant capital are wholly independent of his laborers and have nothing at all to do with them. On the other hand, the capitalist is always well aware that the laborer has something to do with the fact whether the employer buys much or little labor with the same amount of money (for this is the form in which this transaction between the laborer and the capitalist appears in the mind of the latter). The economies realized in the application of constant capital, this method of getting a certain result out of the means of production with the smallest possible expense, is regarded more than any other power inherent in labor as a peculiar gift of capital and as a method characteristic of the capitalist mode of production.

This conception is so much less surprising as it seems to be borne out by facts. For the conditions of capitalist production conceal the internal connection of things by the utter indifference, alienation, and expropriation practiced against the laborer in the matter of the material means in which his labor must be incorporated.

In the first place, the means of production constituting the constant capital represent only the money of the capitalist (just as the body of the Roman debtor represented the money of his creditor, according to Linguet). The laborer comes in contact with them only in the direct process of production, in which he handles them as use-values of production, as instruments of labor and materials of production. The increase or decrease of the value of these things are matters which affect his relation to the capitalist no more than the fact that he may be working up either copper or iron. Occasionally, however, the capitalist likes to profess a different conception of the matter. . . . He does so whenever the means of production become dearer and thereby reduce his rate of profit.

In the second place, so far as these means of production in the capitalist process of labor are at the same time means of exploiting labor, the laborer is no more concerned in the relative dearness or cheapness of these means of exploitation than a horse is concerned in the dearness or cheapness of the bit and bridle by which it is steered.

In the third place, we have seen previously that the social nature of labor, the combination of the labor of a certain individual laborer with that of other laborers for a common purpose, stands opposed to that laborer and his comrades as a foreign power, as the property of a stranger which he would not care particularly to save if he were not compelled to economize with it. It is entirely different in the factories owned by the laborers themselves, for instance, in Rochdale.

It requires hardly any special mention, then, that the general interconnection of social labor, so far as it expresses the productivity of labor in one line of industry by a cheapening and improvement of the means of production in another line, and thereby a raising of the rate of profit, affects the laborers as a matter foreign to them and concerning only the capitalists, since they are the ones who buy and own these means of production. The fact that the capitalist buys the product of the laborers of another line of industry with the product of the laborers in his own line, and that he disposes of the product of the laborers of another capitalist by virtue of having appropriated the unpaid products of his own laborers, is mercifully concealed for him by the process of circulation and its attending circumstances.

This state of things is further complicated by the fact that these economies in the employment of constant capital assume the guise of being due to the peculiar nature of the capitalist mode of production, and to the special function of the capitalist in particular. The thirst for profits and the demands of competition tend toward the greatest possible cheapening of the production of commodities, just as production on a large scale first develops in its capitalistic form.

Capitalist production promotes on the one hand the development of the productive powers of social labor, and on the other it enforces economies in the employment of constant capital.

However, capitalist production does not stop at the alienation and expropriation of the laborer, the bearer of living labor, from his interest in the economical, that is to say, rational and thrifty, use of the material requirements of his labor. In conformity with its contradictory and antagonistic nature, capitalist production proceeds to add to the economies in the use of constant capital, and thus to the means of increasing the rate of profit, a prodigality in the use of the life and health of the laborer himself.

Since the laborer passes the greater portion of his life in the process of production, the conditions of this productive process constitute the greater part of the fundamental conditions of his vital activity, his requirements of life. Economies in these requirements constitute a method of raising the rate of profit, just as we observed on previous occasions that overwork, the transformation of the laborers into laboring cattle, constitutes a means of self-expanding capital, of speeding up the production of surplus-value. Such economies are: The overcrowding of narrow and unsanitary rooms with laborers, or, in the language of the capitalist, a saving in buildings; a crowding of dangerous machinery into one and the same room without means of protection against this danger; a neglect of precautions in productive processes which are dangerous to health or life, such as mining, etc.; not to mention the absence of all provisions to render the process of production human, agreeable, or even bearable, for the laborer. From the capitalist point of view, such measures would be quite useless and senseless. No matter how economical capitalist production may be in other respects, it is utterly prodigal with human life. And its saving in one direction is offset by a waste in another, owing to the distribution of its products through trade and the competitive method. Capitalism loses on one side for society what it gains on another for the individual capitalist.

Just as capital endeavors to reduce the direct application of living labor to necessary labor, and to abbreviate the labor required for the production of any commodity by the exploitation of the social productiveness of labor and thus to use as little living labor as possible, so it has also the tendency to apply this minimized labor under the most economical conditions, that is to say, to reduce the value of the employed constant capital to its minimum. While the value of commodities is determined by the necessary labor-time contained in them, not by all of the labor-time incorporated in them, it is the capital which gives reality to this determination and at the same time reduces continually the labor-time socially necessary for the production of a certain commodity. The price of that commodity is thereby lowered to its minimum, since every portion of the labor required for its production is reduced to its minimum.

It is necessary to make a distinction in the economies realized in the employment of constant capital. If the mass, and consequently the amount of the value, of the employed capital increases, it means primarily a concentration of more capital in one hand. Now, it is precisely this greater mass in one hand, going hand in hand, as a rule, with an absolute increase but relative decrease of the number of employed laborers, which permits economies in constant capital. From the point of view of the individual capitalist the volume of the necessary investment of capital, especially of its fixed portion, increases. But compared to the mass of the worked-up materials and of the exploited labor the value of the invested capital relatively decreases.

12

CAPITAL ACCUMULATION
AND THE CREATION OF AN
INDUSTRIAL RESERVE ARMY

THE ACCUMULATION of capital, though originally appearing as its quantitative extension only, is effected, as we have seen, under a progressive qualitative change in its composition, under a constant increase of its constant, at the expense of its variable constituent.

The specifically capitalist mode of production, the development of the productive power of labor corresponding to it, and the change thence resulting in the organic composition of capital, do not merely keep pace with the advance of accumulation, or with the growth of social wealth. They develop at a much quicker rate, because mere accumulation, the absolute increase of the total social capital, is accompanied by the centralization of the individual capitals of which that total is made up; and because the change in the technological composition of the additional capital goes hand in hand with a similar change in the technological composition of the original capital. With the advance of accumulation, therefore, the proportion of constant to variable capital changes. If it was originally say 1: 1, it now becomes successively 2: 1, 3: 1, 4: 1, 5: 1, 7: 1, etc., so that, as the capital increases, instead of ½ of its total value, only ⅓, ¼, ⅕, ⅙, ⅛, etc., is transformed into labor-power, and, on the other hand, ⅔, ¾, ⅘, ⅚, ⅞ into means of production. Since the demand for labor is determined not by the amount of capital as a whole, but by its variable constituent alone, that demand falls progressively with the increase of the total capi-

From *Capital*, 1:642–60.

tal, instead of, as previously assumed, rising in proportion to it. It falls relatively to the magnitude of the total capital, and at an accelerated rate, as this magnitude increases. With the growth of the total capital, its variable constituent or the labor incorporated in it, also does increase, but in a constantly diminishing proportion. The intermediate pauses are shortened, in which accumulation works as simple extension of production, on a given technical basis. It is not merely that an accelerated accumulation of total capital, accelerated in a constantly growing progression, is needed to absorb an additional number of laborers, or even, on account of the constant metamorphosis of old capital, to keep employed those already functioning. In its turn, this increasing accumulation and centralization becomes a source of new changes in the composition of capital, of a more accelerated diminution of its variable, as compared with its constant constituent. This accelerated relative diminution of the variable constituent, that goes along with the accelerated increase of the total capital, and moves more rapidly than this increase, takes the inverse form, at the other pole, of an apparently absolute increase of the laboring population, an increase always moving more rapidly than that of the variable capital or the means of employment. But in fact, it is capitalistic accumulation itself that constantly produces, and produces in the direct ratio of its own energy and extent, a relatively redundant population of laborers, i.e., a population of greater extent than suffices for the average needs of the self-expansion of capital, and therefore a surplus population.

Considering the social capital in its totality, the movement of its accumulation now causes periodical changes, affecting it more or less as a whole, now distributes its various phases simultaneously over the different spheres of production. In some spheres a change in the composition of capital occurs without increase of its absolute magnitude, as a consequence of simple centralization; in others the absolute growth of capital is connected with absolute diminution of its variable constituent, or of the labor-power absorbed by it; in others again, capital continues growing for a time on its given technical basis, and attracts additional labor-power in proportion to its increase, while at other times it undergoes organic change,

and lessens its variable constituent; in all spheres, the increase of
the variable part of capital, and therefore of the number of laborers
employed by it, is always connected with violent fluctuations and
transitory production of surplus population, whether this takes the
more striking form of the repulsion of laborers already employed,
or the less evident but not less real form of the more difficult absorption of the additional laboring population through the usual
channels.[1] With the magnitude of social capital already functioning, and the degree of its increase, with the extension of the scale
of production, and the mass of the laborers set in motion, with the
development of the productiveness of their labor, with the greater
breadth and fullness of all sources of wealth, there is also an extension of the scale on which greater attraction of laborers by capital
is accompanied by their greater repulsion; the rapidity of the
change in the organic composition of capital, and in its technical
form increases, and an increasing number of spheres of production
becomes involved in this change, now simultaneously, now alternately. The laboring population therefore produces, along with the
accumulation of capital produced by it, the means by which itself is
made relatively superfluous, is turned into a relative surplus popu-

1   The census of England and Wales shows: all persons employed
in agriculture (landlords, farmers, gardeners, shepherds, etc., included):
1851, 2,011,447: 1861, 1,924,110. Fall, 87,337. Worsted manufacture: 1851,
102,714 persons: 1861, 79,242. Silk weaving: 1851, 111,940: 1861, 101,678.
Calico-printing: 1851, 12,098: 1861, 12,556. A small rise that, in the face
of the enormous extension of this industry and implying a great fall proportionally in the number of laborers employed. Hat-making: 1851,
15,957: 1861, 13,814. Straw hat and bonnet-making: 1851, 20,393: 1861,
18,176. Malting: 1851, 10,566: 1861, 10,677. Chandlery, 1851, 4949: 1861,
4686. This fall is due, besides other causes, to the increase in lighting by
gas. Comb-making: 1851, 2,038: 1861, 1,478. Sawyers: 1851, 30,552: 1861,
31,647—a small rise in consequence of the increase of sawing machines.
Nail-making: 1851, 26,940: 1861, 26,130—fall in consequence of the competition of machinery. Tin and copper-mining: 1851, 31,360: 1861, 32,041.
On the other hand: Cotton-spinning and weaving: 1851, 371,777: 1861,
456,646. Coal-mining: 1851, 183,389: 1861, 246,613. "The increase of
labourers is generally greatest, since 1851, in such branches of industry in
which machinery has not up to the present been employed with success."
(Census of England and Wales, 1862. Vol. III. London, 1863, p. 36.)

lation; and it does this to an always increasing extent.[2] This is a law of population peculiar to the capitalist mode of production; and in fact every special historic mode of production has its own special laws of population, historically valid within its limits alone. An abstract law of population exists for plants and animals only, and only insofar as man has not interfered with them.

But if a surplus laboring population is a necessary product of accumulation or of the development of wealth on a capitalist basis, this surplus population becomes, conversely, the lever of capitalistic accumulation, nay, a condition of existence of the capitalist mode of production. It forms a disposable industrial reserve army,

[2]   "The demand for labour depends on the increase of circulating, and not of fixed capital. Were it true that the proportion between these two sorts of capital is the same at all times, and in all circumstances, then, indeed, it follows that the number of labourers employed is in proportion to the wealth of the state. But such a proposition has not the semblance of probability. As arts are cultivated, and civilization is extended, fixed capital bears a larger and larger proportion to circulating capital. The amount of fixed capital employed in the production of a piece of British muslin is at least a hundred, probably a thousand times greater than that employed in a similar piece of Indian muslin. And the proportion of circulating capital is a hundred or thousand times less. . . . the whole of the annual savings, added to the fixed capital, would have no effect in increasing the demand for labour." (John Barton. "Observations on the Circumstances Which Influence the Condition of the Labouring Classes of Society." London, 1817, pp. 16, 17.) "The same cause which may increase the net revenue of the country may at the same time render the population redundant, and deteriorate the condition of the labourer." (David Ricardo, *On the Principles of Political Economy and Taxation*, 3d Edition, London, 1821, p. 469.) With increase of capital, "the demand [for labor] will be in a diminishing ratio." (ibid. p. 480, Note.) "The amount of capital devoted to the maintenance of labour may vary, independently of any changes in the whole amount of capital. . . . Great fluctuations in the amount of employment, and great suffering may become more frequent as capital itself becomes more plentiful." (Richard Jones. "An Introductory Lecture on Pol. Econ., Lond. 1833," p. 13.) "Demand [for labor] will rise . . . not in proportion to the accumulation of the general capital. . . . Every augmentation, therefore, in the national stock destined for reproduction, comes, in the progress of society, to have less and less influence upon the condition of the labourer." (George Ramsay, *An Essay on the Distribution of Wealth*, Edinburgh, 1836, pp. 90, 91.)

that belongs to capital quite as absolutely as if the latter had bred it at its own cost. Independently of the limits of the actual increase of population, it creates, for the changing needs of the self-expansion of capital, a mass of human material always ready for exploitation. With accumulation, and the development of the productiveness of labor that accompanies it, the power of sudden expansion of capital grows also; it grows, not merely because the elasticity of the capital already functioning increases, not merely because the absolute wealth of society expands, of which capital only forms an elastic part, not merely because credit, under every special stimulus, at once places an unusual part of this wealth at the disposal of production in the form of additional capital; it grows, also, because the technical conditions of the process of production themselves—machinery, means of transport, etc.—now admit of the rapidest transformation of masses of surplus product into additional means of production. The mass of social wealth, overflowing with the advance of accumulation, and transformable into additional capital, thrusts itself frantically into old branches of production, whose market suddenly expands, or into newly formed branches, such as railways, etc., the need for which grows out of the development of the old ones. In all such cases, there must be the possibility of throwing great masses of men suddenly on the decisive points without injury to the scale of production in other spheres. Overpopulation supplies these masses. The course characteristic of modern industry, viz., a decennial cycle (interrupted by smaller oscillations), of periods of average activity, production at high pressure, crisis and stagnation, depends on the constant formation, the greater or less absorption, and the re-formation of the industrial reserve army or surplus population. In their turn, the varying phases of the industrial cycle recruit the surplus population, and become one of the most energetic agents of its reproduction. This peculiar course of modern industry, which occurs in no earlier period of human history, was also impossible in the childhood of capitalist production. The composition of capital changed but very slowly. With its accumulation, therefore, there kept pace, on the whole, a corresponding growth in the demand for labor. Slow as was the advance of accumulation compared with that of more modern times, it found a check in the natural limits of the exploitable laboring population, limits which could only be got rid of by forcible means to be mentioned later. The expansion by fits and starts of the scale of production is the preliminary to its equally sudden contraction; the latter again evokes the former, but the former is impossible without disposable human material, without an increase in the number of laborers independently of the absolute growth of the population. This increase is effected by the simple process that constantly "sets free" a part of the laborers; by methods which lessen the number of laborers employed in proportion to the increased production. The whole form of the movement of modern industry depends, therefore, upon the constant transformation of a part of the laboring population into unemployed or half-employed hands. The superficiality of Political Economy shows itself in the fact that it looks upon the expansion and contraction of credit, which is a mere symptom of the periodic changes of the industrial cycle, as their cause. As the heavenly bodies, once thrown into a certain definite motion, always repeat this, so is it with social production as soon as it is once thrown into this movement of alternate expansion and contraction. Effects, in their turn, become causes, and the varying accidents of the whole process, which always reproduces its own conditions, take on the form of periodicity. When this periodicity is once consolidated, even Political Economy then sees that the production of a relative surplus population—i.e., surplus with regard to the average needs of the self-expansion of capital—is a necessary condition of modern industry.

"Suppose," says H. Merivale, formerly Professor of Political Economy at Oxford, subsequently employed in the English Colonial Office,

suppose that, on the occasion of some of these crises, the nation were to rouse itself to the effort of getting rid by emigration of some hundreds of thousands of superfluous arms, what would be the consequence? That, at the first return in demand for labor, there would be a deficiency. However rapid reproduction may be, it takes, at all events, the space of a generation to replace the loss of adult labor. Now, the profits of our manufacturers depend mainly on the power of making use of the prosperous moment when demand is brisk, and thus compensating themselves for the interval during which it is slack. This power is secured to them only by the command of machinery and of manual labor. They must have hands ready by them, they must be able to increase the activity of their operations when required, and to slacken it again, according to the state of the market, or they cannot possibly maintain that pre-eminence in the race of competition on which the wealth of the country is founded.[3]

Even Malthus recognizes overpopulation as a necessity of modern industry, though, after his narrow fashion, he explains it by the absolute over-growth of the laboring population, not by their becoming relatively supernumerary. He says:

Prudential habits with regard to marriage, carried to a considerable extent among the laboring class of a country mainly depending upon manufactures and commerce, might injure it. . . . From the nature of a population, an increase of laborers cannot be brought into market in consequence of a particular demand till after the lapse of 16 or 18 years, and the conversion of revenue into capital, by saving, may take place much more rapidly; a country is always liable to an increase in the quantity of the funds for the maintenance of labor faster than the increase of population.[4]

After Political Economy has thus demonstrated the constant production of a relative surplus population of laborers to be a necessity of capitalistic accumulation, she very aptly, in the guise of an old maid, puts in the mouth of her "beau ideal" of a capitalist the following words addressed to those supernumeraries thrown on the streets by their own creation of additional capital: "We manufacturers do what we can for you, whilst we are increasing that capital on which you must subsist, and you must do the rest by accommodating your numbers to the means of subsistence."[5]

3   H. Merivale: "Lectures on Colonization and Colonies, 1841." Vol. I., p. 146.
4   Malthus. "Principles of Political Economy," pp. 254, 319, 320. In this work, Malthus finally discovers, with the help of Sismondi, the beautiful Trinity of capitalistic production: overproduction, overpopulation, overconsumption—three very delicate monsters, indeed. Cf. F. Engels. "Umrisse zu einer Kritik der National-Oekonomie," l. c., p. 107, et seq.
5   Harriet Martineau, "The Manchester Strike," 1842, p. 101.

Capitalist production can by no means content itself with the quantity of disposable labor-power which the natural increase of population yields. It requires for its free play an industrial reserve army independent of these natural limits.

Up to this point it has been assumed that the increase or diminution of the variable capital corresponds rigidly with the increase or diminution of the number of laborers employed.

The number of laborers commanded by capital may remain the same, or even fall, while the variable capital increases. This is the case if the individual laborer yields more labor, and therefore his wages increase, and this although the price of labor remains the same or even falls, only more slowly than the mass of labor rises. Increase of variable capital, in this case, becomes an index of more labor, but not of more laborers employed. It is the absolute interest of every capitalist to press a given quantity of labor out of a smaller, rather than a greater number of laborers, if the cost is about the same. In the latter case, the outlay of constant capital increases in proportion to the mass of labor set in action; in the former that increase is much smaller. The more extended the scale of production, the stronger this motive. Its force increases with the accumulation of capital.

We have seen that the development of the capitalist mode of production and of the productive power of labor—at once the cause and effect of accumulation—enables the capitalist, with the same outlay of variable capital, to set in action more labor by greater exploitation (extensive or intensive) of each individual labor-power. We have further seen that the capitalist buys with the same capital a greater mass of labor-power, as he progressively replaces skilled laborers by less skilled, mature labor-power by immature, male by female, that of adults by that of young persons or children.

On the one hand, therefore, with the progress of accumulation, a larger variable capital sets more labor in action without enlisting more laborers; on the other, a variable capital of the same magnitude sets in action more labor with the same mass of labor-power; and, finally, a greater number of inferior labor-powers by displacement of higher.

The production of a relative surplus population, or the setting free of laborers, goes on therefore yet more rapidly than the technical revolution of the process of production that accompanies, and is accelerated by, the advance of accumulation; and more rapidly than the corresponding diminution of the variable part of capital as compared with the constant. If the means of production, as they increase in extent and effective power, become to a less extent means of employment of laborers, this state of things is again modified by the fact that in proportion as the productiveness of labor increases, capital increases its supply of labor more quickly than its demand for laborers. The overwork of the employed part of the working class swells the ranks of the reserve, while conversely the greater pressure that the latter by its competition exerts on the former, forces these to submit to overwork and to subjugation under the dictates of capital. The condemnation of one part of the working-class to enforced idleness by the overwork of the other part, and the converse, becomes a means of enriching the individual capitalists,[6] and accelerates at the same time the production of

6   Even in the cotton famine of 1863 we find, in a pamphlet of the operative cotton-spinners of Blackburn, fierce denunciation of overwork, which, in consequence of the Factory Acts, of course only affected adult male laborers. "The adult operatives at this mill have been asked to work from 12 to 13 hours per day, while there are hundreds who are compelled to be idle who would willingly work partial time, in order to maintain their families and save their brethren from a premature grave through being overworked. . . . We," it goes on to say, "would ask if the practice of working overtime by a number of hands, is likely to create a good feeling between masters and servants. Those who are worked overtime feel the injustice equally with those who are condemned to forced idleness. There is in the district almost sufficient work to give to all partial employment if fairly distributed. We are only asking what is right in requesting the masters generally to pursue a system of short hours, particularly until a better state of things begins to dawn upon us, rather than to work a portion of the hands overtime, while others, for want of work, are compelled to exist upon charity." (Reports of Insp. of Fact., Oct. 31, 1863, p. 8.) The author of the "Essay on Trade and Commerce" grasps the effect of a relative surplus population on the employed laborers with his usual unerring bourgeois instinct. "Another cause of idleness in this kingdom is the want of a sufficient number of labouring hands. . . . Whenever from an extraordinary demand for manufactures, labour grows scarce, the labourers

the industrial reserve army on a scale corresponding with the advance of social accumulation. How important is this element in the formation of the relative surplus population, is shown by the example of England. Her technical means for saving labor are colossal. Nevertheless, if tomorrow morning labor generally were reduced to a rational amount, and proportioned to the different sections of the working class according to age and sex, the working population to hand would be absolutely insufficient for the carrying on of national production on its present scale. The great majority of the laborers now "unproductive" would have to be turned into "productive" ones.

Taking them as a whole, the general movements of wages are exclusively regulated by the expansion and contraction of the industrial reserve army, and these again correspond to the periodic changes of the industrial cycle. They are, therefore, not determined by the variations of the absolute number of the working population, but by the varying proportions in which the working class is divided into active and reserve army, by the increase or diminution in the relative amount of the surplus population, by the extent to which it is now absorbed, now set free. For Modern Industry with its decennial cycles and periodic phases, which, moreover, as accumulation advances, are complicated by irregular oscillations following each other more and more quickly, that would indeed be a beautiful law, which pretends to make the action of capital dependent on the absolute variation of the population, instead of regulating the demand and supply of labor by the alternate expansion and contraction of capital, the labor-market now appearing relatively underfull, because capital is expanding, now again overfull, because it is contracting. Yet this is the dogma of the economists. According to them, wages rise in consequence of accumulation of capital. The higher wages stimulate the working population to more rapid multiplication, and this goes on until the labor-

feel their own consequence, and will make their masters feel it likewise—it is amazing; but so depraved are the dispositions of these people, that in such cases a set of workmen have combined to distress the employer, by idling a whole day together." (Essay, etc., pp. 27, 28.) The fellows in fact were hankering after a rise in wages.

market becomes too full, and therefore capital, relatively to the supply of labor, becomes insufficient. Wages fall, and now we have the reverse of the medal. The working population is little by little decimated as the result of the fall in wages, so that capital is again in excess relatively to them, or, as others explain it, falling wages and the corresponding increase in the exploitation of the laborer again accelerates accumulation, while, at the same time, the lower wages hold the increase of the working class in check. Then comes again the time, when the supply of labor is less than the demand, wages rise, and so on. A beautiful mode of motion this for developed capitalist production! Before, in consequence of the rise of wages, any positive increase of the population really fit for work could occur, the time would have been passed again and again, during which the industrial campaign must have been carried through, the battle fought and won.

Between 1849 and 1859, a rise of wages practically insignificant, though accompanied by falling prices of corn, took place in the English agricultural districts. In Wiltshire, e.g., the weekly wages rose from 7s. to 8s.; in Dorsetshire from 7s. or 8s., to 9s., etc. This was the result of an unusual exodus of the agricultural surplus population caused by the demands of war, the vast extension of railroads, factories, mines, etc. The lower the wages, the higher is the proportion in which ever so insignificant a rise of them expresses itself. If the weekly wage, e.g., is 20s. and it rises to 22s., that is a rise of 10 per cent.; but if it is only 7s. and it rises to 9s., that is a rise of 28⁴⁄₇ per cent., which sounds very fine. Everywhere the farmers were howling, and the "London Economist," with reference to these starvation-wages, prattled quite seriously of "a general and substantial advance."[7] What did the farmers do now? Did they wait until, in consequence of this brilliant remuneration, the agricultural laborers had so increased and multiplied that their wages must fall again, as prescribed by the dogmatic economic brain? They introduced more machinery, and in a moment the laborers were redundant again in a proportion satisfactory even to the farmers. There was now "more capital" laid out in agriculture

[7]   Economist, Jan. 21, 1860.

than before, and in a more productive form. With this the demand for labor fell, not only relatively, but absolutely.

The above economic fiction confuses the laws that regulate the general movement of wages, or the ratio between the working class —i.e., the total labor-power—and the total social capital, with the laws that distribute the working population over the different spheres of production. If, e.g., in consequence of favorable circumstances, accumulation in a particular sphere of production becomes especially active, and profits in it, being greater than the average profits, attract additional capital, of course the demand for labor rises and wages also rise. The higher wages draw a larger part of the working population into the more favored sphere, until it is glutted with labor-power, and wages at length fall again to their average level or below it, if the pressure is too great. Then, not only does the immigration of laborers into the branch of industry in question cease; it gives place to their emigration. Here the political economist thinks he sees the why and wherefore of an absolute increase of workers accompanying an increase of wages, and of a diminution of wages accompanying an absolute increase of laborers. But he sees really only the local oscillation of the labor-market in a particular sphere of production—he sees only the phenomena accompanying the distribution of the working population into the different spheres of outlay of capital, according to its varying needs.

The industrial reserve army, during the periods of stagnation and average prosperity, weighs down the active labor-army; during the periods of overproduction and paroxysm, it holds its pretensions in check. Relative surplus population is therefore the pivot upon which the law of demand and supply of labor works. It confines the field of action of this law within the limits absolutely convenient to the activity of exploitation and to the domination of capital.

This is the place to return to one of the grand exploits of economic apologetics. It will be remembered that if through the introduction of new, or the extension of old, machinery, a portion of variable capital is transformed into constant, the economic apologist interprets this operation which "fixes" capital and by that very act set laborers "free," in exactly the opposite way, pretending that it sets free capital for the laborers. Only now can one fully understand the effrontery of these apologists. What are set free are not only the laborers immediately turned out by the machines, but also their future substitutes in the rising generation, and the additional contingent, that with the usual extension of trade on the old basis would be regularly absorbed. They are now all "set free," and every new bit of capital looking out for employment can dispose of them. Whether it attracts them or others, the effect on the general labor demand will be nil, if this capital is just sufficient to take out of the market as many laborers as the machines threw upon it. If it employs a smaller number, that of the supernumeraries increases; if it employs a greater, the general demand for labor only increases to the extent of the excess of the employed over those "set free." The impulse that additional capital, seeking an outlet, would otherwise have given to the general demand for labor, is therefore in every case neutralized to the extent of the laborers thrown out of employment by the machine. That is to say, the mechanism of capitalistic production so manages matters that the absolute increase of capital is accompanied by no corresponding rise in the general demand for labor. And this the apologist calls a compensation for the misery, the sufferings, the possible death of the displaced laborers during the transition period that banishes them into the industrial reserve army! The demand for labor is not identical with increase of capital, nor supply of labor with increase of the working class. It is not a case of two independent forces working on one another. Les dés sont pipés. Capital works on both sides at the same time. If its accumulation, on the one hand, increases the demand for labor, it increases on the other the supply of laborers by the "setting free" of them, whilst at the same time the pressure of the unemployed compels those that are employed to furnish more labor, and therefore makes the supply of labor, to a certain extent, independent of the supply of laborers. The action of the law of supply and demand of labor on this basis completes the despotism of capital. As soon, therefore, as the laborers learn the secret, how it comes to pass that in the same measure as they work more, as they produce more wealth for others, and as the productive power of their labor increases, so in the same measure even their function as a means of the self-expansion of capital becomes more and more precarious for them; as soon as they discover that the degree of intensity of the competition among themselves depends wholly on the pressure of the relative surplus population; as soon as, by Trades' Unions, etc., they try to organize a regular co-operation between employed and unemployed in order to destroy or to weaken the ruinous effects of this natural law of capitalistic production on their class, so soon capital and its sycophant, political economy, cry out at the infringement of the "eternal" and so to say "sacred" law of supply and demand. Every combination of employed and unemployed disturbs the "harmonious" action of this law. But, on the other hand, as soon as (in the colonies, e.g.) adverse circumstances prevent the creation of an industrial reserve army and, with it, the absolute dependence of the working class upon the capitalist class, capital, along with its commonplace Sancho Panza, rebels against the "sacred" law of supply and demand, and tries to check its inconvenient action by forcible means and State interference.

The relative surplus population exists in every possible form. Every laborer belongs to it during the time when he is only partially employed or wholly unemployed. Not taking into account the great periodically recurring forms that the changing phases of the industrial cycle impress on it, now an acute form during the crisis, then again a chronic form during dull times—it has always three forms, the floating, the latent, the stagnant.

In the centers of modern industry—factories, manufactures, ironworks, mines, etc.—the laborers are sometimes repelled, sometimes attracted again in greater masses, the number of those employed increasing on the whole, although in a constantly decreasing proportion to the scale of production. Here the surplus population exists in the floating form.

In the automatic factories, as in all the great workshops, where machinery enters as a factor, or where only the modern division of labor is carried out, large numbers of boys are employed up to the age of maturity. When this term is once reached, only a very small number continue to find employment in the same branches of industry, whilst the majority are regularly discharged. This majority forms an element of the floating surplus population, growing with the extension of those branches of industry. Part of them emigrates, following in fact capital that has emigrated. One consequence is that the female population grows more rapidly than the male, *teste* England. That the natural increase of the number of laborers does not satisfy the requirements of the accumulation of capital, and yet all the time is in excess of them, is a contradiction inherent to the movement of capital itself. It wants larger numbers of youthful laborers, a smaller number of adults. The contradiction is not more glaring than that other one that there is a complaint of the want of hands, while at the same time many thousands are out of work, because the division of labor chains them to a particular branch of industry.[8]

The consumption of labor-power by capital is, besides, so rapid that the laborer, half-way through his life, has already more or less completely lived himself out. He falls into the ranks of the supernumeraries, or is thrust down from a higher to a lower step in the scale. It is precisely among the workpeople of modern industry that we meet with the shortest duration of life. Dr. Lee, Medical Officer of Health for Manchester, stated "that the average age at death of the Manchester . . . upper middle class was 38 years, while the average age at death of the laboring class was 17; while at Liverpool those figures were represented as 35 against 15. It thus appeared that the well-to-do classes had a lease of life which was more than double the value of that which fell to the lot of the less favored citizens."[9] In order to conform to these circumstances, the absolute increase of this section of the proletariat must take place under

8   While during the last six months of 1866, 80–90,000 working people in London were thrown out of work, the Factory Report for that same half-year says: "It does not appear absolutely true to say that demand will always produce supply just at the moment when it is needed. It has not done so with labour, for much machinery has been idle last year for want of hands." (Rep. of Insp. of Fact., 31st Oct., 1866, p. 81.)

9   Opening address to the Sanitary Conference, Birmingham, January 15th, 1875, by J. Chamberlain, Mayor of the town, now (1883) President of the Board of Trade.

conditions that shall swell their numbers, although the individual elements are used up rapidly. Hence, rapid renewal of the generations of laborers (this law does not hold for the other classes of the population). This social need is met by early marriages, a necessary consequence of the conditions in which the laborers of modern industry live, and by the premium that the exploitation of children sets on their production.

As soon as capitalist production takes possession of agriculture, and in proportion to the extent to which it does so, the demand for an agricultural laboring population falls absolutely, while the accumulation of the capital employed in agriculture advances, without this repulsion being, as in non-agricultural industries, compensated by a greater attraction. Part of the agricultural population is therefore constantly on the point of passing over into an urban or manufacturing proletariat, and on the look-out for circumstances favorable to this transformation. (Manufacture is used here in the sense of all non-agricultural industries.) [10] This source of relative surplus population is thus constantly flowing. But the constant flow towards the towns presupposes, in the country itself, a constant latent surplus population, the extent of which becomes evident only when its channels of outlet open to exceptional width. The agricultural laborer is therefore reduced to the minimum of wages, and always stands with one foot already in the swamp of pauperism.

The third category of the relative surplus population, the stagnant, forms a part of the active labor-army, but with extremely irregular employment. Hence it furnishes to capital an inexhaustible

[10]   781 Towns given in the census for 1861 for England and Wales "contained 10,960,998 inhabitants, while the villages and country parishes contained 9,105,226. In 1851, 580 towns were distinguished, and the population in them and in the surrounding country was nearly equal. But while in the subsequent ten years the population in the villages and the country increased half a million, the population in the 580 towns increased by a million and a half (1,554,067). The increase of the population of the country parishes is 6.5 per cent., and of the towns 17.3 per cent. The difference in the rates of increase is due to the migration from country to town. Three-fourths of the total increase of population has taken place in the towns. (Census, etc., pp. 11 and 12.)

reservoir of disposable labor-power. Its conditions of life sink below the average normal level of the working class; this makes it at once the broad basis of special branches of capitalist exploitation. It is characterized by maximum of working time, and minimum of wages. We have learned to know its chief form under the rubric of "domestic industry." It recruits itself constantly from the supernumerary forces of modern industry and agriculture, and specially from those decaying branches of industry where handicraft is yielding to manufacture, manufacture to machinery. Its extent grows, as with the extent and energy of accumulation, the creation of a surplus population advances. But it forms at the same time a self-reproducing and self-perpetuating element of the working class, taking a proportionally greater part in the general increase of that class than the other elements. In fact, not only the number of births and deaths, but the absolute size of the families stand in inverse proportion to the height of wages, and therefore to the amount of means of subsistence of which the different categories of laborers dispose. This law of capitalistic society would sound absurd to savages, or even civilized colonists. It calls to mind the boundless reproduction of animals individually weak and constantly hunted down.[11]

The lowest sediment of the relative surplus population finally dwells in the sphere of pauperism. Exclusive of vagabonds, criminals, prostitutes, in a word, the "dangerous" classes, this layer of society consists of three categories. First, those able to work. One need only glance superficially at the statistics of English pauperism to find that the quantity of paupers increases with every crisis, and diminishes with every revival of trade. Second, orphans and pauper

---

[11]   "Poverty seems favourable to generation." (A. Smith.) This is even a specially wise arrangement of God, according to the gallant and witty Abbé Galiani. "Iddio af che gli uomini che esercitano mestieri di prima utilità nascono abbondantemente." (Ferdinando Galiani, *Della Moneta*, Vol. III, Milan, 1803, p. 78.) "Misery up to the extreme point of famine and pestilence, instead of checking, tends to increase population." (S. Laing: National Distress, 1844, p. 69.) After Laing has illustrated this by statistics, he continues: "If the people were all in easy circumstances, the world would soon be depopulated."

children. These are candidates for the industrial reserve-army, and are, in times of great prosperity, as 1860, e.g., speedily and in large numbers enrolled in the active army of laborers. Third, the demoralized and ragged, and those unable to work, chiefly people who succumb to their incapacity for adaptation, due to the division of labor; people who have passed the normal age of the laborer; the victims of industry, whose number increases with the increase of dangerous machinery, of mines, chemical works, etc., the mutilated, the sickly, the widows, etc. Pauperism is the hospital of the active labor-army and the dead weight of the industrial reserve-army. Its production is included in that of the relative surplus population, its necessity in theirs; along with the surplus population, pauperism forms a condition of capitalist production, and of the capitalist development of wealth. It enters into the *faux frais* of capitalist production; but capital knows how to throw these, for the most part, from its own shoulders on to those of the working class and the lower middle class.

The greater the social wealth, the functioning capital, the extent and energy of its growth, and, therefore, also the absolute mass of the proletariat and the productiveness of its labor, the greater is the industrial reserve-army. The same causes which develop the expansive power of capital, develop also the labor-power at its disposal. The relative mass of the industrial reserve-army increases therefore with the potential energy of wealth. But the greater this reserve-army in proportion to the active labor-army, the greater is the mass of a consolidated surplus population, whose misery is in inverse ratio to its torment of labor. The more extensive, finally, the lazarus-layers of the working-class, and the industrial reserve-army, the greater is official pauperism. *This is the absolute general law of capitalist accumulation.* Like all other laws it is modified in its working by many circumstances, the analysis of which does not concern us here.

The folly is now patent of the economic wisdom that preaches to the laborers the accommodation of their number to the requirements of capital. The mechanism of capitalist production and accumulation constantly effects this adjustment. The first word of this adaptation is the creation of a relative surplus population, or industrial reserve-army. Its last word is the misery of constantly extending strata of the active army of labor, and the dead weight of pauperism.

The law by which a constantly increasing quantity of means of production, thanks to the advance in the productiveness of social labor, may be set in movement by a progressively diminishing expenditure of human power, this law, in a capitalist society—where the laborer does not employ the means of production, but the means of production employ the laborer—undergoes a complete inversion and is expressed thus; the higher the productiveness of labor, the greater is the pressure of the laborers on the means of employment, the more precarious, therefore, becomes their condition of existence, viz., the sale of their own labor-power for the increasing of another's wealth, or for the self-expansion of capital. The fact that the means of production, and the productiveness of labor, increase more rapidly than the productive population, expresses itself, therefore, capitalistically in the inverse form that the laboring population always increases more rapidly than the conditions under which capital can employ this increase for its own self-expansion.

13

ECONOMIC CRISES AND

THEIR EFFECTS ON WORKERS

ALL POLITICAL economists of any standing admit that the introduction of new machinery has a baneful effect on the workmen in the old handicrafts and manufactures with which this machinery at first competes. Almost all of them bemoan the slavery of the factory operative. And what is the great trump-card that they play? That machinery, after the horrors of the period of introduction and development have subsided, instead of diminishing, in the long run increases the number of the slaves of labor! Yes, political economy revels in the hideous theory, hideous to every "philanthropist" who believes in the eternal nature-ordained necessity for capitalist production, that after a period of growth and transition, even its crowning success, the factory system based on machinery, grinds down more workpeople than on its first introduction it throws on the streets.[1]

From *Capital*, 1:449–62.

[1] Ganilh, on the contrary, considers the final result of the factory system to be an absolutely less number of operatives, at whose expense an increased number of "gens honnêtes" live and develop their well-known "perfectibilité perfectible." Little as he understands the movement of production, at least he feels, that machinery must needs be a very fatal institution, if its introduction converts busy workmen into paupers, and its development calls more slaves of labor into existence than it has suppressed. It is not possible to bring out the cretinism of his standpoint, except by his own words: "Les classes condamnées à produire et à consommer diminuent, et les classes qui dirigent le travail, qui soulagent, consolent, et éclaírent toute la population, se multiplient . . . et s'approprient tous les

It is true that in some cases, as we saw from instances of English worsted and silk factories, an extraordinary extension of the factory system may, at a certain stage of its development, be accompanied not only by a relative, but by an absolute decrease in the number of operatives employed. In the year 1860, when a special census of all the factories in the United Kingdom was taken by order of Parliament, the factories in those parts of Lancashire, Cheshire, and Yorkshire, included in the district of Mr. Baker, the factory inspector, numbered 652; 570 of these contained 85,622 powerlooms, 6,819,146 spindles (exclusive of doubling spindles), employed 27,439 horse-power (steam), and 1390 (water), and 94,119 persons. In the year 1865, the same factories contained, looms 95,163, spindles 7,025,031, had a steam-power of 28,925 horses, and a water-power of 1445 horses, and employed 88,913 persons. Between 1860 and 1865, therefore, the increase in looms was 11% in spindles 3%, and in engine-power 3%, while the number of persons employed decreased 5½%.[2] Between 1852 and 1862, considerable extension of the English woollen manufacture took place, while the number of hands employed in it remained almost stationary, showing how greatly the introduction of new machines had superseded the labor of preceding periods.[3] In certain

---

bienfaits qui résultent de la diminution des frais du travail, de l'abondance des productions, et du bon marché des consommations. Dans cette direction, l'espèce humaine s'élève aux plus hautes conceptions du génie, pénètre dans les profondeurs mystèrieuses de la religion, établit les principes salutaires de la morale (which consists in 's'approprier tous les bienfaits,' etc.), les lois tutélaires de la liberté (liberty of 'les classes condamnées à produire?') et du pouvoir, de l'obéissance et de la justice, du devoir et de l'humanité." For this twaddle see *Des systèmes d'économie politique* etc., *par M. Ch. Ganilh*, 2d ed., Paris, 1821, vol. II., p. 224, and see p. 212.

[2]   "Reports of Insp. of Fact., 31 Oct., 1865," p. 58, sq. At the same time, however, means of employment for an increased number of hands was ready in 110 new mills with 11,625 looms, 628,756 spindles, and 2695 total horse-power of steam and water (l. c.).

[3]   "Reports, etc., for 31 Oct., 1862," p. 79. At the end of 1871, Mr. A. Redgrave, the factory inspector, in a lecture given at Bradford, in the New Mechanics' Institution, said: "What has struck me for some time past is the altered appearance of the woollen factories. Formerly they were filled with women and children, now machinery seems to do all the work.

cases, the increase in the number of hands employed is only apparent; that is, it is not due to the extension of the factories already established, but to the gradual annexation of connected trades; for instance, the increase in power-looms, and in the hands employed by them between 1838 and 1856, was, in the cotton trade, simply owing to the extension of this branch of industry; but in the other trades to the application of steam-power to the carpet-loom, to the ribbon-loom, and to the linen-loom, which previously had been worked by the power of men.[4] Hence the increase of the hands in these latter trades was merely a symptom of a diminution in the total number employed. Finally, we have considered this question entirely apart from the fact, that everywhere, except in the metal industries, young persons (under 18), and women and children form the preponderating element in the class of factory hands.

Nevertheless, in spite of the mass of hands actually displaced and virtually replaced by machinery, we can understand how the factory operatives, through the building of more mills and the extension of old ones in a given industry, may become more numerous than the manufacturing workmen and handicraftsmen that have been displaced. Suppose, for example, that in the old mode of production, a capital of £500 is employed weekly, two-fifths being constant and three-fifths variable capital, i.e., £200 being laid out in means of production, and £300, say £1 per man, in labor-power. On the introduction of machinery the composition of this capital becomes altered. We will suppose it to consist of four-fifths constant and one-fifth variable, which means that only £100 is now laid out in labor-power. Consequently, two-thirds of the workmen are discharged. If now the business extends, and the total capital employed grows to £1,500 under unchanged conditions, the number of operatives employed will increase to 300, just as many as before the introduction of the machinery. If the capital further grows to

---

At my asking for an explanation of this from a manufacturer, he gave me the following: 'Under the old system I employed 63 persons; after the introduction of improved machinery I reduced my hands to 33, and lately, in consequence of new and extensive alterations, I have been in a position to reduce those 33 to 13.' "

[4]   See "Reports, etc., 31 Oct., 1856," p. 16.

£2,000, 400 men will be employed, or one-third more than under the old system. Their numbers have, in point of fact, increased by 100, but relatively, i.e., in proportion to the total capital advanced, they have diminished by 800, for the £2,000 capital would, in the old state of things, have employed 1,200 instead of 400 men. Hence, a relative decrease in the number of hands is consistent with an actual increase. We assumed above that while the total capital increases, its composition remains the same, because the conditions of production remain constant. But we have already seen that, with every advance in the use of machinery, the constant component of capital, that part which consists of machinery, raw material, etc., increases, while the variable component, the part laid out in labor-power, decreases. We also know that in no other system of production is improvement so continuous, and the composition of the capital employed so constantly changing as in the factory system. These changes are, however, continually interrupted by periods of rest, during which there is a mere quantitative extension of the factories on the existing technical basis. During such periods the operatives increase in number. Thus, in 1835, the total number of operatives in the cotton, woollen, worsted, flax, and silk factories of the United Kingdom was only 354,684; while in 1861 the number of the power-loom weavers alone (of both sexes and of all ages, from eight years upwards), amounted to 230,654. Certainly, this growth appears less important when we consider that in 1838 the hand-loom weavers with their families still numbered 800,000,[5] not to mention those thrown out of work in Asia, and on the continent of Europe.

In the few remarks I have still to make on this point, I shall refer to some actually existing relations, the existence of which our theoretical investigation has not yet disclosed.

5   "The sufferings of the hand-loom weavers were the subject of an inquiry by a Royal Commission, but although their distress was acknowledged and lamented, the amelioration of their condition was left, and probably necessarily so, to the chances and changes of time, which it may now be hoped" [20 years later!] "have *nearly* obliterated those miseries, and not improbably by the present great extension of the power-loom." ("Rep. Insp. of Fact., 31 Oct., 1856," p. 15.)

So long as, in a given branch of industry, the factory system extends itself at the expense of the old handicrafts or of manufacture, the result is as sure as is the result of an encounter between an army furnished with breach-loaders, and one armed with bows and arrows. This first period, during which machinery conquers its field of action, is of decisive importance owing to the extraordinary profits that it helps to produce. These profits not only form a source of accelerated accumulation, but also attract into the favored sphere of production a large part of the additional social capital that is being constantly created, and is ever on the look-out for new investments. The special advantages of this first period of fast and furious activity are felt in every branch of production that machinery invades. So soon, however, as the factory system has gained a certain breadth of footing and a definite degree of maturity, and, especially, so soon as its technical basis, machinery, is itself produced by machinery; so soon as coal mining and iron mining, the metal industries, and the means of transport have been revolutionized, so soon, in short, as the general conditions requisite for production by the modern industrial system have been established, this mode of production acquires an elasticity, a capacity for sudden extension by leaps and bounds that finds no hindrance except in the supply of raw material and in the disposal of the produce. On the one hand, the immediate effect of machinery is to increase the supply of raw material in the same way, for example, as the cotton gin augmented the production of cotton. On the other hand, the cheapness of the articles produced by machinery, and the improved means of transport and communication furnish the weapons for conquering foreign markets. By ruining handicraft production in other countries, machinery forcibly converts them into fields for the supply of its raw material. In this way East India was compelled to produce cotton, wool, hemp, jute, and indigo for Great Britain. By constantly making a part of the hands "supernumerary," modern industry, in all countries where it has taken root, gives a spur to emigration and to the colonization of foreign lands, which are thereby converted into settlements for growing the raw material of the mother country; just as Australia, for example, was converted into a colony for growing wool.[6] A new and international division of labor, a division suited to the requirements of the chief centers of modern industry springs up, and converts one part of the globe into a chiefly agricultural field of production, for supplying the other part which remains a chiefly industrial field. This revolution hangs together with radical changes in agriculture which we need not here further inquire into.[7]

On the motion of Mr. Gladstone, the House of Commons ordered, on the 17th February, 1867, a return of the total quantities of grain, corn, and flour, of all sorts, imported into, and exported from, the United Kingdom, between the years 1831 and 1866. I give below [p. 130] a summary of the result. The flour is given in quarters of corn.

The enormous power, inherent in the factory system, of expanding by jumps, and the dependence of that system on the markets of the world, necessarily beget feverish production, followed by overfilling of the markets, whereupon contraction of the markets brings on crippling of production. The life of modern industry becomes a series of periods of moderate activity, prosperity, overproduction, crisis, and stagnation. The uncertainty and instability to which machinery subjects the employment, and consequently the conditions of existence, of the operatives become normal, owing to these periodic changes of the industrial cycle. Except in the periods of prosperity, there rages between the capitalists the most furious combat for the share of each in the markets. This share is

---

6   Export of Cotton from India to Great Britain
1846—34,540,143 lbs.   1860—204,141,168 lbs.   1865—445,947,600 lbs.
       Export of Wool from India to Great Britain
1846—4,570,581 lbs.   1860—20,214,173 lbs.   1865—20,679,111 lbs.
       Export of Wool from the Cape to Great Britain
1846—2,958,457 lbs.   1860—16,574,345 lbs.   1865—29,920,623 lbs.
       Export of Wool from Australia to Great Britain
1846—21,789,346 lbs.   1860—59,166,616 lbs.   1865—109,734,261 lbs.
7   The economical development of the United States is itself a product of European, more especially of English modern industry. In their present form (1866) the States must still be considered a European colony.

Quinquennial Periods and the Year 1866

Annual Average	1831–35	1836–40	1841–45	1846–50
Import (qrs.)	1,096,373	2,389,729	2,843,865	8,776,552
Export (qrs.)	225,363	251,770	139,056	155,461
Excess of import over export	871,110	2,137,959	2,704,809	8,621,091
Population Yearly average in each period	24,621,107	25,929,507	27,262,569	27,797,598
Average quantity of corn, etc., in qrs., consumed annually per head over and above the home produce consumed	0.036	0.082	0.099	0.310

Export of Cotton from the United States to Great Britain
1846—401,949,393 lbs.   1852—765,630,543 lbs.   1859—961,707,264 lbs.
1860—1,115,890,608 lbs.

Export of Corn, etc., from the United States to Great Britain

				1850			1862
Wheat, cwts.	...	...	...	16,202,312	...	...	41,033,503
Barley, cwts.	...	...	...	3,669,653	...	...	6,624,800
Oats, cwts.	...	...	...	3,174,801	...	...	4,426,994
Rye, cwts.	...	...	...	388,749	...	...	7,108
Flour, cwts.	...	...	...	3,819,440	...	...	7,207,113
Buckwheat, cwts.	...	...	...	1,054	...	...	19,571
Maize, cwts.	...	...	...	5,473,161	...	...	11,694,818
Bere or bigg (a sort of barley), cwts. ...				2,039	...	...	7,675
Peas, cwts.	...	...	...	811,620	...	...	1,024,722
Beans, cwts.	...	...	...	1,822,972	...	...	2,037,137
Total exports	...	...	...	34,365,801	...	...	74,083,351

Annual Average	1851–55	1856–60	1861–65	1866
Import (qrs.)	8,345,237	10,912,612	15,009,871	16,457,340
Export (qrs.)	307,491	341,150	302,754	216,218
Excess of import over export	8,037,746	10,572,462	14,707,117	16,241,122
Population Yearly average in each period	27,572,923	28,391,544	29,381,460	29,935,404
Average quantity of corn, etc., in qrs., consumed annually per head over and above the home produce consumed	0.291	0.372	0.543	0.543

directly proportional to the cheapness of the product. Besides the rivalry that this struggle begets in the application of improved machinery for replacing labor-power, and of new methods of production, there also comes a time in every industrial cycle, when a forcible reduction of wages beneath the value of labor-power, is attempted for the purpose of cheapening commodities.[8]

A necessary condition, therefore, to the growth of the number of factory hands, is a proportionally much more rapid growth of the amount of capital invested in mills. This growth, however, is conditioned by the ebb and flow of the industrial cycle. It is, besides, constantly interrupted by the technical progress that at one time virtually supplies the place of new workmen, at another, ac-

---

[8]   In an appeal made in July, 1866, to the Trade Societies of England, by the shoemakers of Leicester, who had been thrown on the streets by a lock-out, it is stated: "Twenty years ago the Leicester shoe trade was revolutionized by the introduction of riveting in the place of stitching. At that time good wages could be earned. Great competition was shown between the different firms as to which could turn out the neatest article. Shortly afterwards, however, a worse kind of competition sprang up, namely, that of underselling one another in the market. The injurious consequences soon manifested themselves in reduction of wages, and so sweepingly quick was the fall in the price of labour, that many firms now pay only one half of the original wages. And yet, though wages sink lower and lower, profits appear, with each alteration in the scale of wages, to increase." Even bad times are utilized by the manufacturers, for making exceptional profits by excessive lowering of wages, i.e., by a direct robbery of the laborer's means of subsistence. One example (it has reference to the crisis in the Coventry silk weaving): "From information I have received from manufacturers as well as workmen, there seems to be no doubt that wages have been reduced to a greater extent than either the competition of the foreign producers, or other circumstances have rendered necessary . . . the majority of weavers are working at a reduction of 30 to 40 per cent in their wages. A piece of ribbon for making which the weaver got 6s. or 7s. five years back, now only brings them 3s. 3d. or 3s. 6d.; other work is now priced at 2s. and 2s. 3d. which was formerly priced at 4s. and 4s. 3d. The reduction in wage seems to have been carried to a greater extent than is necessary for increasing demand. Indeed, the reduction in the cost of weaving, in the case of many descriptions of ribbons, has not been accompanied by any corresponding reduction in the selling price of the manufactured article." (Mr. F. D. Longe's Report. "Ch. Emp. Com., V. Rep., 1866," p. 114, 1.)

tually displaces old ones. This qualitative change in mechanical industry continually discharges hands from the factory, or shuts its doors against the fresh stream of recruits, while the purely quantitative extension of the factories absorbs not only the men thrown out of work, but also fresh contingents. The workpeople are thus continually both repelled and attracted, hustled from pillar to post, while, at the same time, constant changes take place in the sex, age, and skill of the levies.

The lot of the factory operatives will be best depicted by taking a rapid survey of the course of the English cotton industry.

From 1770 to 1815 this trade was depressed or stagnant for 5 years only. During this period of 45 years the English manufacturers had a monopoly of machinery and of the markets of the world. From 1815 to 1821 depression; 1822 and 1823 prosperity; 1824 abolition of the laws against Trades' Unions, great extension of factories everywhere; 1825 crisis; 1826 great misery and riots among the factory operatives; 1827 slight improvement; 1828 great increase in power-looms, and in exports; 1829 exports, especially to India, surpass all former years; 1830 glutted markets, great distress; 1831 to 1833 continued depression, the monopoly of the trade with India and China withdrawn from the East India Company; 1834 great increase of factories and machinery, shortness of hands. The new poor law furthers the migration of agricultural laborers into the factory districts. The country districts swept of children. White slave trade; 1835 great prosperity, contemporaneous starvation of the handloom weavers; 1836 great prosperity; 1837 and 1838 depression and crisis; 1839 revival; 1840 great depression, riots, calling out of the military; 1841 and 1842 frightful suffering among the factory operatives; 1842 the manufacturers lock the hands out of the factories in order to enforce the repeal of the Corn Laws. The operatives stream in thousands into the towns of Lancashire and Yorkshire, are driven back by the military, and their leaders brought to trial at Lancaster; 1843 great misery; 1844 revival; 1845 great prosperity; 1846 continued improvement at first, then reaction. Repeal of the Corn Laws; 1847 crisis, general reduction of wages by 10 and more percent in honor of the "big loaf;" 1848 continued depression; Manchester under

military protection; 1849 revival; 1850 prosperity; 1851 falling
prices, low wages, frequent strikes; 1852 improvement begins,
strikes continue, the manufacturers threaten to import foreign
hands; 1853 increasing exports. Strike for 8 months, and great
misery at Preston; 1854 prosperity, glutted markets; 1855 news
of failures stream in from the United States, Canada, and the
Eastern markets; 1856 great prosperity; 1857 crisis; 1858 improvement; 1859 great prosperity, increase in factories; 1860
Zenith of the English cotton trade, the Indian, Australian, and
other markets so glutted with goods that even in 1863 they had not
absorbed the whole lot; the French Treaty of Commerce, enormous
growth of factories and machinery; 1861 prosperity continues for
a time, reaction, the American Civil War, cotton famine; 1862 to
1863 complete collapse.

The history of the cotton famine is too characteristic to dispense with dwelling upon it for a moment. From the indications as
to the condition of the markets of the world in 1860 and 1861, we
see that the cotton famine came in the nick of time for the manufacturers, and was to some extent advantageous to them, a fact that
was acknowledged in the reports of the Manchester Chamber of
Commerce, proclaimed in Parliament by Palmerston and Derby,
and confirmed by events.[9] No doubt, among the 2,877 cotton mills
in the United Kingdom in 1861, there were many of small size.
According to the report of Mr. A. Redgrave, out of the 2,109 mills
included in his district, 392 or 19% employed less than ten horse-
power each; 345, or 16% employed 10 horse-power, and less than
20 horse-power; while 1,372 employed upwards of 20 horse-
power.[10] The majority of the small mills were weaving sheds, built
during the period of prosperity after 1858, for the most part by
speculators, of whom one supplied the yarn, another the machinery,
a third the buildings, and were worked by men who had been over-
lookers, or by other persons of small means. These small manufacturers mostly went to the wall. The same fate would have overtaken
them in the commercial crisis that was staved off only by the cotton

9   Conf. Reports of Insp. of Fact. 31st October, 1862, p. 30.
10   L. c., p. 19.

famine. Although they formed one-third of the total number of manufacturers, yet their mills absorbed a much smaller part of the capital invested in the cotton trade. As to the extent of the stoppage, it appears from authentic estimates, that in October 1862, 60.3% of the spindles, and 58% of the looms were standing. This refers to the cotton trade as a whole, and, of course, requires considerable modification for individual districts. Only very few mills worked full time (60 hours a week), the remainder worked at intervals. Even in those few cases where full time was worked, and at the customary rate of piece-wage, the weekly wages of the operatives necessarily shrank, owing to good cotton being replaced by bad, Sea Island by Egyptian (in fine spinning mills), American and Egyptian by Surat, and pure cotton by mixings of waste and Surat. The shorter fibre of the Surat cotton and its dirty condition, the greater fragility of the thread, the substitution of all sorts of heavy ingredients for flour in sizing the warps, all these lessened the speed of the machinery, or the number of the looms that could be superintended by one weaver, increased the labor caused by defects in the machinery, and reduced the piece-wage by reducing the mass of the product turned off. Where Surat cotton was used, the loss to the operatives when on full time, amounted to 20, 30, and more per cent. But besides this, the majority of the manufacturers reduced the rate of piece-wage by 5, 7½, and 10 per cent. We can therefore conceive the situation of those hands who were employed for only 3, 3½, or 4 days a week, or for only 6 hours a day. Even in 1863, after a comparative improvement had set in, the weekly wages of spinners and of weavers were 3s. 4d., 3s. 10d., 4s. 6d., and 5s. 1d.[11] Even in this miserable state of things, however, the inventive spirit of the master never stood still, but was exercised in making deductions from wages. These were to some extent inflicted as a penalty for defects in the finished article that were really due to his bad cotton and to his unsuitable machinery. Moreover, where the manufacturer owned the cottages of the workpeople, he paid himself his rents by deducting the amount from these miserable wages. Mr. Redgrave tells us of self-acting minders

[11]   "Rep. Insp. of Fact., 31st October, 1865," pp. 41–45.

(operatives who manage a pair of self-acting mules) "earning at the end of a fortnight's full work 8s. 11d., and that from this sum was deducted the rent of the house, the manufacturer, however, returning half the rent as a gift. The minders took away the sum of 6s. 11d. In many places the self-acting miders ranged from 5s. to 9s. per week, and the weavers from 2s. to 6s. per week, during the latter part of 1862."[12] Even when working short time the rent was frequently deducted from the wages of the operatives.[13] No wonder that in some parts of Lancashire a kind of famine fever broke out. But more characteristic than all this, was the revolution that took place in the process of production at the expense of the workpeople. Experimenta in corpore vili, like those of anatomists on frogs, were formally made. "Although," says Mr. Redgrave,

I have given the actual earnings of the operatives in the several mills, it does not follow that they earn the same amount week by week. The operatives are subject to great fluctuation from the constant experimentalizing of the manufacturers . . . the earnings of the operatives rise and fall with the quality of the cotton mixings: sometimes they have been within 15 percent of former earnings, and then, in a week or two, they have fallen off from 50 to 60 percent.[14]

These experiments were not made solely at the expense of the workman's means of subsistence. His five senses also had to pay the penalty.

The people who are employed in making up Surat cotton complain very much. They inform me, on opening the bales of cotton there is an intolerable smell, which causes sickness. . . . In the mixing, scribbling and carding rooms, the dust and dirt which are disengaged, irritate the air passages, and give rise to cough and difficulty of breathing. A disease of the skin, no doubt from the irritation of the dirt contained in the Surat cotton, also prevails. . . . The fibre being so short, a great amount of size, both animal and vegetable, is used. . . . Bronchitis is more prevalent owing to the dust. Inflammatory sore throat is common, from the same cause. Sickness and dyspepsia are produced by the

12   "Rep. Insp. of Fact., 31st October, 1863."
13   L. c., p. 51.
14   L. c., pp. 50–51.

frequent breaking of the weft, when the weaver sucks the weft through the eye of the shuttle.

On the other hand, the substitutes for flour were a Fortunatus' purse to the manufacturers, by increasing the weight of the yarn. They caused "15 lbs. of raw material to weigh 26 lbs. after it was woven."[15] In the Report of Inspectors of Factories for 30th April, 1864, we read as follows:

The trade is availing itself of this resource at present to an extent which is even discreditable. I have heard on good authority of a cloth weighing 8 lbs. which was made of 5¼ lbs. cotton and 2¾ lbs. size: and of another cloth weighing 5¼ lbs., of which 2 lbs. was size. These were ordinary export shirtings. In cloths of other descriptions, as much as 50 percent size is sometimes added; so that a manufacturer may, and does truly boast, that he is getting rich by selling cloth for less money per pound that he paid for the mere yarn of which they are composed.[16]

But the workpeople had to suffer, not only from the experiments of the manufacturers inside the mills, and of the municipalities outside, not only from reduced wages and absence of work, from want and from charity, and from the eulogistic speeches of lords and commons. "Unfortunate females who, in consequence of the cotton famine, were at its commencement thrown out of employment, and have thereby become outcasts of society; and now, though trade has revived, and work is plentiful, continue members of that unfortunate class, and are likely to continue so. There are also in the borough more youthful prostitutes than I have known for the last 25 years."[17]

We find then, in the first 45 years of the English cotton trade, from 1770 to 1815, only 5 years of crisis and stagnation; but this was the period of monopoly. The second period from 1815 to 1863 counts, during its 48 years, only 20 years of revival and prosperity against 28 of depression and stagnation. Between 1815 and 1830

---

[15]   L. c., pp. 62–63.
[16]   Rep., etc., 30th April, 1864, p. 27.
[17]   From a letter of Mr. Harris, Chief Constable of Bolton, in Rep. of Insp. of Fact. 31st October, 1865, pp. 61–62.

the competition with the continent of Europe and with the United States sets in. After 1833, the extension of the Asiatic markets is enforced by "destruction of the human race" (the wholesale extinction of Indian handloom weavers). After the repeal of the Corn Laws, from 1846 to 1863, there are 8 years of moderate activity and prosperity against 9 years of depression and stagnation. The condition of the adult male operatives, even during the years of prosperity, may be judged from the note subjoined.[18]

18   In an appeal, dated 1863, of the factory operatives of Lancashire, etc., for the purpose of forming a society for organized emigration, we find the following: "That a large emigration of factory workers is now absolutely essential to raise them from their present prostrate condition, few will deny; but to show that a continuous stream of emigration is at all times demanded, and, without which it is impossible for them to maintain their position in ordinary times, we beg to call attention to the subjoined facts: In 1814 the official value of cotton goods exported was £17,665,378, whilst the real marketable value was £20,070,824. In 1858 the official value of cotton goods exported, was £182,221,681; but the real or marketable value was only £43,001,322, being a ten-fold quantity sold for little more than double the former price. To produce results so disadvantageous to the country generally, and to the factory workers in particular, several causes have co-operated, which, had circumstances permitted, we should have brought more prominently under your notice; suffice it for the present to say that the most obvious one is the constant redundancy of labour, without which a trade so ruinous in its effects never could have been carried on, and which requires a constantly extending market to save it from annihilation. Our cotton mills may be brought to a stand by the periodical stagnation of trade, which, under present arrangements, are as inevitable as death itself; but the human mind is constantly at work, and although we believe we are under the mark in stating that six millions of persons have left these shores during the last 25 years, yet, from the natural increase of population, and the displacement of labour to cheapen production, a large percentage of the male adults in the most prosperous times find it impossible to obtain work in factories on any conditions whatever." ("Reports of Insp. of Fact., 30th April, 1863," pp. 51–52.) We shall, in a later chapter, see how our friends, the manufacturers, endeavored, during the catastrophe in the cotton trade, to prevent by every means, including State interference, the emigration of the operatives.

14

THE INTERNATIONALIZATION
OF CAPITALISM AND
ITS RAMIFICATIONS

I. India

How CAME IT that English supremacy was established in India? The paramount power of the Great Mogul was broken by the Mogul Viceroys. The power of the Viceroys was broken by the Mahrattas. The power of the Mahrattas was broken by the Afghans, and while all were struggling against all, the Briton rushed in and was enabled to subdue them all. A country not only divided between Mohammedan and Hindoo, but between tribe and tribe, between caste and caste; a society whose framework was based on a sort of equilibrium, resulting from a general repulsion and constitutional exclusiveness between all its members. Such a country and such a society, were they not the predestined prey of conquest? If we knew nothing of the past history of Hindostan, would there not be the one great and incontestable fact, that even at this moment India is held in English thralldom by an Indian army maintained at the cost of India? India, then, could not escape the fate of being conquered, and the whole of her past history, if it be anything, is the history of the successive conquests she has undergone. Indian society has no history at all, at least no known history. What we call its history, is but the history of the successive intruders who founded their empires on the passive basis of that unresisting and unchanging society. The question, therefore, is not whether the

---

Section I of this chapter is from "The Future Results of British Rule in India," *New York Daily Tribune*, 8 August 1853; section II is from "Revolution in China and in Europe," *New York Daily Tribune*, 14 June 1853.

138

English had a right to conquer India, but whether we are to prefer India conquered by the Turk, by the Persian, by the Russian, to India conquered by the Briton.

England has to fulfill a double mission in India: one destructive, the other regenerating—the annihilation of old Asiatic society, and the laying of the material foundations of Western society in Asia.

Arabs, Turks, Tartars, Moguls, who had successively overrun India, soon became Hindooized, the barbarian conquerors being, by an eternal law of history, conquered themselves by the superior civilization of their subjects. The British were the first conquerors superior, and therefore, inaccessible to Hindoo civilization. They destroyed it by breaking up the native communities, by uprooting the native industry, and by levelling all that was great and elevated in the native society. The historic pages of their rule in India report hardly anything beyond that destruction. The work of regeneration hardly transpires through a heap of ruins. Nevertheless it has begun.

The political unity of India, more consolidated, and extending farther than it ever did under the Great Moguls, was the first condition of its regeneration. That unity, imposed by the British sword, will now be strengthened and perpetuated by the electric telegraph. The native army, organized and trained by the British drill-sergeant, was the sine qua non of Indian self-emancipation, and of India ceasing to be the prey of the first foreign intruder. The free press, introduced for the first time into Asiatic society, and managed principally by the common offspring of Hindoos and Europeans, is a new and powerful agent of reconstruction. The Zemindaree and Ryotwar themselves, abominable as they are, involve two distinct forms of private property in land—the great desideratum of Asiatic society. From the Indian natives, reluctantly and sparingly educated at Calcutta, under English superintendence, a fresh class is springing up, endowed with the requirements for government and imbued with European science. Steam has brought India into regular and rapid communication with Europe, has connected its chief ports with those of the whole south-eastern ocean, and has revindicated it from the isolated position which was the prime law of its stagnation. The day is not far distant when, by a combination of railways and steam vessels, the distance between England and India, measured by time, will be shortened to eight days, and when that once fabulous country will thus be actually annexed to the Western World.

The ruling classes of Great Britain have had, till now, but an accidental, transitory, and exceptional interest in the progress of India. The aristocracy wanted to conquer it, the moneyocracy to plunder it, and the millocracy to undersell it. But now the tables are turned. The millocracy have discovered that the transformation of India into a reproductive country has become a vital importance to them, and that, to that end, it is necessary, above all, to gift her with means of irrigation and of internal communication. They intend now drawing a net of railroads over India. And they will do it. The results must be inappreciable.

It is notorious that the productive powers of India are paralyzed by the utter want of means for conveying and exchanging its various produce. Nowhere, more than in India, do we meet with social destitution in the midst of natural plenty, for want of the means of exchange. It was proved before a Committee of the British House of Commons, which sat in 1848, that "when grain was selling from 6s. to 8s. a quarter at Khandesh, it was sold 64s. to 70s. at Poonah, where the people were dying in the streets of famine, without the possibility of gaining supplies from Khandesh, because the clay roads were impracticable."

The introduction of railroads may be easily made to subserve agricultural purposes by the formation of tanks, where ground is required for embankment, and by the conveyance of water along the different lines. Thus irrigation, the sine qua non of farming in the East, might be greatly extended, and the frequently recurring local famines, arising from the want of water, would be averted. The general importance of railways, viewed under this head, must become evident, when we remember that irrigated lands, even in the districts near Ghats, pay three times as much in taxes, afford ten or twelve times as much employment, and yield twelve or fifteen times as much profit, as the same area without irrigation.

Railways will afford the means of diminishing the amount and the cost of the military establishments. Col. Warren, Town Major of the Fort St. William, stated before a Select Committee of the House of Commons:

The practicability of receiving intelligence from distant parts of the country in as many hours as at present it requires days and even weeks, and of sending instructions with troops and stores, in the more brief period, are considerations which cannot be too highly estimated. Troops could be kept at more distant and healthier stations than at present, and much loss of life from sickness would by this means be spared. Stores could not to the same extent be required at the various depots, and the loss by decay, and the destruction incidental to the climate, would also be avoided. The number of troops might be diminished in direct proportion to their effectiveness.

We know that the municipal organization and the economical basis of the village communities have been broken up, but their worst feature, the dissolution of society into stereotype and disconnected atoms, has survived their vitality. The village isolation produced the absence of roads in India, and the absence of roads perpetuated the village isolation. On this plan a community existed with a given scale of low conveniences, almost without intercourse with other villages, without the desires and efforts indispensable to social advance. The British having broken up this self-sufficient *inertia* of the villages, railways will provide the new want of communication and intercourse. Besides,

one of the effects of the railway system will be to bring into every village affected by it such knowledge of the contrivances and appliances of other countries, and such means of obtaining them, as will first put the hereditary and stipendiary village artisanship of India to full proof of its capabilities, and then supply its defects.[1]

I know that the English millocracy intend to endow India with railways with the exclusive view of extracting at diminished expenses, the cotton and other raw materials for their manufactures. But when you have once introduced machinery into the locomotion

---

1   John Chapman, *The Cotton and Commerce of India, Considered in Relation to the Interests of Great Britain: With Remarks on Railway Communication in the Bombay Presidency* (London, 1851), p. 91.—Ed.

of a country, which possesses iron and coals, you are unable to withhold it from its fabrication. You cannot maintain a net of railways over an immense country without introducing all those industrial processes necessary to meet the immediate and current wants of railway locomotion, and out of which there must grow the application of machinery to those branches of industry not immediately connected with railways. The railway system will therefore become, in India, truly the forerunner of modern industry. This is the more certain as the Hindoos are allowed by British authorities themselves to possess particular aptitude for accommodating themselves to entirely new labor, and acquiring the requisite knowledge of machinery. Ample proof of this fact is afforded by the capacities and expertness of the native engineers in the Calcutta mint, where they have been for years employed in working the steam machinery, by the natives attached to the several steam-engines in the Hurdwar coal districts, and by other instances. Mr. Campbell himself, greatly influenced as he is by the prejudices of the East India Company, is obliged to avow "that the great mass of the Indian people possesses a great *industrial energy*, is well fitted to accumulate capital, and remarkable for a mathematical clearness of head, and talent for figures and exact sciences." "Their intellects," he says, "are excellent."[2]

Modern industry, resulting from the railway system, will dissolve the hereditary divisions of labor, upon which rest the Indian castes, those decisive impediments to Indian progress and Indian power.

All the English bourgeoisie may be forced to do will neither emancipate nor materially mend the social condition of the mass of the people, depending not only on the development of the productive powers, but of their appropriation by the people. But what they will not fail to do is to lay down the material premises for both. Has the bourgeoisie ever done more? Has it ever effected a progress without dragging individuals and peoples through blood and dirt, through misery and degradation?

[2]   George Campbell, *Modern India: A Sketch of the System of Civil Government* (London, 1852), pp. 59–60.—Ed.

The Indians will not reap the fruits of the new elements of society scattered among them by the British bourgeoisie, till in Great Britain itself the now ruling classes shall have been supplanted by the industrial proletariat, or till the Hindoos themselves shall have grown strong enough to throw off the English yoke altogether. At all events, we may safely expect to see, at a more or less remote period, the regeneration of that great and interesting country, whose gentle natives are, to use the expression of Prince Saltykov, even in the most inferior classes, "plus fins et plus adroits que les Italiens,"[3] whose submission even is counterbalanced by a certain calm nobility, who, notwithstanding their natural languor, have astonished the British officers by their bravery, whose country has been the source of our languages, our religions, and who represent the type of the ancient German in the Jat and the type of the ancient Greek in the Brahmin.

I cannot part with the subject of India without some concluding remarks.

The profound hypocrisy and inherent barbarism of bourgeois civilization lies unveiled before our eyes, turning from its home, where it assumes respectable forms, to the colonies, where it goes naked. They are the defenders of property, but did any revolutionary party ever originate agrarian revolutions like those in Bengal, in Madras, and in Bombay? Did they not, in India, to borrow an expression of that great robber, Lord Clive himself, resort to atrocious extortion, when simple corruption could not keep pace with their rapacity? While they prated in Europe about the inviolable sanctity of the national debt, did they not confiscate in India the dividends of the rajahs, who had invested their private savings in the Company's own funds? While they combatted the French revolution under the pretext of defending "our holy religion," did they not forbid, at the same time, Christianity to be propagated in India, and did they not, in order to make money out of the pilgrims steaming to the temples of Orissa and Bengal, take up the trade in the murder and prostitution perpetrated in the temple of Jugger-

3   More subtle and adroit than the Italians"; Marx quotes from Alexei Dmitriyevich Saltykov's *Lettres sur l'Inde* (Paris, 1848), p. 61. —Ed.

naut? These are the men of "Property, Order, Family, and Religion."

The devastating effects of English industry, when contemplated with regard to India, a country as vast as Europe, and containing 150 millions of acres, are palpable and confounding. But we must not forget that they are only the organic results of the whole system of production as it is now constituted. That production rests on the supreme rule of capital. The centralization of capital is essential to the existence of capital as an independent power. The destructive influence of that centralization upon the markets of the world does not reveal, in the most gigantic dimensions, the inherent organic laws of political economy now at work in every civilized town. The bourgeois period of history has to create the material basis of the new world—on the one hand the universal intercourse founded upon the mutual dependency of mankind, and the means of that intercourse; on the other hand the development of the productive powers of man and the transformation of material production into a scientific domination of natural agencies. Bourgeois industry and commerce create these material conditions of a new world in the same way as geological revolutions have created the surface of the earth. When a great social revolution shall have mastered the results of the bourgeois epoch, the market of the world and the modern powers of production, and subjected them to the common control of the most advanced peoples, then only will human progress cease to resemble that hideous pagan idol, who would not drink the nectar but from the skulls of the slain.

II. China

A most profound yet fantastic speculator on the principles which govern the movements of Humanity was wont to extol as one of the ruling secrets of nature what he called the law of the contact of extremes. The homely proverb that "extremes meet" was, in his view, a grand and potent truth in every sphere of life; an axiom with which the philosopher could as little dispense as the astronomer with the laws of Kepler or the great discovery of Newton.

Whether the "contact of extremes" be such a universal principle or not, a striking illustration of it may be seen in the effect the Chinese revolution seems likely to exercise upon the civilized world. It may seem a very strange, and a very paradoxical assertion that the next uprising of the people of Europe, and their next movement for republican freedom and economy of Government, may depend more probably on what is now passing in the Celestial Empire—the very opposite of Europe—than on any other political cause that now exists—more even than on the menaces of Russia and the consequent likelihood of a general European war. But yet it is no paradox, as all may understand by attentively considering the circumstances of the case.

Whatever be the social causes, and whatever religious, dynastic, or national shape they may assume, that have brought about the chronic rebellions subsisting in China for about ten years past, and now gathered together in one formidable revolution, the occasion of this outbreak has unquestionably been afforded by the English cannon forcing upon China that soporific drug called opium. Before the British arms the authority of the Manchu dynasty fell to pieces; the superstitious faith in the Eternity of the Celestial Empire broke down; the barbarous and hermetic isolation from the civilized world was infringed; and an opening was made for that intercourse which has since proceeded so rapidly under the golden attractions of California and Australia. At the same time the silver coin of the Empire, its life-blood, began to be drained away to the British East Indies.

Up to 1830, the balance of trade being continually in favor of the Chinese, there existed an uninterrupted importation of silver from India, Britain, and the United States into China. Since 1833, and especially since 1840, the export of silver from China to India has become almost exhausting for the Celestial Empire. Hence the strong decrees of the Emperor against the opium trade, responded to by still stronger resistance to his measures. Besides this immediate economical consequence, the bribery connected with opium smuggling has entirely demoralized the Chinese State officers in the Southern provinces. Just as the Emperor was wont to be considered the father of all China, so his officers were looked upon as sustaining the paternal relation to their respective districts. But this patriarchal authority, the only moral link embracing the vast machinery of the State, has gradually been corroded by the corruption of those officers, who have made great gains by conniving at opium smuggling. This has occurred principally in the same Southern provinces where the rebellion commenced. It is almost needless to observe that, in the same measure in which opium has obtained the sovereignty over the Chinese, the Emperor and his staff of pedantic mandarins have become dispossessed of their own sovereignty. It would seem as though history had first to make this whole people drunk before it could rouse them out of their hereditary stupidity.

Though scarcely existing in former times, the import of English cottons, and to a small extent of English woolens, has rapidly risen since 1833, the epoch when the monopoly of trade with China was transferred from the East India Company to private commerce, and on a much greater scale since 1840, the epoch when other nations, and especially our own, also obtained a share in the Chinese trade. This introduction of foreign manufactures has had a similar effect on the native industry to that which it formerly had on Asia Minor, Persia, and India. In China the spinners and weavers have suffered greatly under this foreign competition, and the community has become unsettled in proportion.

The tribute to be paid to England after the unfortunate war of 1840, the great unproductive consumption of opium, the drain of the precious metals by this trade, the destructive influence of foreign competition on native manufacturers, the demoralized condition of the public administration, produced two things: the old taxation became more burdensome and harassing, and new taxation was added to the old. Thus in a decree of the Emperor, dated Pekin, January 5, 1853, we find orders given to the viceroys and governors of the southern provinces of Woo-Chang and Hun-Yang to remit and defer the payment of taxes, and especially not in any case to exact more than the regular amount; for otherwise, says the decree, "how will the poor people be able to bear it?" And "Thus, perhaps," continues the Emperor, "will my people, in a period of general hardship and distress, be exempted from the evils of being pursued and worried by the tax-gatherer." Such language as this, and such concessions we remember to have heard from Australia, the China of Germany, in 1848.

All these dissolving agencies acting together on the finances, the morals, the industry, and political structure of China, received their full development under the English cannon in 1840, which broke down the authority of the Emperor, and forced the Celestial Empire into contact with the terrestrial world. Complete isolation was the prime condition of the preservation of Old China. That isolation having come to a violent end by the medium of England, dissolution must follow as surely as that of any mummy carefully preserved in a hermetically sealed coffin, whenever it is brought into contact with the open air. Now, England having brought about the revolution of China, the question is how that revolution will in time react on England, and through England on Europe. This question is not difficult of solution.

The attention of our readers has often been called to the unparalleled growth of British manufactures since 1850. Amid the most surprising prosperity, it has not been difficult to point out the clear symptoms of an approaching industrial crisis. Notwithstanding California and Australia, notwithstanding the immense and unprecedented emigration, there must ever, without any particular accident, in due time arrive a moment when the extension of the markets is unable to keep pace with the extension of British manufactures, and this disproportion must bring about a new crisis with the same certainty as it has done in the past. But, if one of the great markets suddenly becomes contracted, the arrival of the crisis is necessarily accelerated thereby. Now, the Chinese rebellion must, for the time being, have precisely this effect upon England. The necessity for opening new markets, or for extending the old ones, was one of the principal causes of the reduction of the British tea-duties, as, with an increased importation of tea, an increased exportation of manufactures to China was expected to take place. Now, the value of the annual exports from the United Kingdom to China amounted, before the repeal in 1834 of the trading monopoly possessed by the East India Company, to only £600,000; in 1836, it reached the sum of £1,326,388; in 1845, it had risen to £2,394,827; in 1852 it amounted to about £3,000,000. The quantity of tea imported from China did not exceed, in 1793, 16,167,331 lbs.; but in 1845, it amounted to 50,714,657 lbs.; in 1846, to 57,584,561 lbs.; it is now above 60,000,000 lbs.

The tea crop of the last season will not prove short, as shown already by the export lists from Shanghai, of 2,000,000 lbs. above the preceding year. This excess is to be accounted for by two circumstances. On one hand, the state of the market at the close of 1851 was much depressed, and the large surplus stock left has been thrown into the export of 1852. On the other hand, the recent accounts of the altered British legislation with regard to imports of tea, reaching China, have brought forward all the available teas to a ready market, at greatly enhanced prices. But with respect to the coming crop, the case stands very differently. This is shown by the following extracts from the correspondence of a large tea firm in London:

In Shanghai the terror is extreme. Gold has advanced in value upwards of 25 percent, *being eagerly sought for hoarding;* silver had so far disappeared that *none could be obtained* to pay the Chinese dues on the British vessels requiring port clearance; and in consequence of which Mr. [Consul] Alcock has consented to become responsible to the Chinese authorities for the payment of these dues, on receipt of East India Company's bills, or other approved securities. *The scarcity of the precious metals* is one of the most unfavourable features, when viewed in reference to the immediate future of commerce, as this abstraction occurs precisely at that period when their use is most needed, to enable the tea and silk buyers to go into their interior and effect their purchases, for which a *large portion of bullion is paid in advance, to enable the producers to carry on their operations.*

. . . At this period of the year it is usual to begin making arrangements for the new teas, whereas at present nothing is talked of but the means of protecting persons and property, all transactions being at a stand. . . . If the means are not applied to secure the leaves in April and May, the early crop, which includes all the finer descriptions, both of black and green teas, will be as much lost as unreaped wheat at Christmas.[4]

---

[4]   Marx is quoting a circular of Moffatt & Co., printed in the *Economist*, 21 May 1854. Marx's italics.—Ed.

Now the means for securing the tea leaves will certainly not be given by the English, American, or French squadrons stationed in the Chinese seas, but these may easily, by their interference, produce such complications as to cut off all transactions between the tea-producing interior and the tea-exporting sea ports. Thus, for the present crop, a rise in the prices must be expected—speculation has already commenced in London—and for the crop to come a large deficit is as good as certain. Nor is this all. The Chinese, ready though they may be, as are all people in periods of revolutionary convulsion, to sell off to the foreigner all the bulky commodities they have on hand, will, as the Orientals are used to do in the apprehension of great changes, set to hoarding, not taking much in return for their tea and silk, except hard money. England has accordingly to expect a rise in the price of one of her chief articles of consumption, a drain of bullion, and a great contraction of an important market for her cotton and woollen goods. Even the *Economist*, that optimist conjurer of all things menacing the tranquil minds of the mercantile community, is compelled to use language like this:

We must not flatter ourselves with finding as extensive a market as formerly for our exports to China. . . . It is more probable, therefore, that our export trade to China should suffer, and that there should be a diminished demand for the produce of Manchester and Glasgow.[5]

It must not be forgotten that the rise in the price of so indispensable an article as tea, and the contraction of so important a market as China, will coincide with a deficient harvest in Western Europe, and, therefore, with rising prices of meat, corn, and all other agricultural produce. Hence contracted markets for manufacturers, because every rise in the prices of the first necessaries of life is counter-balanced, at home and abroad, by a corresponding reduction in the demand for manufactures. From every part of Great Britain complaints have been received on the backward state of most of the crops. The *Economist* says on this subject:

In the South of England "not only will there be left much land unsown, until too late for a crop of any sort, but much of the sown

5   *Economist*, 21 May 1853.—Ed.

land will prove to be foul, or otherwise in a bad state for corn-growing." On the wet or poor soils destined for wheat, signs that mischief is going on are apparent. "The time for planting mangel-wurzel may now be said to have passed away, and very little has been planted, while the time for preparing land for turnips is rapidly going by, without any adequate preparation for this important crop having been accomplished . . . oat-sowing has been much interfered with by the snow and rain. Few oats were sown early, and late-sown oats seldom produce a large crop."[6]

In many districts losses among the breeding flocks have been considerable. The price of other farm-produce than corn is from 20 to 30, and even 50 per cent higher than last year. On the Continent, corn has risen comparatively more than in England. Rye has risen in Belgium and Holland a full 100 per cent. Wheat and other grains are following suit.

Under these circumstances, as the greater part of the regular commercial circle has already been run through by British trade, it may safely be augured that the Chinese revolution will throw the spark into the overloaded mine of the present industrial system and cause the explosion of the long-prepared general crisis, which, spreading abroad, will be closely followed by political revolutions on the Continent. It would be a curious spectacle, that of China sending disorder into the Western World while the Western Powers, by English, French, and American war-steamers, are conveying "order" to Shanghai, Nankin, and the mouths of the Great Canal. Do these order-mongering Powers, which would attempt to support the wavering Manchu dynasty, forget that the hatred against foreigners and their exclusion from the Empire, once the mere result of China's geographical and ethnographical situation, have become a political system only since the conquest of the country by the race of the Manchu Tartars? There can be no doubt that the turbulent dissensions among the European nations who, at the later end of the seventeenth century, rivaled each other in the trade with China, lent a mighty aid to the exclusive policy adopted by the Manchus. But more than this was done by the fear of the new dynasty, lest the foreigners might favor the discontent existing among a large proportion of the Chinese during the first half-century or thereabouts of their subjection to the Tartars. From these considerations, foreigners were then prohibited from all communication with the Chinese, except through Canton, a town at a great distance from Pekin and the tea-districts, and their commerce restricted to intercourse with the Hong merchants, licensed by the Government expressly for the foreign trade, in order to keep the rest of its subjects from all connection with the odious strangers. In any case an interference on the part of the Western Governments at this time can only serve to render the revolution more violent, and protract the stagnation of trade.

At the same time it is to be observed with regard to India that the British Government of that country depends for full one-seventh of its revenue on the sale of opium to the Chinese while a considerable proportion of the Indian demand for British manufactures depends on the production of that opium in India. The Chinese, it is true, are no more likely to renounce the use of opium than are the Germans to foreswear tobacco. But as the new Emperor is understood to be favorable to the culture of the poppy and the preparation of opium in China itself, it is evident that a death-blow is very likely to be struck at once at the business of opium-raising in India, the Indian revenue, and the commercial resources of Hindostan. Though this blow would not immediately be felt by the interests concerned, it would operate effectually in due time, and would come in to intensify and prolong the universal financial crisis whose horoscope we have cast above.

Since the commencement of the eighteenth century there has been no serious revolution in Europe which had not been preceded by a commercial and financial crisis. This applies no less to the revolution of 1789 than to that of 1848. It is true, not only that we every day behold more threatening symptoms of conflict between the ruling powers and their subjects, between the State and society, between the various classes; but also the conflict of the existing powers among each other gradually reaching that height where the sword must be drawn, and the *ultima ratio* of princes be recurred to. In the European capitals, every day brings despatches big with universal war, vanishing under the despatches of the following day, bearing the assurance of peace for a week or so. We may be sure, nevertheless, that to whatever height the conflict between the European powers may rise, however threatening the aspect of the diplomatic horizon may appear, whatever movements may be attempted by some enthusiastic fraction in this or that country, the rage of princes and the fury of the people are alike enervated by the breath of prosperity. Neither wars nor revolutions are likely to put Europe by the ears, unless in consequence of a general commercial and industrial crisis, the signal of which has, as usual, to be given by England, the representative of European industry in the market of the world.

It is unnecessary to dwell on the political consequences such a crisis must produce in these times, with the unprecedented extension of factories in England, with the utter dissolution of her official parties, with the whole State machinery of France transformed into one immense swindling and stock-jobbing concern, with Austria on the eve of bankruptcy, with wrongs everywhere accumulated to be revenged by the people, with the conflicting interests of the reactionary powers themselves, and with the Russian dream of conquest once more revealed to the world.

15

THE HISTORICAL SPECIFICS

OF THE CLASS STRUGGLE

I. *The Conflict between Machinery and Workmen*

THE CONTEST between the capitalist and the wage-laborer dates back to the very origin of capital. It raged on throughout the whole manufacturing period.[1] But only since the introduction of machinery has the workman fought against the instrument of labor itself, the material embodiment of capital. He revolts against this particular form of the means of production, as being the material basis of the capitalist mode of production.

In the seventeenth century nearly all Europe experienced revolts of the workpeople against the ribbon-loom, a machine for weaving ribbons and trimmings, called in Germany Bandmühle,

---

Section I of this chapter is from *Capital*, 1:427–38; section II from *The Eighteenth Brumaire of Louis Bonaparte*, pp. 15–26 and 118–35; section III from Friedrich Engels, *Germany: Revolution and Counter-Revolution*, pp. 9–17.

[1]   See among others, John Houghton: "Husbandry and Trade improved. London, 1727." "The Advantages of the East India Trade, 1720." John Bellers, l. c. "The masters and their workmen are, unhappily, in a perpetual war with each other. The invariable object of the former is to get their work done as cheaply as possible; and they do not fail to employ every artifice to this purpose, whilst the latter are equally attentive to every occasion of distressing their masters into a compliance with higher demands." ("An Inquiry into the Causes of the Present High Prices of Provisions," p. 61–62. Author, the Rev. Nathaniel Forster, quite on the side of the workmen.)

Schnurmühle, and Mühlenstuhl. These machines were invented in Germany. Abbé Lancellotti, in a work that appeared in Venice in 1636, but which was written in 1579, says as follows: "Anthony Müller of Danzig, saw about 50 years ago in that town, a very ingenious machine, which weaves 4 to 6 pieces at once. But the Mayor being apprehensive that this invention might throw a large number of workmen on the streets, caused the inventor to be secretly strangled or drowned." In Leyden, this machine was not used till 1629; there the riots of the ribbon-weavers at length compelled the Town Council to prohibit it. "In hac urbe," says Boxhorn (Inst. Pol., 1663), referring to the introduction of this machine into Leyden, "ante hos viginti circiter annos instrumentum quidam invenerunt textorium, quo solus plus panni et facilius conficere poterat, quam plures aequali tempore. Hinc turbae ortae et querulae textorum, tandemque usus hujus instrumenti a magistratu prohibitus est." After making various decrees more or less prohibitive against this loom in 1632, 1639, etc., the States General of Holland at length permitted it to be used, under certain conditions, by the decree of the 15th December, 1661. It was also prohibited in Cologne in 1676, at the same time that its introduction into England was causing disturbances among the workpeople. By an imperial Edict of 19th February, 1685, its use was forbidden throughout all Germany. In Hamburg it was burnt in public by order of the Senate. The Emperor Charles VI., on 9th February, 1719, renewed the edict of 1685, and not till 1765 was its use openly allowed in the Electorate of Saxony. This machine, which shook Europe to its foundations, was in fact the precursor of the mule and the power-loom, and of the industrial revolution of the eighteenth century. It enabled a totally inexperienced boy, to set the whole loom with all its shuttles in motion, by simply moving a rod backwards and forwards, and in its improved form produced from 40 to 50 pieces at once.

About 1630, a wind-sawmill, erected near London by a Dutchman, succumbed to the excesses of the populace. Even as late as the beginning of the eighteenth century, sawmills driven by water overcame the opposition of the people, supported as it was by parliament, only with great difficulty. No sooner had Everet in 1758 erected the first wool-shearing machine that was driven by water-power, than it was set on fire by 100,000 people who had been thrown out of work. Fifty thousand workpeople, who had previously lived by carding wool, petitioned parliament against Arkwright's scribbling mills and carding engines. The enormous destruction of machinery that occurred in the English manufacturing districts during the first 15 years of this century, chiefly caused by the employment of the power-loom, and known as the Luddite movement, gave the anti-jacobin governments of a Sidmouth, a Castlereagh, and the like, a pretext for the most reactionary and forcible measures. It took both time and experience before the workpeople learnt to distinguish between machinery and its employment by capital, and to direct their attacks, not against the material instruments of production, but against the mode in which they are used.[2]

The contests about wages in manufacture, presuppose manufacture, and are in no sense directed against its existence. The opposition against the establishment of new manufactures, proceeds from the guilds and privileged towns, not from the workpeople. Hence the writers of the manufacturing period treat the division of labor chiefly as a means of virtually supplying a deficiency of laborers, and not as a means of actually displacing those in work. This distinction is self-evident. If it be said that 100 millions of people would be required in England to spin with the old spinning-wheel the cotton that is now spun with mules by 500,000 people, this does not mean that the mules took the place of those millions who never existed. It means only this, that many millions of workpeople would be required to replace the spinning machinery. If, on the other hand, we say, that in England the power-loom threw 800,000 weavers on the streets, we do not refer to existing machinery, that would have to be replaced by a definite number of workpeople, but to a number of weavers in existence who were actually replaced or displaced by the looms. During the manufacturing period, handicraft labor, altered though it was by division of labor, was yet the

2   In old-fashioned manufactures the revolts of the workpeople against machinery, even to this day, occasionally assume a savage character, as in the case of the Sheffield file cutters in 1865.

basis. The demands of the new colonial markets could not be satisfied owing to the relatively small number of town operatives handed down from the Middle Ages, and the manufactures proper opened out new fields of production to the rural population, driven from the land by the dissolution of the feudal system. At that time, therefore, division of labor and co-operation in the workshops, were viewed more from the positive aspect, that they made the workpeople more productive.[3] Long before the period of Modern Industry, co-operation and the concentration of the instruments of labor in the hands of a few, gave rise, in numerous countries where these methods were applied in agriculture, to great, sudden, and forcible revolutions in the modes of production, and consequentially, in the conditions of existence, and the means of employment of the rural populations. But this contest at first takes place more between the large and the small landed proprietors, than between capital and wage-labor; on the other hand, when the laborers are displaced by the instruments of labor, by sheep, horses, etc., in this case force is directly resorted to in the first instance as the prelude to the industrial revolution. The laborers are first driven from the land, and then come the sheep. Land grabbing on a great scale, such as was perpetrated in England, is the first step in creating a field for the establishment of agriculture on a great scale.

[3]   Sir James Stewart also understands machinery quite in this sense. "Je considère donc les machines comme des moyens d'augmenter (virtuellement) le nombre des gens industrieux qu'on n'est pas obligé de nourrir. . . . En quoi l'effet d'une machine diffère-t-il de celui de nouveaux habitants?" (French trans. t. I., l. I., ch. XIX.) More naïve is Petty, who says, it replaces "Polygamy." The above point of view is, at the most, admissible only for some parts of the United States. On the other hand, "machinery can seldom be used with success to abridge the labour of an individual; more time would be lost in its construction than could be saved by its application. It is only really useful when it acts on great masses, when a single machine can assist the work of thousands. It is accordingly in the most populous countries, where there are most idle men, that it is most abundant. . . . It is not called into use by a scarcity of men, but by the facility with which they can be brought to work in masses." (Piercy Ravenstone, "Thoughts on the Funding System and Its Effects." London, 1824, p. 15.)

Hence this subversion of agriculture puts on, at first, more the appearance of a political revolution.

The instrument of labor, when it takes the form of a machine, immediately becomes a competitor of the workman himself.[4] The self-expansion of capital by means of machinery is thenceforward directly proportional to the number of the workpeople, whose means of livelihood have been destroyed by that machinery. The whole system of capitalist production is based on the fact that the workman sells his labor-power as a commodity. Division of labor specializes this labor-power, by reducing it to skill in handling a particular tool. So soon as the handling of this tool becomes the work of a machine, then, with the use-value, the exchange-value too, of the workman's labor-power vanishes; the workman becomes unsaleable, like paper money thrown out of currency by legal enactment. That portion of the working class, thus by machinery rendered superfluous, i.e., no longer immediately necessary for the self-expansion of capital, either goes to the wall in the unequal contest of the old handicrafts and manufactures with machinery, or else floods all the more easily accessible branches of industry, swamps the labor market, and sinks the price of labor-power below its value. It is impressed upon the workpeople, as a great consolation, first, that their sufferings are only temporary ("a temporary inconvenience"), secondly, that machinery acquires the mastery over the whole of a given field of production, only by degrees, so that the extent and intensity of its destructive effect is diminished. The first consolation neutralizes the second. When machinery seizes on an industry by degrees, it produces chronic misery among the operatives who compete with it. Where the transition is rapid, the effect is acute and felt by great masses. History discloses no tragedy more horrible than the gradual extinction of the English hand-loom weavers, an extinction that was spread over several decades, and finally sealed in 1838. Many of them died of starvation, many with families vegetated for a long time on 2½d.

[4]   "Machinery and labour are in constant competition." David Ricardo, *On the Principles of Political Economy and Taxation*, 3d ed., London, 1821, p. 479.

a day.[5] On the other hand, the English cotton machinery produced an accute effect in India. The Governor General reported 1834–35 "The misery hardly finds a parallel in the history of commerce. The bones of the cotton-weavers are bleaching the plains of India." No doubt, in turning them out of this "temporal" world, the machinery caused them no more than "a temporary inconvenience." For the rest, since machinery is continually seizing upon new fields of production, its temporary effect is really permanent. Hence, the character of independence and estrangement which the capitalist mode of production as a whole gives to the instruments of labor and to the product, as against the workman, is developed by means of machinery into a thorough antagonism.[6] Therefore, it is with the advent of machinery, that the workman for the first time brutally revolts against the instruments of labor.

[5]   The competition between hand-weaving and power-weaving in England, before the passing of the Poor Law of 1833, was prolonged by supplementing the wages, which had fallen considerably below the minimum, with parish relief. "The Rev. Mr. Turner was, in 1827, rector of Wilmslow, in Cheshire, a manufacturing district. The questions of the Committee of Emigration, and Mr. Turner's answers, show how the competition of human labour is maintained against machinery. Question: 'Has not the use of the power-loom superseded the use of the hand-loom?' Answer: 'Undoubtedly; it would have superseded them much more than it has done, if the hand-loom weavers were not enabled to submit to a reduction of wages.' Question: 'But in submitting he has accepted wages which are insufficient to support him, and looks to parochial contribution as the remainder of his support?' Answer: 'Yes, and in fact the competition between the hand-loom and the power-loom is maintained out of the poor-rates.' Thus degrading pauperism or expatriation, is the benefit which the industrious receive from the introduction of machinery, to be reduced from the respectable and in some degree independent mechanic, to the cringing wretch who lives on the debasing bread of charity. This they call a temporary inconvenience." ("A Prize Essay on the Comparative Merits of Competition and Co-operation," Lond., 1834, p. 29.)

[6]   "The same cause which may increase the revenue of the country" (i.e., as Ricardo explains in the same passage, the revenues of landlords and capitalists, whose wealth, from the economical point of view, forms the Wealth of the Nation), "may at the same time render the population redundant and deteriorate the condition of the labourer." (Ricardo, l. c., p. 469.) "The constant aim and the tendency of every improvement in machinery is, in fact, to do away entirely with the labour of man, or to lessen

The instrument of labor strikes down the laborer. This direct antagonism between the two comes out most strongly, whenever newly introduced machinery competes with handicrafts or manufactures, handed down from former times. But even in Modern Industry the continual improvement of machinery, and the development of the automatic system, has an analogous effect. "The object of improved machinery is to diminish manual labor, to provide for the performance of a process or the completion of a link in a manufacture by the aid of an iron instead of the human apparatus."[7] "The adaptation of power to machinery heretofore moved by hand, is almost of daily occurrence . . . the minor improvements in machinery having for their object economy of power, the production of better work, the turning off more work in the same time, or in supplying the place of a child, a female, or a man, are constant, and although sometimes apparently of no great moment, have somewhat important results."[8] "Whenever a process requires peculiar dexterity and steadiness of hand, it is withdrawn, as soon as possible, from the cunning workman, who is prone to irregularities of many kinds, and it is placed in charge of a peculiar mechanism, so self-regulating that a child can superint it."[9] "On the

---

its price by substituting the labour of women and children for that of grown-up men, or of unskilled for that of skilled workmen." (Andrew Ure, *The Philosophy of Manufactures*, 2d edition, London, 1835, t. I., p. 35).

7   "Rep. Insp. Fact. for 31st October, 1858," p. 43.

8   "Rep. Insp. Fact., for 31st October, 1856." p. 15.

9   Ure, l. c., p. 19. "The great advantage of the machinery employed in brickmaking consists in this, that the employer is made entirely independent of skilled labourers." ("Ch. Empl. Comm. V. Report," Lond., 1866, p. 180, n. 46.) Mr. A. Sturrock, superintendent of the machine department of the Great Northern Railway, says, with regard to the building of locomotives, etc.: "Expensive English workmen are being less used every day. The production of the workshops of England is being increased by the use of improved tools and these tools are again served by a low class of labour. . . . Formerly their skilled labour necessarily produced all the parts of engines. Now the parts of engines are produced by labour with less skill, but with good tools. By tools, I mean engineer's machinery, lathes, planing machines, drills, and so on." ("Royal Com. on Railways." Lond., 1867, Minutes of Evidence, n. 17,862 and 17,863.)

automatic plan skilled labor gets progressively superseded."[10] "The effect of improvements in machinery, not merely in superseding the necessity for the employment of the same quantity of adult labor as before, in order to produce a given result, but in substituting one description of human labor for another, the less skilled for the more skilled, juvenile for adult, female for male, causes a fresh disturbance in the rate of wages."[11] "The effect of substituting the self-acting mule for the common mule, is to discharge the greater part of the men spinners, and to retain adolescents and children."[12] The extraordinary power of expansion of the factory system owing to accumulated practical experience, to the mechanical means at hand, and to constant technical progress, was proved to us by the giant strides of that system under the pressure of a shortened working day. But who in 1860, the Zenith year of the English cotton industry, would have dreamt of the galloping improvements in machinery, and the corresponding displacement of working people, called into being during the following 3 years, under the stimulus of the American Civil War? A couple of examples from the Reports of the Inspectors of Factories will suffice on this point. A Manchester manufacturer states: "We formerly had 75 carding engines, now we have 12, doing the same quantity of work. . . . We are doing with fewer hands by 14, at a saving in wages of £10 a-week. Our estimated saving in waste is about 10% in the quantity of cotton consumed." "In another fine spinning mill in Manchester, I was informed that through increased speed, and the adoption of some self-acting processes, a reduction had been made, in number, of a fourth in one department, and of above half in another, and that the introduction of the combing machine in place of the second carding, had considerably reduced the number of hands formerly employed in the carding-room." Another spinning mill is estimated to effect a saving of labor of 10%. The Messrs. Gilmour, spinners at Manchester, state:

In our blowing-room department we consider our expense with new machinery is fully one-third less in wages and hands . . . in the jack-

---

10   Ure, l. c., p. 20.
11   Ure, l. c., p. 321.
12   Ure, l. c., p. 23.

frame and drawing-frame room, about one-third less in expense, and likewise one-third less in hands; in the spinning-room about one-third less in expenses. But this is not all; when our yarn goes to the manufacturers, it is so much better by the application of our new machinery, that they will produce a greater quantity of cloth, and cheaper than from the yarn produced by old machinery.[13]

Mr. Redgrave further remarks in the same Report: "The reduction of hands against increased production is, in fact, constantly taking place; in woollen mills the reduction commenced some time since, and is continuing; a few days since, the master of a school in the neighborhood of Rochdale said to me, that the great falling off in the girls' school is not only caused by the distress, but by the changes of machinery in the woollen mills, in consequence of which a reduction of 70 short-timers had taken place."[14]

The following table shows the total result of the mechanical improvements in the English cotton industry due to the American Civil War.

Number of Factories			
	1858	1861	1868
England and Wales	2,046	2,715	2,405
Scotland	152	163	131
Ireland	12	9	13
United Kingdom	2,210	2,887	2,549

Number of Power-Looms			
	1858	1861	1868
England and Wales	275,590	368,125	344,719
Scotland	21,624	30,110	31,864
Ireland	1,633	1,757	2,746
United Kingdom	298,847	399,992	379,329

13   "Rep. Insp. Fact., 31st Oct., 1863," pp. 108, 109.
14   L. c., p. 109. The rapid improvement of machinery, during the crisis, allowed the English manufacturers, immediately after the termination of the American Civil War, and almost in no time, to glut the markets of the world again. Cloth, during the last six months of 1866, was almost unsaleable. Thereupon began the consignment of goods to India and China, thus naturally making the glut more intense. At the beginning of 1867 the manufacturers resorted to their usual way out of the difficulty, viz., reducing wages 5 per cent. The workpeople resisted and said that the only remedy was to work short time, 4 days a-week; and their theory was

Number of Spindles

	1858	1861	1868
England and Wales	25,818,576	28,352,152	30,478,228
Scotland	2,041,129	1,915,398	1,397,546
Ireland	150,512	119,944	124,240
United Kingdom	28,010,217	30,387,494	32,000,014

Number of Persons Employed

	1858	1861	1868
England and Wales	341,170	407,598	357,052
Scotland	34,698	41,237	39,809
Ireland	3,345	2,734	4,203
United Kingdom	379,213	451,569	401,064

Hence, between 1861 and 1868, 338 cotton factories disappeared, in other words more productive machinery on a larger scale was concentrated in the hands of a smaller number of capitalists. The number of power-looms decreased by 20,663; but since their product increased in the same period, an improved loom must have yielded more than an old one. Lastly the number of spindles increased by 1,612,541, while the number of operatives decreased by 50,505. The "temporary" misery, inflicted on the workpeople by the cotton-crisis, was heightened, and from being temporary made permanent, by the rapid and persistent progress of machinery.

But machinery not only acts as a competitor who gets the better of the workman, and is constantly on the point of making him superfluous. It is also a power inimical to him, and as such capital proclaims it from the roof tops and as such makes use of it. It is the most powerful weapon for repressing strikes, those periodical revolts of the working class against the autocracy of capital.[15] According to Gaskell, the steam engine was from the very first an an-

---

the correct one. After holding out for some time, the self-elected captains of industry had to make up their minds to short time, with reduced wages in some places and in others without.

[15]   "The relation of master and man in the blown-flint bottle trades amounts to a chronic strike." Hence the impetus given to the manufacture of pressed glass, in which the chief operations are done by machinery. One firm in Newcastle, who formerly produced 350,000 lbs. of brown-flint glass, now producs in its place 3,000,500 lbs. of pressed glass. ("Ch. Empl. Comm., Fourth Rep.," 1865, pp. 262, 263.)

tagonist of human power, an antagonist that enabled the capitalist to tread under foot the growing claims of the workmen, who threatened the newly born factory system with a crisis.[16] It would be possible to write quite a history of the inventions, made since 1830, for the sole purpose of supplying capital with weapons against the revolts of the working class. At the head of these in importance, stands the self-acting mule, because it opened up a new epoch in the automatic system.[17]

Nasmyth, the inventor of the steam hammer, gives the following evidence before the Trades Union Commission, with regard to the improvements made by him in machinery and introduced in consequence of the wide-spread and long strikes of the engineers in 1851.

The characteristic feature of our modern mechanical improvements, is the introduction of self-acting tool machinery. What every mechanical workman has now to do, and what every boy can do, is not to work himself but to superintend the beautiful labour of the machine. The whole class of workmen that depend exclusively on their skill, is now done away with. Formerly, I employed four boys to every mechanic. Thanks to these new mechanical combinations, I have reduced the number of grown-up men from 1500 to 750. The result was a considerable increase in my profits.

Ure says of a machine used in calico printing: "At length capitalists sought deliverance from this intolerable bondage" [namely the, in their eyes, burdensome terms of their contracts with the workmen] "in the resources of science, and were speedily re-instated in their legitimate rule, that of the head over the inferior members." Speaking of an invention for dressing warps: "Then the combined malcontents, who fancied themselves impregnably intrenched behind the old lines of division of labour, found their flanks turned and their defences rendered useless by the new me-

---

16   Gaskell. "The Manufacturing Population of England, London, 1833," pp. 3, 4.
17   W. Fairbairn discovered several very important applications of machinery to the construction of machines, in consequence of strikes in his own workshops.

chanical tactics, and were obliged to surrender at discretion." With regard to the invention of the self-acting mule, he says: "A creation destined to restore order among the industrious classes. . . . This invention confirms the great doctrine already propounded, that when capital enlists science into her service, the refractory hand of labour will always be taught docility."[18] Although Ure's work appeared 30 years ago, at a time when the factory system was comparatively but little developed, it still perfectly expresses the spirit of the factory, not only by its undisguised cynicism, but also by the naïveté with which it blurts out the stupid contradictions of the capitalist brain. For instance, after propounding the "doctrine" stated above, that capital, with the aid of science taken into its pay, always reduces the refractory hand of labor to docility, he grows indignant because "it (physico-mechanical science) has been accused of lending itself to the rich capitalist as an instrument for harassing the poor." After preaching a long sermon to show how advantageous the rapid development of machinery is to the working classes, he warns them, that by their obstinacy and their strikes they hasten that development. "Violent revulsions of this nature," he says, "display short-sighted man in the contemptible character of a self-tormentor." A few pages before he states the contrary. "Had it not been for the violent collisions and interruptions resulting from erroneous views among the factory operatives, the factory system would have been developed still more rapidly and beneficially for all concerned." Then he exclaims again: "Fortunately for the state of society in the cotton districts of Great Britain, the improvements in machinery are gradual." "It" (improvement in machinery) "is said to lower the rate of earnings of adults by displacing a portion of them, and thus rendering their number superabundant as compared with the demand for their labour. It certainly augments the demand for the labour of children and increases the rate of *their* wages." On the other hand, this same dispenser of consolation defends the lowness of the children's wages on the ground that it prevents parents from sending their children at too early an age into the factory. The whole of his book

18   Ure, l. c., pp. 368–70.

is a vindication of a working day of unrestricted length; that Parliament should forbid children of 13 years to be exhausted by working 12 hours a day, reminds his liberal soul of the darkest days of the Middle Ages. This does not prevent him from calling upon the factory operatives to thank Providence, who by means of machinery has given them the leisure to think of their "immortal interests."[19]

II. Class and Political Conflict in France, 1848–51

Hegel remarks somewhere that all facts and personages of great importance in world history occur, as it were, twice. He forgot to add: the first time as tragedy, the second as farce. Caussidière for Danton, Louis Blanc for Robespierre, the *Montagne* of 1848 to 1851 for the *Montagne* of 1793 to 1795, the Nephew for the Uncle. And the same caricature occurs in the circumstances attending the second edition of the eighteenth Brumaire![20]

Men make their own history, but they do not make it just as they please; they do not make it under circumstances chosen by themselves, but under circumstances directly encountered, given, and transmitted from the past. The tradition of all the dead generations weighs like a nightmare on the brain of the living. And just when they seem engaged in revolutionizing themselves and things, in creating something that has never yet existed, precisely in such periods of revolutionary crisis they anxiously conjure up the spirits of the past to their service and borrow from them names, battle cries, and costumes in order to present the new scene of world history in this time-honored disguise and this borrowed language. Thus Luther donned the mask of the Apostle Paul, the Revolution of 1789 to 1814 draped itself alternately as the Roman republic and the Roman empire, and the Revolution of 1848 knew nothing

---

19   Ure, l. c. pp. 368, 7, 370, 280, 321, 281, 370, 475.
20   *The Eighteenth Brumaire* (November 9, 1799): the coup d'etat, which took place on this day, completed the bourgeois counterrevolutionary development in France and resulted in the establishment of Napoleon Bonaparte's military dictatorship.—Ed.

better to do than to parody, now 1789, now the revolutionary tradition of 1793 to 1795. In like manner a beginner who has learned a new language always translates it back into his mother tongue, but he has assimilated the spirit of the new language and can freely express himself in it only when he finds his way in it without recalling the old and forgets his native tongue in the use of the new.

Consideration of this conjuring up of the dead of world history reveals at once a salient difference. Camille Desmoulins, Danton, Robespierre, Saint-Just, Napoleon, the heroes as well as the parties and the masses of the old French Revolution, performed the task of their time in Roman costume and with Roman phrases, the task of unchaining and setting up modern *bourgeois* society. The first ones knocked the feudal basis to pieces and mowed off the feudal heads which had grown on it. The other created inside France the conditions under which alone free competition could be developed, parcelled landed property exploited and the unchained industrial productive power of the nation employed; and beyond the French borders he everywhere swept the feudal institutions away, so far as was necessary to furnish bourgeois society in France with a suitable up-to-date environment on the European Continent. The new social formation once established, the antediluvian Colossi disappeared and with them resurrected Romanity—the Brutuses, Gracchi, Publicolas, the tribunes, the senators, and Caesar himself. Bourgeois society in its sober reality had begotten its true interpreters and mouthpieces in the Says, Cousins, Royer-Collards, Benjamin Constants and Guizots; its real military leaders sat behind the office desks, and the hog-headed Louis XVIII was its political chief. Wholly absorbed in the production of wealth and in peaceful competitive struggle, it no longer comprehended that ghosts from the days of Rome had watched over its cradle. But unheroic as bourgeois society is, it nevertheless took heroism, sacrifice, terror, civil war, and battles of peoples to bring it into being. And in the classically austere traditions of the Roman republic its gladiators found the ideals and the art forms, the self-deceptions that they needed in order to conceal from themselves the bourgeois limitations of the content of their struggles and to keep their enthusiasm on the high plane of the great historical tragedy. Similarly, at another stage of development, a century earlier, Cromwell and the English people had borrowed speech, passions, and illusions from the Old Testament for their bourgeois revolution. When the real aim had been achieved, when the bourgeois transformation of English society had been accomplished, Locke supplanted Habakkuk.

Thus the awakening of the dead in those revolutions served the purpose of glorifying the new struggles, not of parodying the old; of magnifying the given task in imagination, not of fleeing from its solution in reality; of finding once more the spirit of revolution, not of making its ghost walk about again.

From 1848 to 1851 only the ghost of the old revolution walked about, from Marrast, the *républicain en gants jaunes*,[21] who disguised himself as the old Bailly, down to the adventurer, who hides his commonplace repulsive features under the iron death mask of Napoleon. An entire people, which had imagined that by means of a revolution it had imparted to itself an accelerated power of motion, suddenly finds itself set back into a defunct epoch and, in order that no doubt as to the relapse may be possible, the old dates arise again, the old chronology, the old names, the old edicts, which had long become a subject of antiquarian erudition, and the old minions of the law, who had seemed long decayed. The nation feels like that mad Englishman in Bedlam who fancies that he lives in the times of the ancient Pharaohs and daily bemoans the hard labor that he must perform in the Ethiopian mines as a gold digger, immured in this subterranean prison, a dimly burning lamp fastened to his head, the overseer of the slaves behind him with a long whip, and at the exits a confused welter of barbarian mercenaries, who understand neither the forced laborers in the mines nor one another, since they speak no common language. "And all this is expected of me," sighs the mad Englishman, "of me, a freeborn Briton, in order to make gold for the old Pharaohs." "In order to pay the debts of the Bonaparte family," sighs the French nation. The Englishman, so long as he was in his right mind, could not get rid of the fixed idea of making gold. The French, so long as they

21   Republican in kid gloves.—Ed.

were engaged in revolution, could not get rid of the memory of Napoleon, as the election of December 10 proved. They hankered to return from the perils of revolution to the fleshpots of Egypt, and December 2, 1851 was the answer. They have not only a caricature of the old Napoleon, they have the old Napoleon himself, caricatured as he must appear in the middle of the nineteenth century.

The social revolution of the nineteenth century cannot draw its poetry from the past, but only from the future. It cannot begin with itself before it has stripped off all superstition in regard to the past. Earlier revolutions required recollections of past world history in order to drug themselves concerning their own content. In order to arrive at its own content, the revolution of the nineteenth century must let the dead bury their dead. There the phrase went beyond the content; here the content goes beyond the phrase.

The February Revolution was a surprise attack, a *taking* of the old society *unawares*, and the people proclaimed this unexpected *strok*e as a deed of world importance, ushering in a new epoch. On December 2 the February Revolution is conjured away by a cardsharper's trick, and what seems overthrown is no longer the monarchy but the liberal concessions that were wrung from it by centuries of struggle. Instead of *society* having conquered a new content for itself, it seems that the *state* only returned to its oldest form, to the shamelessly simple domination of the sabre and the cowl. This is the answer to the *coup de main*[22] of February 1848, given by the *coup de tête*[23] of December 1851. Easy come, easy go. Meanwhile the interval of time has not passed by unused. During the years 1848 to 1851 French society has made up, and that by an abbreviated because revolutionary method, for the studies and experiences which, in a regular, so to speak, textbook course of development would have had to precede the February Revolution, if it was to be more than a ruffling of the surface. Society now seems to have fallen back behind its point of departure; it has in truth first to create for itself the revolutionary point of departure, the

[22]   *Coup de main:* Unexpected stroke.—Ed.
[23]   *Coup de tête:* Rash act.—Ed.

situation, the relations, the conditions under which alone modern revolution becomes serious.

Bourgeois revolutions, like those of the eighteenth century, storm swiftly from success to success; their dramatic effects outdo each other; men and things seem set in sparkling brilliants; ecstasy is the everyday spirit; but they are short-lived; soon they have attained their zenith, and a long crapulent depression lays hold of society before it learns soberly to assimilate the results of its storm-and-stress period. On the other hand, proletarian revolutions, like those of the nineteenth century, criticize themselves constantly, interrupt themselves continually in their own course, come back to the apparently accomplished in order to begin it afresh, deride with unmerciful thoroughness the inadequacies, weaknesses, and paltrinesses of their first attempts, seem to throw down their adversary only in order that he may draw new strength from the earth and rise again, more gigantic, before them, recoil ever and anon from the indefinite prodigiousness of their own aims, until a situation has been created which makes all turning back impossible, and the conditions themselves cry out:

> *Hic Rhodus, hic salta!*
> *Here is the rose, here dance!*

For the rest, every fairly competent observer, even if he had not followed the course of French developments step by step, must have had a presentiment that an unheard-of fiasco was in store for the revolution. It was enough to hear the self-complacent howl of victory with which Messieurs the Democrats congratulated each other on the expected gracious consequences of the second Sunday in May 1852.[24] In their minds the second Sunday in May 1852 had become a fixed idea, a dogma, like the day on which Christ should reappear and the millennium begin, in the minds of the Chiliasts. As ever, weakness had taken refuge in a belief in miracles, fancied the enemy overcome when he was only conjured away in imagination, and it lost all understanding of the present in a

---

[24]   In May 1852 Louis Bonaparte's term of office as president expired. According to the French Constitution of 1848 presidential elections had to take place every four years on the second Sunday in May.—Ed.

passive glorification of the future that was in store for it and of the deeds it had *in petto* but which it merely did not want to carry out as yet. Those heroes who seek to disprove their demonstrated incapacity by mutually offering each other their sympathy and getting together in a crowd had tied up their bundles, collected their laurel wreaths in advance, and were just then engaged in discounting on the exchange market the republics *in partibus* for which they had already providently organized the government personnel with all the calm of their unassuming disposition. December 2 struck them like a thunderbolt from a clear sky, and the peoples that in periods of pusillanimous depression gladly let their inward apprehension be drowned by the loudest bawlers will perchance have convinced themselves that the times are past when the cackle of geese could save the Capitol.

The Constitution, the National Assembly, the dynastic parties, the blue and the red republicans, the heroes of Africa, the thunder from the platform, the sheet lightning of the daily press, the entire literature, the political names and the intellectual reputations, the civil law and the penal code, the *liberté, égalité, fraternité* and the second Sunday in May 1852—all has vanished like a phantasmagoria before the spell of a man whom even his enemies do not make out to be a sorcerer. Universal suffrage seems to have survived only for a moment, in order that with its own hand it may make its last will and testament before the eyes of all the world and declare in the name of the people itself: All that exists deserves to perish.

It is not enough to say, as the French do, that their nation was taken unawares. A nation and a woman are not forgiven the unguarded hour in which the first adventurer that came along could violate them. The riddle is not solved by such turns of speech, but merely formulated differently. It remains to be explained how a nation of thirty-six millions can be surprised and delivered unresisting into captivity by three *chevaliers d'industrie*.

Let us recapitulate in general outline the phases that the French Revolution went through from February 24, 1848, to December 1851.

Three main periods are unmistakable: *the February period;* May 4, 1848, to May 28, 1849: *the period of the constitution of the republic,* or *of the Constituent National Assembly;* May 28, 1849, to December 2, 1851: *the period of the constitutional repub-lic* or *of the Legislative National Assembly.*

The *first period,* from February 24, or the overthrow of Louis Philippe, to May 4, 1848, the meeting of the Constituent Assem-bly, the *February period* proper, may be described as the *prologue* to the revolution. Its character was officially expressed in the fact that the government improvised by it itself declared that it was *provisional* and, like the government, everything that was mooted, attempted, or enunciated during this period proclaimed itself to be only *provisional.* Nothing and nobody ventured to lay claim to the right of existence and of real action. All the elements that had prepared or determined the revolution, the dynastic opposition, the republican bourgeoisie, the democratic-republican petty bour-geoisie, and the social-democratic workers, provisionally found their place in the February *government.*

It could not be otherwise. The February days originally in-tended an electoral reform, by which the circle of the politically privileged among the possessing class itself was to be widened and the exclusive domination of the aristocracy of finance over-thrown. When it came to the actual conflict, however, when the people mounted the barricades, the National Guard maintained a passive attitude, the army offered no serious resistance, and the monarchy ran away, the republic appeared to be a matter of course. Every party construed it in its own way. Having secured it arms in hand, the proletariat impressed its stamp upon it and proclaimed it to be a *social republic.* There was thus indicated the general content of the modern revolution, a content which was in most singular contradiction to everything that, with the material available, with the degree of education attained by the masses, un-der the given circumstances and relations, could be immediately realized in practice. On the other hand, the claims of all the remain-ing elements that had collaborated in the February Revolution were recognized by the lion's share that they obtained in the govern-ment. In no period do we, therefore, find a more confused mixture of high-flown phrases and actual uncertainty and clumsiness, of more enthusiastic striving for innovation and more deeply-rooted domination of the old routine, of more apparent harmony of the whole of society and more profound estrangement of its elements. While the Paris proletariat still revelled in the vision of the wide prospects that had opened before it and indulged in seriously meant discussions on social problems, the old powers of society had grouped themselves, assembled, reflected, and found unexpected support in the mass of the nation, the peasants, and petty bourgeois, who all at once stormed on to the political stage, after the barriers of the July Monarchy had fallen.

The *second period*, from May 4, 1848, to the end of May 1849, is the period of the *constitution*, the *foundation, of the bourgeois republic*. Directly after the February days not only had the dynastic opposition been surprised by the republicans and the republicans by the Socialists, but all France by Paris. The National Assembly, which met on May 4, 1848, had emerged from the national elections and represented the nation. It was a living protest against the pretensions of the February days and was to reduce the results of the revolution to the bourgeois scale. In vain the Paris proletariat, which immediately grasped the character of this National Assembly, attempted on May 15, a few days after it met, forcibly to negate its existence, to dissolve it, to disintegrate again into its constituent parts the organic form in which the proletariat was threatened by the reacting spirit of the nation. As is known, May 15 had no other result save that of removing Blanqui and his comrades, that is, the real leaders of the proletarian party, from the public stage for the entire duration of the cycle we are considering.

The *bourgeois monarchy* of Louis Philippe can be followed only by a *bourgeois republic*, that is to say, whereas a limited section of the bourgeoisie ruled in the name of the king, the whole of the bourgeoisie will now rule in the name of the people. The demands of the Paris proletariat are utopian nonsense, to which an end must be put. To this declaration of the Constituent National Assembly the Paris proletariat replied with the *June Insurrection*, the most colossal event in the history of European civil wars. The bourgeois republic triumphed. On its side stood the aristocracy of finance, the industrial bourgeoisie, the middle class, the petty bourgeois, the army, the *lumpenproletariat* organized as the Mobile

Guard, the intellectual lights, the clergy, and the rural population. On the side of the Paris proletariat stood none but itself. More than three thousand insurgents were butchered after the victory, and fifteen thousand were transported without trial. With this defeat the proletariat passes into the *background* of the revolutionary stage. It attempts to press forward again on every occasion, as soon as the movement appears to make a fresh start, but with ever decreased expenditure of strength and always slighter results. As soon as one of the social strata situated above it gets into revolutionary ferment, the proletariat enters into an alliance with it and so shares all the defeats that the different parties suffer, one after another. But these subsequent blows become the weaker, the greater the surface of society over which they are distributed. The more important leaders of the proletariat in the Assembly and in the press successively fall victims to the courts, and ever more equivocal figures come to head it. In part it throws itself into *doctrinaire experiments, exchange banks and workers' associations, hence into a movement in which it renounces the revolutionizing of the old world by means of the latter's own great, combined resources, and seeks, rather, to achieve its salvation behind society's back, in private fashion, within its limited conditions of existence, and hence necessarily suffers shipwreck.* It seems to be unable either to rediscover revolutionary greatness in itself or to win new energy from the connections newly entered into, until *all classes* with which it contended in June themselves lie prostrate beside it. But at least it succumbs with the honors of the great, world-historic struggle; not only France, but all Europe trembles at the June earthquake, while the ensuing defeats of the upper classes are so cheaply bought that they require bare-faced exaggeration by the victorious party to be able to pass for events at all, and become the more ignominious the further the defeated party is removed from the proletarian party.

The defeat of the June insurgents, to be sure, had now prepared, had levelled the ground on which the bourgeois republic could be founded and built up, but it had shown at the same time that in Europe the questions at issue are other than that of "republic or monarchy." It had revealed that here *bourgeois republic* signifies the unlimited despotism of one class over other classes. It had proved that in countries with an old civilization, with a developed formation of classes, with modern conditions of production and with an intellectual consciousness in which all traditional ideas have been dissolved by the work of centuries, *the republic* signifies *in general only the political form of revolution of bourgeois society* and not its *conservative form of life*, as, for example, in the United States of North America, where, though classes already exist, they have not yet become fixed, but continually change and interchange their elements in constant flux, where the modern means of production, instead of coinciding with a stagnant surplus population, rather compensate for the relative deficiency of heads and hands, and where, finally, the feverish, youthful movement of material production, which has to make a new world its own, has left neither time nor opportunity for abolishing the old spirit world.

During the June days all classes and parties had united in the *party of Order* against the proletarian class as the *party of Anarchy*, of Socialism, of Communism. They had "saved" society from *"the enemies of society."* They had given out the watchwords of the old society, *"property, family, religion, order,"* to their army as passwords and had proclaimed to the counter-revolutionary crusaders: "In this sign thou shalt conquer!" From that moment, as soon as one of the numerous parties which had gathered under this sign against the June insurgents seeks to hold the revolutionary battlefield in its own class interest, it goes down before the cry: "Property, family, religion, order." Society is saved just as often as the circle of its rulers contracts, as a more exclusive interest is maintained against a wider one. Every demand of the simplest bourgeois financial reform, of the most ordinary liberalism, of the most formal republicanism, of the most shallow democracy, is simultaneously castigated as an "attempt on society" and stigmatized as "Socialism." And, finally, the high priests of "the religion and order" themselves are driven with kicks from their Pythian tripods, hauled out of their beds in the darkness of night, put in prison-vans, thrown into dungeons or sent into exile; their temple is razed to the ground, their mouths are sealed, their pens broken, their law torn to pieces in the name of religion, of property, of the family, of order. Bourgeois fanatics for order are shot down on their balconies by mobs of drunken soldiers, their domestic sanctuaries profaned, their houses bombarded for amusement—in the name of property, of the family, of religion, and of order. Finally, the scum of bourgeois society forms the *holy phalanx of order* and the hero Crapulinski installs himself in the Tuileries as the *"saviour of society."*

On the threshold of the February Revolution, the *social republic* appeared as a phrase, as a prophecy. In the June days of 1848, it was drowned in the blood of the *Paris proletariat,* but it haunts the subsequent acts of the drama like a ghost. The *democratic republic* announces its arrival. On June 13, 1849, it is dissipated together with its *petty bourgeois,* who have taken to their heels, but in its flight it blows its own trumpet with redoubled boastfulness. The *parliamentary republic,* together with the bourgeoisie, takes possession of the entire stage; it enjoys its existence to the full, but December 2, 1851 buries it to the accompaniment of the anguished cry of the royalists in coalition: "Long live the Republic!"

The French bourgeoisie balked at the domination of the working proletariat; it has brought the *lumpenproletariat* to domination, with the chief of the Society of December 10 at the head. The bourgeoisie kept France in breathless fear of the future terrors of red anarchy; Bonaparte discounted this future for it when, on December 4, he had the eminent bourgeois of the Boulevard Montmartre and the Boulevard des Italiens shot down at their windows by the liquor-inspired army of order. It apotheosized the sword; the sword rules it. It destroyed the revolutionary press; its own press has been destroyed. It placed popular meetings under police supervision; its salons are under the supervision of the police. It disbanded the democratic National Guards; its own National Guard is disbanded. It imposed a state of siege; a state of siege is imposed upon it. It supplanted the juries by military commissions; its juries are supplanted by military commissions. It subjected public education to the sway of the priests; the priests subject it to their own education. It transported people without trial; it is being transported without trial. It repressed every stirring in society by means of the state power; every stirring in its society is suppressed by means of the state power. Out of enthusiasm for its purse, it rebelled against its own politicians and men of letters; its politicians and men of letters are swept aside, but its purse is being plundered now that its mouth has been gagged and its pen broken. The bourgeoisie never wearied of crying out to the revolution what Saint Arsenius cried out to the Christians: *"Fuge, tace, quiesce!* Flee, be silent, keep still!"* Bonaparte cries to the bourgeoisie: *"Fuge, tace, quiesce!* Flee, be silent, keep still!"*

The French bourgeoisie had long ago found the solution to Napoleon's dilemma: *"Dans cinquante ans l'Europe sera républicaine ou cosaque."*[25] It had found the solution to it in the *"république cosaque."*[26] No Circe, by means of black magic, has distorted that work of art, the bourgeois republic, into a monstrous shape. That republic has lost nothing but the semblance of respectability. Present-day France[27] was contained in a finished state within the parliamentary republic. It only required a bayonet thrust for the bubble to burst and the monster to spring forth before our eyes.

Why did the Paris proletariat not rise in revolt after December 2?

The overthrow of the bourgeoisie had as yet been only decreed; the decree had not been carried out. Any serious insurrection of the proletariat would at once have put fresh life into the bourgeoisie, would have reconciled it with the army, and ensured a second June defeat for the workers.

On December 4 the proletariat was incited by bourgeois and *épicier* to fight. On the evening of that day several legions of the National Guard promised to appear, armed and uniformed, on the scene of battle. For the bourgeois and the *épicier* had got wind of the fact that in one of his decrees of December 2 Bonaparte abolished the secret ballot and enjoined them to record their "yes" or "no" in the official registers after their names. The resistance of December 4 intimidated Bonaparte. During the night he caused placards to be posted on all the street corners of Paris, announcing the restoration of the secret ballot. The bourgeois and the

[25]   "In fifty years Europe will be republican or Cossack."—Ed.
[26]   "Cossack republic."—Ed.
[27]   I.e., France after the coup d'état of December 2, 1851.—Ed.

épicier believed that they had gained their end. Those who failed to appear next morning were the bourgeois and the *épicier*.

By a *coup de main* during the night of December 1 to 2, Bonaparte had robbed the Paris proletariat of its leaders, the barricade commanders. An army without officers, averse to fighting under the banner of the *Montagnards* because of the memories of June 1848 and 1849 and May 1850, it left to its vanguard, the secret societies, the task of saving the insurrectionary honor of Paris, which the bourgeoisie had so unresistingly surrendered to the soldiery that, later on, Bonaparte could sneeringly give as his motive for disarming the National Guard—his fear that its arms would be turned against it itself by the anarchists!

"C'est le triomphe complet et définitif du socialisme!"[28] Thus Guizot characterized December 2. But if the overthrow of the parliamentary republic contains within itself the germ of the triumph of the proletarian revolution, its immediate and palpable result was *the victory of Bonaparte over parliament, of the executive power over the legislative power, of force without phrases over the force of phrases.* In parliament the nation made its general will the law, that is, it made the law of the ruling class its general will. Before the executive power it renounces all will of its own and submits to the superior command of an alien will, to authority. The executive power, in contrast to the legislative power, expresses the heteronomy of a nation, in contrast to its autonomy. France, therefore, seems to have escaped the despotism of a class only to fall back beneath the despotism of an individual, and, what is more, beneath the authority of an individual without authority. The struggle seems to be settled in such a way that all classes, equally impotent and equally mute, fall on their knees before the rifle butt.

But the revolution is thoroughgoing. It is still journeying through purgatory. It does its work methodically. By December 2, 1851, it had completed one-half of its preparatory work; it is now completing the other half. First it perfected the parliamentary power, in order to be able to overthrow it. Now that it has attained this, it perfects the *executive power*, reduces it to its purest expres-

---

[28]   "This is the complete and final triumph of Socialism!"—Ed.

sion, isolates it, sets it up against itself as the sole target, in order to concentrate all its forces of destruction against it. And when it has done this second half of its preliminary work, Europe will leap from its seat and exultantly exclaim: Well grubbed, old mole!

This executive power with its enormous bureaucratic and military organization, with its ingenious state machinery, embracing wide strata, with a host of officials numbering half a million, besides an army of another half million, this appalling parasitic body, which enmeshes the body of French society like a net and chokes all its pores, sprang up in the days of the absolute monarchy, with the decay of the feudal system, which it helped to hasten. The seignorial privileges of the landowners and towns became transformed into so many attributes of the state power, the feudal dignitaries into paid officials, and the motley pattern of conflicting medieval plenary powers into the regulated plan of a state authority whose work is divided and centralized as in a factory. The first French Revolution, with its task of breaking all separate local, territorial, urban, and provincial powers in order to create the civil unity of the nation, was bound to develop what the absolute monarchy had begun: centralization, but at the same time the extent, the attributes, and the agents of governmental power. Napoleon perfected this state machinery. The Legitimist Monarchy and the July Monarchy added nothing but a greater division of labor, growing in the same measure as the division of labor within bourgeois society created new groups of interests, and, therefore, new material for state administration. Every *common* interest was straightway severed from society, counterposed to it as a higher, *general* interest, snatched from the activity of society's members themselves and made an object of government activity, from a bridge, a schoolhouse, and the communal property of a village community to the railways, the national wealth, and the national university of France. Finally, in its struggle against the revolution, the parliamentary republic found itself compelled to strengthen, along with the repressive measures, the resources and centralization of governmental power. All revolutions perfected this machine instead of smashing it. The parties that contended in turn for domination regarded the possession of this huge state edifice as the principal spoils of the victor.

But under the absolute monarchy, during the first Revolution, under Napoleon, bureaucracy was only the means of preparing the class rule of the bourgeoisie. Under the Restoration, under Louis Philippe, under the parliamentary republic, it was the instrument of the ruling class, however much it strove for power of its own.

Only under the second Bonaparte does the state seem to have made itself completely independent. As against civil society, the state machine has consolidated its position so thoroughly that the chief of the Society of December 10 suffices for its head, an adventurer blown in from abroad, raised on the shield by a drunken soldiery, which he has bought with liquor and sausages, and which he must continually ply with sausage anew. Hence the downcast despair, the feeling of most dreadful humiliation and degradation that oppresses the breast of France and makes her catch her breath. She feels dishonored.

And yet the state power is not suspended in midair. Bonaparte represents a class, and the most numerous class of French society at that, the *small-holding* [*Parzellen*] *peasants*.

Just as the Bourbons were the dynasty of big landed property and just as the Orleans were the dynasty of money, so the Bonapartes are the dynasty of the peasants, that is, the mass of the French people. Not the Bonaparte who submitted to the bourgeois parliament, but the Bonaparte who dispersed the bourgeois parliament is the chosen of the peasantry. For three years the towns had succeeded in falsifying the meaning of the election of December 10 and in cheating the peasants out of the restoration of the empire. The election of December 10, 1848, has been consummated only by the coup d'état of December 2, 1851.

The small-holding peasants form a vast mass, the members of which live in similar conditions but without entering into manifold relations with one another. Their mode of production isolates them from one another instead of bringing them into mutual intercourse. The isolation is increased by France's bad means of communication and by the poverty of the peasants. Their field of production, the small holding, admits of no division of labor in its cultivation, no application of science and, therefore, no diversity of development, no variety of talent, no wealth of social relationships. Each individual peasant family is almost self-sufficient; it itself directly produces the major part of its consumption and thus acquires its means of life more through exchange with nature than in intercourse with society. A small holding, a peasant and his family; alongside them another small holding, another peasant and another family. A few score of these make up a village, and a few score of villages make up a Department. In this way, the great mass of the French nation is formed by simple addition of homologous magnitudes, much as potatoes in a sack form a sack of potatoes. Insofar as millions of families live under economic conditions of existence that separate their mode of life, their interests, and their culture from those of the other classes, and put them in hostile opposition to the latter, they form a class. Insofar as there is merely a local interconnection among these small-holding peasants, and the identity of their interests begets no community, no national bond, and no political organization among them, they do not form a class. They are consequently incapable of enforcing their class interest in their own name, whether through a parliament or through a convention. They cannot represent themselves, they must be represented. Their representative must at the same time appear as their master, as an authority over them, as an unlimited governmental power that protects them against the other classes and sends them rain and sunshine from above. The political influence of the small-holding peasants, therefore, finds its final expression in the executive power subordinating society to itself.

Historical tradition gave rise to the belief of the French peasants in the miracle that a man named Napoleon would bring all the glory back to them. And an individual turned up who gives himself out as the man because he bears the name of Napoleon, in consequence of the *Code Napoléon,* which lays down that *la recherche de la paternité est interdite.*[29] After a vagabondage of twenty years and after a series of grotesque adventures, the legend finds fulfillment and the man becomes Emperor of the French. The fixed idea of the Nephew was realized, because it coincided with the fixed idea of the most numerous class of the French people.

But, it may be objected, what about the peasant risings in half

[29]   Enquiry into paternity is forbidden.—Ed.

of France, the raids on the peasants by the army, the mass incarceration and transportation of peasants?

Since Louis XIV, France has experienced no similar persecution of the peasants "on account of demagogic practices."

But let there be no misunderstanding. The Bonaparte dynasty represents not the revolutionary, but the conservative peasant; not the peasant that strikes out beyond the condition of his social existence, the small holding, but rather the peasant who wants to consolidate this holding, not the country folk who, linked up with the towns, want to overthrow the old order through their own energies, but on the contrary those who, in stupefied seclusion within this old order, want to see themselves and their small holdings saved and favored by the ghost of the empire. It represents not the enlightenment, but the superstition of the peasant; not his judgment, but his prejudice; not his future, but his past; not his modern Cevennes, but his modern Vendée.

The three years' rigorous rule of the parliamentary republic had freed a part of the French peasants from the Napoleonic illusion and had revolutionized them, even if only superficially; but the bourgeoisie violently repressed them, as often as they set themselves in motion. Under the parliamentary republic the modern and the traditional consciousness of the French peasant contended for mastery. This progress took the form of an incessant struggle between the schoolmasters and the priests. The bourgeoisie struck down the schoolmasters. For the first time the peasants made efforts to behave independently in the face of the activity of the government. This was shown in the continual conflict between the *maires* and the prefects. The bourgeoisie deposed the *maires*. Finally, during the period of the parliamentary republic, the peasants of different localities rose against their own offspring, the army. The bourgeoisie punished them with states of siege and punitive expeditions. And this same bourgeoisie now cries out about the stupidity of the masses, the vile multitude, that has betrayed it to Bonaparte. It has itself forcibly strengthened the empire sentiments of the peasant class, it conserved the conditions that form the birthplace of this peasant religion. The bourgeoisie, to be sure, is bound to fear the stupidity of the masses as long as they remain conservative, and the insight of the masses as soon as they become revolutionary.

In the risings after the coup d'état, a part of the French peasants protested, arms in hand,. against their own vote of December 10, 1848. The school they had gone through since 1848 had sharpened their wits. But they had made themselves over to the underworld of history; history held them to their word, and the majority was still so prejudiced that in precisely the reddest Departments the peasant population voted openly for Bonaparte. In its view, the National Assembly had hindered his progress. He had now merely broken the fetters that the towns had imposed on the will of the countryside. In some parts the peasants even entertained the grotesque notion of a convention side by side with Napoleon.

After the first revolution had transformed the peasants from semi-villeins into freeholders, Napoleon confirmed and regulated the conditions on which they could exploit undisturbed the soil of France which had only just fallen to their lot and slake their youthful passion for property. But what is now causing the ruin of the French peasant is his small holding itself, the division of the land, the form of property which Napoleon consolidated in France. It is precisely the material conditions which made the feudal peasant a small-holding peasant and Napoleon an emperor. Two generations have sufficed to produce the inevitable result: progressive deterioration of agriculture, progressive indebtedness of the agriculturist. The "Napoleonic" form of property, which at the beginning of the nineteenth century was the condition for the liberation and enrichment of the French country folk, has developed in the course of this century into the law of their enslavement and pauperization. And precisely this law is the first of the *"idées napoléoniennes"* which the second Bonaparte has to uphold. If he still shares with the peasants the illusion that the cause of their ruin is to be sought, not in this small-holding property itself, but outside it, in the influence of secondary circumstances, his experiments will burst like soap bubbles when they come in contact with the relations of production.

The economic development of small-holding property has radically changed the relation of the peasants to the other classes of society. Under Napoleon, the fragmentation of the land in the countryside supplemented free competition and the beginning of big industry in the towns. The peasant class was the ubiquitous protest against the landed aristocracy which had just been overthrown. The roots that small-holding property struck in French soil deprived feudalism of all nutriment. Its landmarks formed the natural fortifications of the bourgeoisie against any surprise attack on the part of its old overlords. But in the course of the nineteenth century the feudal lords were replaced by urban usurers; the feudal obligation that went with the land was replaced by the mortgage; aristocratic landed property was replaced by bourgeois capital. The small holding of the peasant is now only the pretext that allows the capitalist to draw profits, interest, and rent from the soil, while leaving it to the tiller of the soil himself to see how he can extract his wages. The mortgage debt burdening the soil of France imposes on the French peasantry payment of an amount of interest equal to the annual interest on the entire British national debt. Small-holding property, in this enslavement by capital to which its development inevitably pushes forward, has transformed the mass of the French nation into troglodytes. Sixteen million peasants (including women and children) dwell in hovels, a large number of which have but one opening, others only two and the most favored only three. And windows are to a house what the five senses are to the head. The bourgeois order, which at the beginning of the century set the state to stand guard over the newly arisen small holding and manured it with laurels, has become a vampire that sucks out its blood and brains and throws it into the alchemistic cauldron of capital. The *Code Napoléon* is now nothing but a *codex* of distraints, forced sales, and compulsory auctions. To the four million (including children, etc.) officially recognized paupers, vagabonds, criminals, and prostitutes in France must be added five million who hover on the margin of existence and either have their haunts in the countryside itself or, with their rags and their children, continually desert the countryside for the towns and the towns for the countryside. The interests of the peasants, therefore, are no longer, as under Napoleon, in accord with, but in opposition to the interests of the bourgeoisie, to capital. Hence the peasants find their natural ally and leader in the *urban proletariat*, whose task is the overthrow of the bourgeois order. But *strong and unlimited government*—and this is the second *"idée napoléonienne,"* which the second Napoleon has to carry out—is called upon to defend this "material" order by force. This *"ordre matériel"* also serves as the catchword in all of Bonaparte's proclamations against the rebellious peasants.

Besides the mortgage which capital imposes on it, the small holding is burdened by *taxes*. Taxes are the source of life for the bureaucracy, the army, the priests, and the court, in short, for the whole apparatus of the executive power. Strong government and heavy taxes are identical. By its very nature, small-holding property forms a suitable basis for an all-powerful and innumerable bureaucracy. It creates a uniform level of relationships and persons over the whole surface of the land. Hence it also permits of uniform action from a supreme center on all points of this uniform mass. It annihilates the aristocratic intermediate grades between the mass of the people and the state power. On all sides, therefore, it calls forth the direct interference of this state power and the interposition of its immediate organs. Finally, it produces an unemployed surplus population for which there is no place either on the land or in the towns, and which accordingly reaches out for state offices as a sort of respectable alms, and provokes the creation of state posts. By the new markets which he opened at the point of the bayonet, by the plundering of the Continent, Napoleon repaid the compulsory taxes with interest. These taxes were a spur to the industry of the peasant, whereas now they rob his industry of its last resources and complete his inability to resist pauperism. And an enormous bureaucracy, well gallooned and well fed, is the *"idée napoléonienne"* which is most congenial of all to the second Bonaparte. How could it be otherwise, seeing that alongside the actual classes of society he is forced to create an artificial caste, for which the maintenance of his regime becomes a bread-and-butter question? Accordingly, one of his first financial operations was the raising of officials' salaries to their old level and the creation of new sinecures.

Another *"idée napoléonienne"* is the domination of the *priests* as an instrument of government. But while in its accord with society, in its dependence on natural forces and its submission to the authority which protected it from above, the small holding that had newly come into being was naturally religious, the small holding that is ruined by debts, at odds with society and authority, and driven beyond its own limitations naturally becomes irreligious. Heaven was quite a pleasing accession to the narrow strip of land just won, more particularly as it makes the weather; it becomes an insult as soon as it is thrust forward as substitute for the small holding. The priest then appears as only the anointed bloodhound of the earthly police—another *"idée napoléonienne."* On the next occasion, the expedition against Rome will take place in France itself, but in a sense opposite to that of M. de Montalembert.

Lastly, the culminating point of the *"idées napoléoniennes"* is the preponderance of the *army.* The army was the *point d'honneur*[30] of the small-holding peasants, it was they themselves transformed into heroes, defending their new possessions against the outer world, glorifying their recently won nationhood, plundering and revolutionizing the world. The uniform was their own state dress; war was their poetry; the small holding, extended and rounded off in imagination, was their fatherland, and patriotism the ideal form of the sense of property. But the enemies against whom the French peasant has now to defend his property are not the Cossacks; they are the *huissiers*[31] and the tax collectors. The small holding lies no longer in the so-called fatherland, but in the register of mortgages. The army itself is no longer the flower of the peasant youth; it is the swamp-flower of the peasant *lumpenproletariat.* It consists in large measure of *remplaçants,* of substitutes, just as the second Bonaparte is himself only a *remplaçant,* the substitute for Napoleon. It now performs its deeds of valor by hounding the peasants in masses like chamois, by doing *gendarme* duty, and if the internal contradictions of his system chase the chief of the Society of December 10 over the French border, his army, after some acts of brigandage, will reap, not laurels, but thrashings.

One sees: *all* "idées napoléoniennes" *are ideas of the undevel-*

30   Matter of honor, a point of special touch.—Ed.
31   *Huissiers:* Bailiffs.—Ed.

oped small holding in the freshness of its youth; for the small holding that has outlived its day they are an absurdity. They are only
the hallucinations of its death struggle, words that are transformed
into phrases, spirits transformed into ghosts. But the parody of the
empire was necessary to free the mass of the French nation from
the weight of tradition and to work out in pure form the opposition
between the state power and society. With the progressive undermining of small-holding property, the state structure erected upon
it collapses. The centralization of the state that modern society requires arises only on the ruins of the military-bureaucratic government machinery which was forged in opposition to feudalism.

The condition of the French peasants provides us with the answer to the riddle of the *general elections of December 20 and 21,*
which bore the second Bonaparte up Mount Sinai, not to receive
laws, but to give them.

Manifestly, the bourgeoisie had now no choice but to elect
Bonaparte. When the puritans at the Council of Constance com-
plained of the dissolute lives of the popes and wailed about the
necessity of moral reform, Cardinal Pierre d'Ailly thundered at
them: "Only the devil in person can still save the Catholic Church,
and you ask for angels." In like manner, after the coup d'état, the
French bourgeoisie cried: Only the chief of the Society of December 10 can still save bourgeois society! Only theft can still save
property; only perjury, religion; bastardy, the family; disorder,
order!

As the executive authority which has made itself an independent power, Bonaparte feels it to be his mission to safeguard "bourgeois order." But the strength of this bourgeois order lies in the
middle class. He looks on himself, therefore, as the representative
of the middle class and issues decrees in this sense. Nevertheless,
he is somebody solely due to the fact that he has broken the political
power of this middle class and daily breaks it anew. Consequently,
he looks on himself as the adversary of the political and literary
power of the middle class. But by protecting its material power, he
generates its political power anew. The cause must accordingly be
kept alive; but the effect, where it manifests itself, must be done
away with. But this cannot pass off without slight confusions of

cause and effect, since in their interaction both lose their distinguishing features. New decrees that obliterate the border line. As against the bourgeoisie, Bonaparte looks on himself, at the same time, as the representative of the peasants and of the people in general, who wants to make the lower classes of the people happy within the frame of bourgeois society. New decrees that cheat the "True Socialists" of their statecraft in advance. But, above all, Bonaparte looks on himself as the chief of the Society of December 10, as the representative of the *lumpenproletariat* to which he himself, his *entourage*, his government, and his army belong, and whose prime consideration is to benefit itself and draw California lottery prizes from the state treasury. And he vindicates his position as chief of the Society of December 10 with decrees, without decrees, and despite decrees.

This contradictory task of the man explains the contradictions of his government, the confused groping about which seeks now to win, now to humiliate first one class and then another and arrays all of them uniformly against him, whose practical uncertainty forms a highly comical contrast to the imperious, categorical style of the government decrees, a style which is faithfully copied from the Uncle.

Industry and trade, hence the business affairs of the middle class, are to prosper in hothouse fashion under the strong government. The grant of innumerable railway concessions. But the Bonapartist *lumpenproletariat* is to enrich itself. The initiated play *tripotage*[32] on the *bourse* with the railway concessions. But no capital is forthcoming for the railways. Obligation of the Bank to make advances on railway shares. But, at the same time, the Bank is to be exploited for personal ends and therefore must be cajoled. Release of the Bank from the obligation to publish its report weekly. Leonine agreement of the Bank with the government. The people are to be given employment. Initiation of public works. But the public works increase the obligations of the people in respect of taxes. Hence reduction of the taxes by an onslaught on the *rentiers*, by conversion of the 5 percent bonds to 4½ percent. But, once

[32]   *Tripotage:* Hanky-panky.—Ed.

more, the middle class must receive a *douceur*.[33] Therefore doubling of the wine tax for the people, who buy it *en détail*,[34] and halving of the wine tax for the middle class, who drink it *en gros*.[35] Dissolution of the actual workers' associations, but promises of miracles of association in the future. The peasants are to be helped. Mortgage banks that expedite their getting into debt and accelerate the concentration of property. But these banks are to be used to make money out of the confiscated estates of the House of Orleans. No capitalist wants to agree to this condition, which is not in the decree, and the mortgage bank remains a mere decree, etc., etc.

Bonaparte would like to appear as the patriarchal benefactor of all classes. But he cannot give to one class without taking from another. Just as at the time of the Fronde it was said of the Duke of Guise that he was the most *obligeant* man in France because he had turned all his estates into his partisans' obligations to him, so Bonaparte would fain be the most *obligeant* man in France and turn all the property, all the labor of France into a personal obligation to himself. He would like to steal the whole of France in order to be able to make a present of her to France or, rather, in order to be able to buy France anew with French money, for as the chief of the Society of December 10 he must needs buy what ought to belong to him. And all the state institutions, the Senate, the Council of State, the legislative body, the Legion of Honor, the soldiers' medals, the washhouses, the public works, the railways, the *état major*[36] of the National Guard to the exclusion of privates, and the confiscated estates of the House of Orleans—all become parts of the institution of purchase. Every place in the army and in the government machine becomes a means of purchase. But the most important feature of this process, whereby France is taken in order to give to her, is the percentages that find their way into the pockets of the head and the members of the Society of December 10 during the turnover. The witticism with which Countess L., the mistress of M. de Morney, characterized the confiscation of the Orleans es-

33   *Douceur:* Sop.—Ed.
34   *En détail:* By retail.—Ed.
35   *En gros:* Wholesale.—Ed.
36   *Etat major:* General Staff.—Ed.

tates: *"C'est le premier vol*[37] *de l'aigle"*[38] is applicable to every flight of this *eagle*, which is more like a *raven*. He himself and his adherents call out to one another daily like that Italian Carthusian admonishing the miser who, with boastful display, counted up the goods on which he could yet live for years to come: *"Tu fai conto sopra i beni, bisogna prima far il conto sopra gli anni."*[39] Lest they make a mistake in the years, they count the minutes. A bunch of blokes push their way forward to the court, into the ministries, to the head of the administration and the army, a crowd of the best of whom it must be said that no one knows whence he comes, a noisy, disreputable, rapacious bohème that crawls into gallooned coats with the same grotesque dignity as the high dignitaries of Soulouque. One can visualize clearly this upper stratum of the society of December 10, if one reflects that *Véron-Crevel* is its preacher of morals and *Granier de Cassagnac* its thinker. When Guizot, at the time of his ministry, utilized this Granier on a hole-and-corner newspaper against the dynastic opposition, he used to boast of him with the quip: *"C'est le roi des drôles,"* "he is the king of buffoons." One would do wrong to recall the Regency or Louis XV in connection with Louis Bonaparte's court and clique. For "often already, France has experienced a government of mistresses; but never before a government of *hommes entretenus.*"[40]

Driven by the contradictory demands of his situation and being at the same time, like a conjurer, under the necessity of keeping the public gaze fixed on himself, as Napoleon's substitute, by springing constant surprises, that is to say, under the necessity of executing a coup d'état *en miniature* every day, Bonaparte throws the entire bourgeois economy into confusion, violates everything that seemed inviolable to the Revolution of 1848, makes some tolerant of revolution, others desirous of revolution, and produces actual anarchy in the name of order, while at the same time stripping its halo from the entire state machine, profanes it and makes it at once loathsome and ridiculous. The cult of the Holy Tunic of Treves he dupli-

37   *Vol* means flight and theft.
38   "It is the first flight (theft) of the eagle."—Ed.
39   "Thou countest thy goods, thou shouldst first count thy years."
40   *Hommes entretenus:* Kept men.—Ed.

cates at Paris in the cult of the Napoleonic imperial mantle. But when the imperial mantle finally falls on the shoulders of Louis Bonaparte, the bronze statue of Napoleon will crash from the top of the Vendôme Column.

III. *Class and Political Conflict in Germany, 1848–51*

The first act of the revolutionary drama on the continent of Europe has closed. The "powers that were" before the hurricane of 1848 are again the "powers that be," and the more or less popular rulers of a day, provisional governors, triumvirs, dictators, with their tail of representatives, civil commissioners, military commissioners, prefects, judges, generals, officers, and soldiers, are thrown upon foreign shores, and "transported beyond the seas" to England or America, there to form new governments *in partibus infidelium*, European committees, central committees, national committees, and to announce their advent with proclamations quite as solemn as those of any less imaginary potentates.

A more signal defeat than that undergone by the continental revolutionary party—or rather parties—upon all points of the line of battle, cannot be imagined. But what of that? Has not the struggle of the British middle classes for their social and political supremacy embraced forty-eight, that of the French middle classes forty, years of unexampled struggles? And was their triumph ever nearer than at the very moment when restored monarchy thought itself more firmly settled than ever? The times of that superstition which attributed revolutions to the ill will of a few agitators have long passed away. Everyone knows nowadays that wherever there is a revolutionary convulsion, there must be some social want in the background, which is prevented, by outworn institutions, from satisfying itself. The want may not yet be felt as strongly, as generally, as might ensure immediate success; but every attempt at forcible repression will only bring it forth stronger and stronger, until it bursts its fetters. If, then, we have been beaten, we have nothing else to do but to begin again from the beginning. And, fortunately, the probably very short interval of rest which is allowed us between the close of the first and the beginning of the second act of the movement, gives us time for a very necessary piece of work: the study of the causes that necessitated both the late outbreak and its defeat; causes that are not to be sought for in the accidental efforts, talents, faults, errors, or treacheries of some of the leaders, but in the general social state and conditions of existence of each of the convulsed nations. That the sudden movements of February and March 1848 were not the work of single individuals, but spontaneous, irresistible manifestations of national wants and necessities, more or less clearly understood, but very distinctly felt by numerous classes in every country, is a fact recognized everywhere; but when you inquire into the causes of the counterrevolutionary successes, there you are met on every hand with the ready reply that it was Mr. This or Citizen That who "betrayed" the people. Which reply may be very true or not, according to circumstances, but under no circumstances does it explain anything—not even show how it came to pass that the "people" allowed themselves to be thus betrayed. And what a poor chance stands a political party whose entire stock-in-trade consists in a knowledge of the solitary fact that Citizen So-and-so is not to be trusted.

The inquiry into, and the exposition of, the causes, both of the revolutionary convulsion and its suppression, are, besides, of paramount importance from a historical point of view. All these petty, personal quarrels and recriminations—all these contradictory assertions that it was Marrast, or Ledru-Rollin, or Louis Blanc, or any other member of the Provisional Government, or the whole of them, that steered the Revolution amid the rocks upon which it foundered—of what interest can they be, what light can they afford, to the American or Englishman who observed all these various movements from a distance too great to allow of his distinguishing any of the details of operations? No man in his senses will ever believe that eleven men, mostly of very indifferent capacity either for good or evil, were able in three months to ruin a nation of thirty-six millions, unless those thirty-six millions saw as little of their way before them as the eleven did. But how it came to pass that thirty-six millions were at once called upon to decide for themselves which way to go, although partly groping in dim twilight, and how then they got lost and their old leaders were for a moment allowed to return to their leadership, that is just the question.

If, then, we try to lay [out] the causes which, while they necessitated the German Revolution of 1848, led quite as inevitably to its momentary repression in 1849 and 1850, we shall not be expected to give a complete history of events as they passed in that country. Later events, and the judgment of coming generations, will decide what portion of that confused mass of seemingly accidental, incoherent, and incongruous facts is to form a part of the world's history. The time for such a task has not yet arrived; we must confine ourselves to the limits of the possible, and be satisfied, if we can find rational causes, based upon undeniable facts, to explain the chief events, the principal vicissitudes of that movement, and to give us a clue as to the direction which the next, and perhaps not very distant, outbreak will impart to the German people.

And firstly, what was the state of Germany at the outbreak of the Revolution?

The composition of the different classes of the people which form the groundwork of every political organization was, in Germany, more complicated than in any other country. While in England and France feudalism was entirely destroyed, or, at least, reduced, as in the former country, to a few insignificant forms, by a powerful and wealthy middle class, concentrated in large towns, and particularly in the capital, the feudal nobility in Germany had retained a great portion of their ancient privileges. The feudal system of tenure was prevalent almost everywhere. The lords of the land had even retained the jurisdiction over their tenants. Deprived of their political privileges, of the right to control the princes, they had preserved almost all their mediaeval supremacy over the peasantry of their demesnes, as well as their exemption from taxes. Feudalism was more flourishing in some localities than in others, but nowhere except on the left bank of the Rhine was it entirely destroyed. This feudal nobility, then extremely numerous and partly very wealthy, was considered, officially, the first "Order" in the country. It furnished the higher Government officials, it almost exclusively officered the army.

The bourgeoisie of Germany was by far not as wealthy and

concentrated as that of France or England. The ancient manufactures of Germany had been destroyed by the introduction of steam, and the rapidly extending supremacy of English manufactures; the more modern manufactures, started under the Napoleonic continental system, established in other parts of the country, did not compensate for the loss of the old ones, nor suffice to create a manufacturing interest strong enough to force its wants upon the notice of Governments jealous of every extension of nonnoble wealth and power. If France carried her silk manufactures victorious through fifty years of revolutions and wars, Germany, during the same time, all but lost her ancient linen trade. The manufacturing districts, besides, were few and far between; situated far inland, and using, mostly, foreign, Dutch, or Belgian ports for their imports and exports, they had little or no interest in common with the large seaport towns on the North Sea and the Baltic; they were, above all, unable to create large manufacturing and trading centers, such as Paris and Lyons, London and Manchester. The causes of this backwardness of German manufactures were manifold, but two will suffice to account for it: the unfavorable geographical situation of the country, at a distance from the Atlantic, which had become the great highway for the world's trade, and the continuous wars in which Germany was involved, and which were fought on her soil, from the sixteenth century to the present day. It was this want of numbers, and particularly of anything like concentrated numbers, which prevented the German middle classes from attaining that political supremacy which the English bourgeoisie has enjoyed ever since 1688, and which the French conquered in 1789. And yet, ever since 1815, the wealth, and with the wealth the political importance of the middle class in Germany, was continually growing. Governments were, although reluctantly, compelled to bow, at least to its more immediate material interests. It may even be truly said that from 1815 to 1830, and from 1832 to 1840, every particle of political influence, which, having been allowed to the middle class in the constitutions of the smaller States, was again wrested from them during the above two periods of political reaction, that every such particle was compensated for by some more practical advantage allowed to them. Every political defeat of the middle class drew after it a victory on the field of commercial legislation. And, certainly, the Prussian Protective Tariff of 1818, and the formation of the Zollverein, were worth a good deal more to the traders and manufacturers of Germany than the equivocal right of expressing in the chambers of some diminutive dukedom their want of confidence in ministers who laughed at their votes. Thus, with growing wealth and extending trade, the bourgeoisie soon arrived at a stage where it found the development of its most important interests checked by the political constitution of the country; by its random division among thirty-six princes with conflicting tendencies and caprices; by the feudal fetters upon agriculture and the trade connected with it; by the prying superintendence to which an ignorant and presumptuous bureaucracy subjected all its transactions. At the same time the extension and consolidation of the Zollverein, the general introduction of steam communication, the growing competition in the home trade, brought the commercial classes of the different States and Provinces closer together, equalized their interests, centralized their strength. The natural consequence was the passing of the whole mass of them into the camp of the Liberal Opposition, and the gaining of the first serious struggle of the German middle class for political power. This change may be dated from 1840, from the moment when the bourgeoisie of Prussia assumed the lead of the middle-class movement of Germany. We shall hereafter revert to this Liberal Opposition movement of 1840–47.

The great mass of the nation, which neither belonged to the nobility nor to the bourgeoisie, consisted in the towns of the small trading and shopkeeping class and the working people, and in the country of the peasantry.

The small trading and shopkeeping class is exceedingly numerous in Germany, in consequence of the stinted development which the large capitalists and manufacturers as a class have had in that country. In the larger towns it forms almost the majority of the inhabitants; in the smaller ones it entirely predominates, from the absence of wealthier competitors or influence. This class, a most important one in every body politic, and in all modern revolutions, is still more important in Germany, where, during the recent struggles, it generally played the decisive part. Its intermediate position between the class of larger capitalists, traders, and manufacturers, the bourgeoisie properly so-called, and the proletarian or industrial class, determines its character. Aspiring to the position of the first, the least adverse turn of fortune hurls the individuals of this class down into the ranks of the second. In monarchical and feudal countries the custom of the court and aristocracy becomes necessary to its existence; the loss of this custom might ruin a great part of it. In the smaller towns a military garrison, a county government, a court of law with its followers, form very often the base of its prosperity; withdraw these, and down go the shopkeepers, the tailors, the shoemakers, the joiners. Thus eternally tossed about between the hope of entering the ranks of the wealthier class, and the fear of being reduced to the state of proletarians or even paupers; between the hope of promoting their interests by conquering a share in the direction of public affairs, and the dread of rousing, by ill-timed opposition, the ire of a Government which disposes of their very existence, because it has the power of removing their best customers; possessed of small means, the insecurity of the possession of which is in the inverse ratio of the amount, this class is extremely vacillating in its views. Humble and crouchingly submissive under a powerful feudal or monarchical Government, it turns to the side of Liberalism when the middle class is in the ascendant; it becomes seized with violent democratic fits as soon as the middle class has secured its own supremacy, but falls back into the abject despondency of fear as soon as the class below itself, the proletarians, attempts an independent movement. We shall by and by see this class, in Germany, pass alternately from one of these stages to the other.

The working class in Germany is, in its social and political development, as far behind that of England and France as the German bourgeoisie is behind the bourgeoisie of those countries. Like master, like man. The evolution of the conditions of existence for a numerous, strong, concentrated, and intelligent proletarian class goes hand in hand with the development of the conditions of existence for a numerous, wealthy, concentrated, and powerful middle class. The working-class movement itself never is independent, never is of an exclusively proletarian character until all the different factions of the middle class, and particularly its most progressive faction, the large manufacturers, have conquered political power, and remodeled the State according to their wants. It is then that the inevitable conflict between the employer and the employed becomes imminent, and cannot be adjourned any longer; that the working class can no longer be put off with delusive hopes and promises never to be realized; that the great problem of the nineteenth century, the abolition of the proletariat, is at last brought forward fairly and in its proper light. Now, in Germany the mass of the working class were employed, not by those modern manufacturing lords of which Great Britain furnishes such splendid specimens, but by small tradesmen, whose entire manufacturing system is a mere relic of the Middle Ages. And as there is an enormous difference between the great cotton lord and the petty cobbler or master tailor, so there is a corresponding distance from the wide-awake factory operative of modern manufacturing Babylons to the bashful journeyman tailor or cabinet-maker of a small country town, who lives in circumstances and works after a plan very little different from those of the like sort of men some five hundred years ago. This general absence of modern conditions of life, of modern modes of industrial production, of course, was accompanied by a pretty equally general absence of modern ideas, and it is, therefore, not to be wondered at if, at the outbreak of the Revolution, a large part of the working classes should cry out for the immediate reestablishment of guilds and Mediaeval privileged trades corporations. Yet from the manufacturing districts, where the modern system of production predominated, and in consequence of the facilities of intercommunication and mental development afforded by the migratory life of a large number of the working men, a strong nucleus formed itself, whose ideas about the emancipation of their class were far clearer and more in accordance with existing facts and historical necessities; but they were a mere minority. If the active movement of the middle classes may be dated from 1840, that of the working class commences its advent by the insurrections of the Silesian and Bohemian factory operatives in 1844, and we shall soon have occasion to pass in review the different stages through which this movement passed.

Lastly, there was the great class of the small farmers, the peasantry, which, with its appendix of farm laborers, constitutes a considerable majority of the entire nation. But this class again sub-divided itself into different fractions. There were, firstly, the more wealthy farmers, what is called in Germany *Gross* and *Mittel-Bauern*, proprietors of more or less extensive farms, and each of them commanding the services of several agricultural laborers. This class, placed between the large untaxed feudal landowners, and the smaller peasantry and farm laborers, for obvious reasons found in an alliance with the antifeudal middle class of the towns its most natural political course. Then there were, secondly, the small free-holders, predominating in the Rhine country, where feudalism had succumbed before the mighty strokes of the great French Revolution. Similar independent small freeholders also existed here and there in other provinces, where they had succeeded in buying off the feudal charges formerly due upon their lands. This class, how-ever, was a class of freeholders by name only, their property being generally mortgaged to such an extent, and under such onerous conditions, that not the peasant, but the usurer who had advanced the money, was the real landowner. Thirdly, the feudal tenants, who could not be easily turned out of their holdings, but who had to pay a perpetual rent, or to perform in perpetuity a certain amount of labor in favor of the lord of the manor. Lastly, the agricultural laborers, whose condition, in many large farming concerns, was exactly that of the same class in England, and who in all cases lived and died poor, ill-fed, and the slaves of their employers. These three latter classes of the agricultural population, the small freeholders, the feudal tenants, and the agricultural laborers, never troubled their heads much about politics before the Revolution, but it is evi-dent that this event must have opened to them a new career, full of brilliant prospects. To every one of them the Revolution offered advantages, and the movement once fairly engaged in, it was to be expected that each, in their turn, would join it. But at the same time it is quite as evident, and equally borne out by the history of all modern countries, that the agricultural population, in consequence of its dispersion over a great space, and of the difficulty of bringing about an agreement among any considerable portion of it, never can attempt a successful independent movement; they require the initiatory impulse of the more concentrated, more enlightened, more easily moved people of the towns.

The preceding short sketch of the most important of the classes, which in their aggregate formed the German nation at the outbreak of the recent movements, will already be sufficient to explain a great part of the incoherence, incongruence, and apparent contradiction which prevailed in that movement. When interests so varied, so conflicting, so strangely crossing each other, are brought into violent collision; when these contending interests in every district, every province, are mixed in different proportions; when, above all, there is no great center in the country, no London, no Paris, the decisions of which, by their weight, may supersede the necessity of fighting out the same quarrel over and over again in every single locality; what else is to be expected but that the contest will dissolve itself into a mass of unconnected struggles, in which an enormous quantity of blood, energy, and capital is spent, but which for all that remain without any decisive results?

The political dismemberment of Germany into three dozen of more or less important principalities is equally explained by this confusion and multiplicity of the elements which compose the nation, and which again vary in every locality. Where there are no common interests there can be no unity of purpose, much less of action. The German Confederation, it is true, was declared everlastingly indissoluble; yet the Confederation, and its organ, the Diet, never represented German unity. The very highest pitch to which centralization was ever carried in Germany was the establishment of the Zollverein; by this the States on the North Sea were also forced into a Customs Union of their own, Austria remaining wrapped up in her separate prohibitive tariff. Germany had the satisfaction to be, for all practical purposes, divided between three independent powers only, instead of between thirty-six. Of course the paramount supremacy of the Russian Czar, as established in 1814, underwent no change on this account.

16

THE TRANSITION TO COMMUNIST
SOCIETY

WHAT WE HAVE to deal with here is a communist society, not as it has *developed* on its own foundations, but, on the contrary, as it *emerges* from capitalist society; which is thus in every respect, economically, morally and intellectually, still stamped with the birthmarks of the old society from whose womb it emerges. Accordingly the individual producer receives back from society—after the deductions have been made—exactly what he gives to it. What he has given to it is his individual amount of labor. For example, the social working day consists of the sum of the individual labor hours; the individual labor time of the individual producer is the part of the social labor day contributed by him, his share in it. He receives a certificate from society that he has furnished such and such an amount of labor (after deducting his labor for the common fund), and with this certificate he draws from the social stock of means of consumption as much as the same amount of labor costs. The same amount of labor which he has given to society in one form, he receives back in another.

Here obviously the same principle prevails as that which regulates the exchange of commodities, as far as this is exchange of equal values. Content and form are changed, because under the altered circumstances no one can give anything except his labor, and because, on the other hand, nothing can pass into the ownership of individuals except individual means of consumption. But, as far as the distribution of the latter among the individual pro-

From *A Critique of the Gotha Programme*, pp. 8–10, 18.

ducers is concerned, the same principle prevails as in the exchange of commodity-equivalents, so much labor in one form is exchanged for an equal amount of labor in another form.

Hence, *equal right* here is still in principle—*bourgeois right*, although principle and practice are no longer in conflict, while the exchange of equivalents in commodity exchange only exists on the *average* and not in the individual case.

In spite of this advance, this *equal right* is still stigmatized by a bourgeois limitation. The right of the producers is *proportional* to the labor they supply; the equality consists in the fact that measurement is made with an *equal standard*, labor.

But one man is superior to another physically or mentally and so supplies more labor in the same time, or can labor for a longer time; and labor, to serve as a measure, must be defined by its duration or intensity, otherwise it ceases to be a standard of measurement. This *equal* right is an unequal right for unequal labor. It recognizes no class differences, because everyone is only a worker like everyone else; but it tacitly recognizes unequal individual endowment and thus productive capacity as natural privileges. *It is therefore a right of inequality in its content, like every right.* Right by its very nature can only consist in the application of an equal standard; but unequal individuals (and they would not be different individuals if they were not unequal) are only measurable by an equal standard in so far as they are brought under an equal point of view, are taken from one *definite* side only, e.g., in the present case are regarded *only as workers*, and nothing more seen in them, everything else being ignored. Further, one worker is married, another not; one has more children than another and so on and so forth. Thus with an equal output, and hence an equal share in the social consumption fund, one will in fact receive more than another, one will be richer than another, and so on. To avoid all these defects, right, instead of being equal, would have to be unequal.

But these defects are inevitable in the first phase of communist society as it is when it has just emerged after prolonged birth pangs from capitalist society. Right can never be higher than the economic structure of society and the cultural development thereby determined.

In a higher phase of communist society, after the enslaving subordination of individuals under division of labor, and therewith also the antithesis between mental and physical labor, has vanished; after labor, from a mere means of life, has itself become the prime necessity of life; after the productive forces have also increased with the all-round development of the individual, and all the springs of cooperative wealth flow more abundantly—only then can the narrow horizon of bourgeois right be fully left behind and society inscribe on its banners: from each according to his ability, to each according to his needs!

"Present-day society" is capitalist society, which exists in all civilized countries, more or less free from mediaeval admixture, more or less modified by the special historical development of each country and more or less developed. On the other hand, the "present-day state" changes with a country's frontier. It is different in the Prusso-German empire from what it is in Switzerland, it is different in England from what it is in the United States. "*The* present-day state" is therefore a fiction.

Nevertheless, the different states of the different civilized countries, in spite of their manifold diversity of form, all have this in common, that they are based on modern bourgeois society, only one more or less capitalistically developed. They have, therefore, also certain essential features in common. In this sense it is possible to speak of the "present-day state," in contrast to the future in which its present root, bourgeois society, will have died away.

The question then arises: what transformation will the state undergo in communist society? In other words, what social functions will remain in existence there that are analogous to the present functions of the state? This question can only be answered scientifically and one does not get a flea-hop nearer to the problem by a thousandfold combination of the word people with the word state.

Between capitalist and communist society lies the period of the revolutionary transformation of the one into the other. There corresponds to this also a political transition period in which the state can be nothing but *the revolutionary dictatorship of the proletariat.*

Index